PUTTING LIBERALISM
IN ITS PLACE

■   ■   ■   ■

Paul W. Kahn

PRINCETON UNIVERSITY PRESS

Princeton and Oxford

Copyright © 2005 by Princeton University Press
Published by Princeton University Press,
41 William Street, Princeton, New Jersey 08540
In the United Kingdom: Princeton University Press,
3 Market Place, Woodstock, Oxfordshire OX20 1SY

Library of Congress Cataloging-in-Publication Data

Kahn, Paul W., 1952–
Putting liberalism in its place / Paul W. Kahn.
p. cm.
Includes bibliographical references and index.
ISBN 0-691-12024-2 (alk. paper)
1. Liberalism—United States. 2. Communitarianism—United States.
3. Political culture—United States. 4. Social contract. I. Title.
JC574.2.U6K34 2005
320.51′0973—dc22   2004049132

British Library Cataloging-in-Publication Data is available

This book has been composed in Sabon
Printed on acid-free paper. ∞
pup.princeton.edu
Printed in the United States of America
1 3 5 7 9 10 8 6 4 2

CONTENTS

ACKNOWLEDGMENTS

I have been thinking about the arguments in this book for a long time. I have pursued them in many different contexts and with many different scholars. Colleagues, students, and friends have all taken the time to engage my ideas and, often, to point out the errors of my ways. I have learned from all of these engagements, even if I have not always followed the advice. Some people, however, deserve special thanks. Bruce Ackerman and Owen Fiss have been especially helpful, as were Annelise Riles and Jonathan Schell, during their visits at the Yale Law School. I learned much from George Fletcher and Andrzej Rapaczynski when I presented part of chapter six at Columbia Law School. Michael Ignatieff, of the Kennedy Center, also provided very useful comments when I presented part of the work in his project on American Exceptionalism. I have benefited greatly from the graduate student seminar I conduct at Yale. Participants in that seminar have included Daniel Bonilla, Hugo Cyr, Ming-sung Kuo, Marcio Grandchamp, Alejandro Madrazo, and Benjamin Berger. Of this group, I want especially to thank Daniel Bonilla for helping me to understand contemporary views on multiculturalism and for a very close reading of the entire manuscript. I also owe a substantial debt to a number of very fine research assistants: Wes Kelman, Zachary Richter, Bradley Klein, and Miriam Ingber. Ian Malcolm, of Princeton University Press, has been exceptionally helpful, as was an anonymous reviewer for the Press. I owe much to Barbara Mianzo, whose administrative skills make it possible for me to do what I do. Finally, my debts to my family are unending. I hope that they can see themselves at the center of this book about love and politics.

INTRODUCTION

■ ■ ■ ■

PUTTING LIBERALISM
IN ITS PLACE

Every age has its own point of access to ethical and political deliberation. For us, that point is the problem of cultural pluralism. Lacking
a conviction in the absolute truth of our own beliefs and practices, we
are uncertain how to respond to those who live by different norms.
We are all too aware that such differences exist, as we interact with
cultures that put different values on life and death, family and society,
religion and the state, men and women. We constantly confront the
question of whether some of the practices supported by these values
are beyond the limits of our own commitment to a liberal moral philosophy and a political practice of tolerance. We worry about moral
cowardice when we fail to respond critically, and about cultural imperialism when we do respond. The problem is both theoretical and
practical: theoretical, when we struggle to find a form of reasoning
that can occupy a position between a discredited claim to universal
moral truth and an incapacitating moral relativism; practical, when
we must decide how to respond to groups and individuals that offend
our own values.

THE CHALLENGE OF CULTURAL PLURALISM

The problem of cultural pluralism has both an internal and an external
face. Internally, we confront cultural differences within our own society. These differences arise only in part from the historical legacy of
waves of immigrants who brought diverse traditions to the nation-
building project. More importantly, differences arise because of contemporary critiques of traditional practice and beliefs. These critiques
purport to expose the manner in which the traditions carry forward

entrenched status relationships. Is the traditional family, for example, a cultural inheritance to be treasured and preserved, or does it perpetuate gendered role differentiation and patriarchal values that should be rejected? Is religion a source of values to be protected or of irrationality to be cabined? Is ethnicity a legitimate or an illegitimate source of political difference? Confronting this internal pluralism, we wonder how much normative difference can be absorbed by a single political culture and what common principles can hold together a multicultural society.[1]

Externally, it is difficult to find any area of the world with which we do not interact, and about whose customs and practices we can express either ignorance or indifference. In fact, the larger the degree of dissonance between a foreign culture's values and our own, the more likely those practices will come to our attention. Differences between ourselves and others are not mere matters of degree or of interpretation of common standards. Rather, we have radically different understandings of the appropriate social norms and, consequently, very different expectations of politics. Europeans may be drawing together in a common political and moral order, but much of the rest of the world, from Africa to Asia, is following other patterns of order— or disorder. These cultural differences are deeply entwined with differences in material circumstances as well as political organization. Since these material and organizational differences are not likely to decrease as populations increase under conditions of material scarcity, it would be futile to try to disentangle cultural from material differences.[2] Each inevitably shapes and is shaped by the other.

Aware that Western aspirations for a single global order are not universally accepted, we are thrown back again on the question of difference. We are forced to think critically about our own claims for universal norms. We are no longer quite so confident of the status of our own truths. We find Islamic states today—and even a Jewish state—but we do not find Christian states. The contemporary truths

[1] Compare, e.g., K. Karst, "The Bonds of American Nationhood," 21 *Cardozo L. Rev.* 1141 (2000), with S. Huntington, *The Clash of Civilizations and the Remaking of World Order* (1996).

[2] See R. Kaplan, *The Coming Anarchy: Shattering the Dreams of the Post-Cold War* (2000).

of the West are procedural and economic: the rule of law, democracy, and free markets. We wonder whether any of these constitutes adequate grounds for rejecting the moral truths of others. We appeal to the idea of human rights—"It is the law," we say—but beneath the legal rhetoric we find disagreement about the nature of the individual and his or her relationship to the community. Disagreement, we fear, may go all the way down.[3]

Western states, including our own, have traditionally been quite willing to force people to comply with moral truth. The theoretical project, in the form of theological and philosophical inquiry, was to defend and elaborate that truth. Once the truth was grasped, there was no more difficulty in making it compulsory than there was in making individuals follow the rules of mathematics. As long as the good and the true were believed to be one and the same, moral science had the same status as natural science. Even as tolerant a country as our own has a past marked by little toleration for deep religious difference (consider the treatment, at various times, of Mormons, Catholics, and Muslims), for claims of racial and gender equality, or for the beliefs of non-Western immigrants and Native Americans.

Yet forcing people to follow our truths has never been our only strategy for dealing with difference. Across a broad domain, we have tolerated difference. Toleration for some religious differences is deeply embedded in American history. Free speech, too, rests on a principle of liberal tolerance for difference. Intolerance appears at the margins of a field of tolerance. Those margins have moved substantially over the course of our history.

Within our own community, we reach a rough compromise between the universal and the particular. Compromise is possible because the background values of the culture are not widely or deeply opposed. As a matter of law, we protect certain fundamental rights. Individuals and groups are free to live as they wish, as long as they respect fundamental norms protective of individual dignity. This still leaves a wide range within which ordinary political forces, as well as individuals, make choices among competing norms. At times, certain values or norms become so important that they shift from the domain of choice

[3] See M. Ignatieff, *Human Rights as Politics and Idolatry* 54–55 (2001).

to that of constitutional law; that is, they are taken out of the ongoing political and moral debate and protected as a matter of fundamental law. This, for example, was the process marked by *Roe v. Wade* with respect to the right to choose an abortion.

The most difficult internal clashes that we confront tend to emerge from minority religious groups outside of this broad value consensus. With respect to these groups, we inevitably feel a double-pull: an instinct toward charitable toleration—it seems to cost us little to tolerate difference—and an opposite impulse toward the universalization of norms. When the Amish will not send their children to high school, or when Seventh-Day Adventists say they need unemployment compensation because they cannot accept jobs that require Saturday work, the Supreme Court has generally been willing to grant exemptions.[4] Recently, however, it has inclined in the opposite direction, toward universalization.[5] Even then, Congress has generally responded in the opposite way.[6] Our own liberal political culture, in these cases, is uncertain where to draw the line between uniformity and toleration.

Even when it costs little, the toleration of such group difference is always precarious. A shift of perspective from the adults to the children in these groups, or from the group's relationship to the dominant culture to its relationship to dissident minorities within its own geographic reach, is likely to produce just the opposite reactions even in a broadly tolerant community. We want to protect the right of the child to choose his or her own cultural community or of minorities to their own choice of lifestyle.[7] We reason that if we do not protect the rights of the individual against the group here, we will do so nowhere.

---

[4] See *Wisconsin v. Yoder* 406 U.S. 205 (1972); *Sherbert v. Verner*, 374 U.S. 398 (1963).

[5] See *Employment Division, Dept. of Human Resources v. Smith*, 494 U.S. 872 (1990) (refusing to exempt religious use of peyote from state laws of general applicability). For an earlier example of the same tension, but with movement in the opposite direction, compare *Minersville School District v. Gobitis*, 310 U.S. 586 (1940), and *West Va. State Bd. of Ed. v. Barnette*, 319 U.S. 624 (1943). All of these cases are discussed in chap. 2 *infra*.

[6] See the Religious Freedom Restoration Act of 1993, 42 U.S.C. §2000bb et seq. This act was, in turn, declared unconstitutional by the Supreme Court. *City of Boerne v. Flores*, 521 U.S. 507 (1997).

[7] See, e.g., *Yoder*, 406 U.S. at 244 (Douglas, J., dissenting) (arguing that Amish children have cognizable interests that may depart from those of their parents).

A tolerance based on respect for choice easily becomes a reverse image of itself: intolerance for the actual choices made.

Theoretical approaches to the problems of cultural pluralism reflect a similar conceptual *aporia* between universalism and tolerance as competing first principles. We can articulate a set of universal values and supporting norms, against which cultural practices and belief systems are to be measured. This is the approach pursued by contemporary advocates of human-rights law. Alternatively, we can begin from the perception of difference among groups. The intuition of difference is no less fundamental than that of commonality. This is the approach of those who perceive in human rights discourse a neocolonial, Western enterprise.[8]

Each approach, when released from the practical compromises of an ongoing enterprise, can push to an extreme. Pursuing the fundamental dignity and equality of each individual, claims of human rights can proliferate endlessly. In response to every need—food, health, work, education, and well-being more generally—some group is willing to formulate a claim of right. On the other hand, an approach that begins from the perception of difference can quickly dissolve into an extreme moral relativism. In this extreme form, there is no foundation from which one can gain sufficient purchase to make any compelling criticism of different cultures. Every criticism is thought to rest on a particular community's values; there is no way to make cross-cultural comparisons of value. To condemn another's practices is simply to produce a kind of tautological affirmation of one's own values.

Moral relativism, however, offers no more support for tolerance than for intolerance. From the fact of difference, nothing follows about whether to accept it or reject it. There may be no common ground upon which to justify condemnation, but neither is there a common ground upon which to justify acceptance.[9] Intervention may be an imposition of one's own values, but failure to intervene may be a violation of those values. For this reason, the same classical system

---

[8] See, e.g., Bangkok Declaration, adopted at the World Human Rights Conference Regional Preparatory Meeting (1993); M. Mutua, "Savages, Victims, and Saviors: The Metaphor of Human Rights," 42 *Harv. Int'l. L.J.* 201 (2001).

[9] See e.g., R. Rorty, "Human Rights, Rationality, and Sentimentality," in *On Human Rights: The Oxford Amnesty Lectures* 111 (S. Shute and S. Hurley, eds., 1995).

of international law that made state sovereignty a fundamental norm placed no legal constraint on the decisions of states to go to war. War and peace were matters of sovereign choice. The move from recognition of difference to intervention was not a large move at all.[10] Neither the universal nor the particular seems firm ground from which theory can direct practice.

Multiculturalism would not pose a problem if the plurality of values could simply be aggregated—like adding another wing to a museum. The problem of cultural difference is not like that of difference among cuisines, in which each culture values some distinct set of flavors and tastes. Rather, different cultures affirm values that others reject. Some reject what others insist upon as a matter of right—for example, gender equality. Affirmation and rejection are not abstractions. They invoke passions and these passions run into each other, sometimes in a violent way. Societies may be defined by their hatreds as much as by their attachments.

It is often difficult for Americans to know how to react to these social hatreds. Not only our religious traditions but also our political culture pursues a practice of proselytizing. Other people never appear as permanently alien; they appear instead as the object for our efforts at conversion. Of course, we have had—and still have—our own hatreds. Nevertheless, that history of hatred tends to be understood within a narrative of progressive toleration, accepting the hated group into the political community or into that larger community of nations with which we maintain friendly relations. We try to distinguish a people, capable of redemption, from its leadership, lost to evil. Our enemies regularly become our allies—for example, the Japanese and the Germans for the last generation, and today, the Russians.

Our contemporary missionaries preach democracy, free markets, and the rule of law—all institutions founded on our belief in the equality and liberty of every person. This dogged commitment to a universal community is a product of both our Christian and Enlightenment tra-

---

[10] This political antinomy had an epistemic reflection in the practice of ethnography, which formally suggested political indifference across boundaries, but posed a danger of offering ideological support for colonial exploitation. See A. Riles, "The Empty Place: Legal Formalities and the Cultural State," in *The Place of Law* (A. Sarat, ed., 2002).

ditions. We experience this commitment simultaneously as a kind of open-ended love and as a faith in the capacity of each individual to enter a rational debate that will result in mutual agreement. No one, we believe, is beyond conversion to our values. When we dream of a global order, we project our own values onto it. We do not imagine that the global community of the future will be led by an Islamic cleric.

Other cultures do not necessarily share this proselytizing attitude toward the alien other. They do not pursue a universal mission of either love or reason. Difference, for them, may not be understood as a problem to be overcome, but as a border establishing identity. Ours, after all, is an era marked by the simultaneous, but opposing, development of globalization and ethnic nationalism. From the latter perspective, Western universalism may appear as yet another form of cultural imperialism. For the West, the story of colonialism was one of Christian proselytizing and the progress of civilization; it was simultaneously a project of imperial destruction.[11]

We can retreat in the face of these problems to our own traditions and the limits of our own community. That community is now defined by those who accept our truths; that is, those who accept the conditions that limit the domain of tolerable difference. But this strategy just returns us to the very practical problem from which we started: the problem of cultural pluralism.[12] Normative systems are plural because there is no agreement about the substantive or procedural bases upon which they are constructed. Individual moral autonomy may be a bedrock first principle for us and an immoral denial of the primacy of a community of faith for others.

Are we forced to say either too much or too little? As long as we focus on difference itself, we cannot solve the problem. We will alternate between a rhetoric of the universal and a rhetoric of the particular, each of which can collapse into the other. Proving yet again that liberalism follows from a certain understanding of the autonomy of

[11] For a skeptical view of statements of Christian ends, see A. Hochschild, *King Leopold's Ghost* (1999); see also, E. Said, *Reflections on Exile and Other Essays* 411, 429 (2000).

[12] A good example is Huntington, *The Clash of Civilizations*, which begins by looking at geopolitical conflict, but is led to a critique of cultural pluralism within the United States.

the moral subject is hardly a convincing argument to those who accept neither that view of the subject nor the primacy of reason among the possible forms of argument. But for those who find that autonomy an obvious and undeniable first principle, no claims by the other— whether the parishioner, the communitarian or the multiculturalist— will shake that faith.

If arguments from first principles will always come too late because there is no agreement on these principles, how can we make any progress? Instead of searching for resources that are not already marked by their own culturally contingent character, we must directly confront the contingent character of our own position. Our ambition must be to create a space from within which to assess our own normative beliefs and practices, which include, but are hardly exhausted by, liberalism. This is not a neutral space from which to judge others, nor a space from within which we can pursue a program of reform. Its end is neither to make others like ourselves nor to remake ourselves. Rather, it is a space of suspended commitments from which to apprehend the self. Cultural pluralism is not a problem to be solved, as if we could finally articulate the *right* set of universal values or the appropriate scope of the particular. It is, instead, a warning that normative inquiry can no longer take the form of proscription, but must turn to self-exploration.[13]

CULTURAL STUDY AND LIBERALISM

Cultural difference is such a prominent problem today because it presses against some of the most basic assumptions of our own broadly liberal culture. My ambition is to expose these assumptions and show how they fail to account for central aspects of our experience of ourselves and of our relationship to the political community. The assumptions within which liberalism operates generate the familiar oppositions that have dominated modern political theory, including that between the universal and the particular, the public and the private, and reason and interest. None of these oppositions can be resolved

---

[13] I have developed this conception of self-exploration in P. Kahn, *The Cultural Study of Law: Reconstructing Legal Scholarship* (2000).

on its own terms. Part I of my inquiry exposes the structure of these oppositions, explains why they arise, and the particular content they assume in modern American political culture. Part II investigates what the debate framed by these oppositions leaves out or fails to see.

Most of all, liberalism fails to see the way in which citizens committed to American political culture occupy a meaningful world. It fails to see what I will describe as the erotic foundations of modern political life. We cannot understand the character of the relationship between self and polity without first understanding love. To understand love, however, we need to explore the character of the will in dimensions that are beyond the imagination of liberal thought. This linking of will to love, and both to meaning, expresses the Christian inheritance of our political tradition. This is Christianity not as a source of religious doctrine but as a form of understanding of self and community. Much of this study is an effort to explore the way in which our political life draws as much upon the Christian tradition of love and will as on the Enlightenment tradition of reason. Modern American political practices and beliefs have achieved a kind of stable synthesis of these two sources. That stability, I will argue in the conclusion, is under considerable stress today as the erotic conception of the citizen's body is displaced by a more plastic and disembodied conception of a subject who locates the self in a variety of networked relationships: economic, informational, and communicative. Many of the tensions in contemporary political life, and particularly the tension between the United States and its European allies, arise from the fact that Americans generally remain embedded in a modern conception of the citizen and the nation-state in an increasingly postmodern world.

To understand our own political culture, we need to begin by putting liberalism in its proper place. To put liberalism in its proper place, I need to emphasize, is not to put liberalism down or to dismiss its norms. I take for granted that most of my readers share—as I do—a commitment to basic liberal values. These include respect for the dignity and equality of individuals, a skepticism toward fixed hierarchies, broad acceptance of diverse social groupings whether religious or ethnic, a demand for representative government limited by a doctrine of individual rights embodied in a rule of law administered by courts, and a general sense of the need for well-regulated markets to satisfy material wants. These liberal values do not, however, explain the conditions that bind a community into one sustained historical project. They do not explain why citizens will put survival of a particular political community ahead of their own survival.

Liberal theorists tend to take the political community as given and set out to construct the rules that should operate within that community. Rather than look to the origins of the particular community, they are more likely to look to an original position that is a kind of prepolitical abstraction. The same failure to attend to the unity of the particular historical community leads many liberals—not just theoreticians—uncritically to accept the global reach of liberal norms, whether of legal rights or market transactions. All individuals, not just citizens, should live under conditions of equality and autonomy; all should have their rights respected and all should be able to participate in open markets and in the institutions of governance. The boundaries of the state often appear as a problem to be overcome.

To put liberalism in its proper place is to take up the question of the nature of the unity of the political community—in particular, of our political community. It is to turn from the rules of governance to the character of political meaning. Charles Taylor usefully labels this distinction as advocacy versus ontology.[14] Taylor notes that to criticize liberalism's understanding of the nature of the subject (the ontological perspective) does not commit one to a similar criticism of liberal politics (the advocacy perspective). In his terms, this is a work in political ontology. Yet the distinction is not without problems and offers only a rough approximation of the scope of the inquiry.

First, the terms suggest a kind of priority for the ontological, as if here we deal with the real or essential, while advocacy deals with the contingent or incidental. This is not a helpful way to understand the distinction. Liberalism generally ignores certain forms of commitment and beliefs, but they are no more real than that which it does see. At best, we are talking about different kinds of necessity, not an ontological priority in these different perspectives. We live our lives within symbolic domains; we never get beyond the categories of our own imaginations, whether we are speaking of who we are or what we

---

[14] See C. Taylor, "Cross-Purposes: The Liberal-Communitarian Debate," in *Liberalism and the Moral Life* 159 (N. Rosenblum, ed., 1989).

should do. Second, the distinction is consistently transgressed in both directions. Beliefs about the character of the subject and about policies reciprocally affect each other. The pursuit of liberal norms as a matter of advocacy may really have a tendency to build citizen character in the way liberals conceive of the self—as an autonomous subject who applies reason to individual choices. Conversely, belief that community relationships are constitutive of individual identity may lead to the advocacy of traditional values. My argument is not that the ontological character of the subject undermines the liberal project, but that the range of our beliefs and commitments is broader than the liberal project perceives. Third, the ontological, as I treat it, is better understood as the product of history than of being. We find ourselves with a certain range of possibilities because we are the bearers of particular historical traditions. While I do argue for some very abstract categories of self-understanding, the content of these categories is always a function of history. Ontology and genealogy are not separate inquiries.

Rather than speak of advocacy and ontology with respect to the political subject, I will speak of the rule of law and political sovereignty. The rule of law is the normative ideal of a liberal politics: it guarantees individual rights against the state, organizes and limits the exercise of state power, and provides the conditions for market transactions. Issues of advocacy concern the content and character of the norms given expression and life in the rule of law. Rights, markets, and limited government are transnational norms. The liberal discourse of law easily becomes a universal discourse, that is, the rule of law is not bound to a particular political space. Political sovereignty, on the other hand, is always bound to a particular community temporally and geographically. Claims of sovereignty reflect a community's understanding of itself as embodying a distinct set of meanings that are substantive not formal, realized at a particular historical moment, and limited to members. Traditionally, sovereignty was thought to precede law in two senses: first, the sovereign is the source of law; and second, sovereignty defines a political community, establishing the jurisdictional reach of law.[15] This is the sense in which sovereignty was thought an "ontological" condition of law.

---

[15] This conception of the relationship of sovereignty to law raises particular problems for international law. See P. Kahn, "American Hegemony and International

Contemporary liberal thought—particularly in the form of the human rights movement—has challenged both of these ontological claims: law is to be freed from sovereignty. But we will never understand the character of the American rule of law without first understanding the way in which it is embedded in a conception of popular sovereignty. More importantly, we will not understand the way in which the nation-state presents itself to the citizen as an ultimate value, that is, one for which the citizen may be asked to sacrifice his or her life. Liberal thought, as well as liberal politics, believes claims for sacrifice are exterior to the purposes and functions of a legitimate political arrangement—a kind of unfortunate, historical accident. I will argue that recognition of the possibility of sacrifice is at the base of our experience of the political and an adequate theory of our political beliefs must offer an explanation of sacrifice.

To speak of sovereignty—in the American case, popular sovereignty—is to speak of a relationship of meaning between the citizen and the community considered as a unified, historical subject. Our liberalism operates within this politics of meaning, but liberal theory lacks the conceptual tools by which to grasp this context. It lacks these tools because of its broad privileging of reason. It believes that political commitments as well as political order can and should be the products of reason. If not literally the products of reason, still our political arrangements should be tested against the standards of reason. Reason may grasp the content of the social contract, but it cannot grasp the erotic character of the experience of political meaning. Attachment to the political community is a matter not of contract but of love. That which we will do for love cannot always find its measure in justice. I do not mean to substitute a politics of sacrifice and love for one of reason and contract; this is not a work in advocacy. Rather, our politics already is one of love and sacrifice; reason finds its place within this experience of self and polity.

A religious analogy can help to clarify the distinction between law and sovereignty. In the Judeo-Christian tradition, God speaks the world into being. There is a difference between God's speaking and

Law—Speaking Law to Power: Popular Sovereignty, Human Rights, and the New International Order," 1 *Chi. J. Int'l Law* 1 (2000).

what it is that He says. To understand the religious experience of the world, we cannot simply dismiss the belief that it is God who spoke; we cannot concentrate only on the content of that speech. For Americans, the polity has its origin in the speech of the popular sovereign. That the sovereign speaks a language of the liberal rule of law does not mean that we can ignore the belief that it is the sovereign who speaks. Liberal theorists generally do just that: they focus on the content of the speech, that is, on what it is the sovereign said or should say. They do not reflect on the significance of the belief that it is the popular sovereign who does the speaking. If the idea of popular sovereignty arises at all, it tends to be equated with majority rule. That conception, however, is hardly adequate to the transhistorical idea of a people creating and maintaining itself. Voting is only a particular act, while participation in the popular sovereign is constitutive of the citizen's self-understanding.

In considering the problems of cultural pluralism, we have been the prisoners of liberalism. The approach of liberalism to difference has been to assume that the thinner the normative standard, the more universal its claim. We will have greater success in understanding the significance of cultural conflict if we start from the opposite end. A thicker description of our own normative order will put us in a better position from which to evaluate difference. Gaining this understanding of ourselves will not tell us directly what to do, as if the problem of theory is to work out a practical calculus of tolerance. But self-awareness is a necessary condition of avoiding the cultural imperialist's mistakes of the past—mistakes made even with the best of intentions—as well as the mistakes of that particular form of academic imperialist: the liberal theorist.

THE LIMITS OF THE LIBERAL SELF

While there is no single theory of liberalism, theories in the tradition share a core set of assumptions about the individual, the role of the polity, and the manner of constructing rules for both. Different liberal philosophers interpret these assumptions differently, and they assign different weights to different aspects of this core. Still, none would place faith above reason in the construction of public norms; none would affirm that some individuals are worth less than others; and all agree that individuals must be relatively free to set for themselves their own conception of the good. Liberal theorists believe in the primacy of autonomous individuals who share a capacity for rational deliberation but do not necessarily share a common set of interests. For most liberal theorists, the autonomous individual always has the capacity to redefine the relationship to his or her culture.[16] Of course, a liberal state need not support equally every individual's conception of the good, and liberal theorists disagree on the appropriate limits of state recognition and support of these diverse conceptions.

Apart from their commitment to autonomy and dignity, liberal theorists also see a world of individuals competing under conditions of moderate scarcity to satisfy their own interests.[17] Scarcity means that individuals of necessity share a common world; they must regulate themselves and deal with others. Unless individuals can take up the perspective of reason, which means temporarily to bracket one's own immediate interests as a source of direction for the will, there will be only competition and chaos. To bracket interest and pursue the common perspective of reason is not, however, to abandon the self. For reason expresses that virtue of the self most emphasized by the modern, liberal theorist. Reason supports autonomy, dignity, and public deliberation, on the one hand, and the liberal philosopher's pursuit of theory, on the other. The centrality of reason means that liberal practice and liberal theory are continuous activities.

My concern in this book is not to elaborate the rich variations on these themes that liberal philosophers have pursued with great creativity—especially since the publication in 1971 of John Rawls's *A Theory of Justice*. Rawls himself struggled to refine his position over the years. While the refinements may improve the theory, they do not improve on his first book's translation of the liberal core of the culture into a philosophical position. *A Theory of Justice* reached a kind of "reflec-

[16] But see C. Larmore, *The Morals of Modernity*, chap. 7 (1996) (arguing that political liberalism must not take a position on the capacity for individual self-definition). In general, however, even those varieties of liberalism concerned with the importance of culture insist on the need for an exit option. See, e.g., W. Kymlicka, *Multicultural Citizenship: A Liberal Theory of Minority Rights* 152–53 (1995).

[17] See, e.g., B. Ackerman, *Social Justice in the Liberal State* 31–33 (1980); J. Rawls, *A Theory of Justice* 127 (1971) (on moderate scarcity); D. Hume, *A Treatise on Human Nature* 486–88 (L. A. Selby-Bigge, ed., [1739] 1951) (on the circumstances of justice.)

tive equilibrium" with the broadly intuited norms of our liberal culture.[18] For that reason, it remains the most important work in political theory of the last fifty years. Many of my examples of liberal attitudes will, therefore, be drawn from Rawls, supplemented by other prominent liberal theorists, including Habermas and Ackerman. All three stand squarely in the Enlightenment tradition, with its faith in reason's capacity to generate a just public order. All three are particularly concerned with the role of reason as public discourse in the liberal polity.

Liberal theory aims to set forth the course of reasonable deliberation that autonomous individuals should pursue in order to give institutional structure and procedural coherence to a common political life. Modern liberal theorists, such as Rawls, Habermas, and Ackerman, often support their claims to normative objectivity by modeling an ideal discourse. Each believes that if he can properly set the conditions of this discourse, then all rational beings will agree with the results.[19] The universal character of the norms that emerge is, therefore, limited only by the particularity of the conditions within which the discourse proceeds. The more generally applicable those conditions, the more universal the norms. Again, this is not the only form of contemporary liberal theory, but it is the dominant form. That, I hope to show, is because it resonates with broadly accepted beliefs about the role of reason in the life of the individual and the state.

Liberalism is a political view that rests on a moral epistemology. It combines a theory of reason and a conception of interest to construct a political world divided between the private and the public. My ambition is to put liberalism in its place by juxtaposing to it other normative strands of our culture that I hope the reader will sympathetically recognize. It is, in other words, to shift the point of reflective equilibrium in a way that allows us better to comprehend the place of liberalism in our self-understanding. My most fundamental claim is that liberalism lacks an adequate conception of the will. This may seem a

---

[18] See Rawls, *Theory of Justice* at 48–51 (on reflective equilibrium).

[19] See *ibid* 138 ("To say that a certain conception of justice would be chosen in the original position is equivalent to saying that rational deliberation satisfying certain conditions and restrictions would reach a certain conclusion."); J. Habermas, *Knowledge and Human Interests* 284 (J. Shapiro, trans., 1971) (collective life must be organized "according to the principle that the validity of every norm of political consequence be made dependent on a consensus arrived at in communication free from domination"); B. Ackerman, *Social Justice in the Liberal State* 4–12 (1980).

strange claim, given that so much of liberalism is built around a model of contract—the social contract, as well as market contracts. Contract, after all, seems to be nothing other than a formalization and stabilization of the individual's will. Liberalism does indeed model its understanding of the will on the paradigm of contract. But this is just the problem. The liberal will is fundamentally without content. When we speak of the social contract, the content of the will comes from reason. When we speak of market contracts, that content comes from interest. The liberal will is a kind of second-order faculty, affirming a relationship either to an object or to others that has its source and justification in these faculties of reason and interest. On this view, the will attaches to the products of reason or the objects of desire, but has nothing of its own to add.[20]

Opposed to this liberal idea of an empty will is a tradition in which the will refers to an experience that combines the universal quality of reason and the particularity of interest, but which is not reducible to either. Reason leads us beyond our particularity to a domain of abstract ideas in which the uniqueness of the self is either irrelevant or a distraction. Interest, on the other hand, leads us in just the opposite direction: our interests have no truth apart from our particularity. Like interest, will is linked to the individual, finite being. There is no abstract or universal will. But will is not exhausted in the particularity of the individual. The will is the faculty by which, or through which, we understand ourselves as participants in a meaningful world. This is not a world of abstract ideas, but rather one in which ideas are always attached to particular subjects. The domain of this conception of the will is history, which refers equally to a meaningful past and a significant future; it is neither the timelessness of reason, nor the present of interest.

We are most familiar with this conception of the will in its Christian form: the will is the faculty that makes possible the experience of

---

[20] See R. Flathman, *Willful Liberalism: Voluntarism and Individuality in Political Theory and Practice* 145 (1992). ("Difficult as it is to find postmedieval philosophers who do not regularly employ the term *will* and its cognates in discussing human action, officially or programmatically many of them treat it as no more than a name for other (putatively?) more tangible things such as desires, intentions, or dispositions, or they seek to banish it altogether.")

grace. This is the will as a capacity to experience an ultimate or transcendent value as an historical experience in the world. Neither reason nor interest provides access to a world that shows itself as an image and product of the divine. Through the will we do not transcend the world, yet we find ourselves in a world of transcendent value. In our own revolutionary-constitutional tradition, we project this conception of the will onto the popular sovereign. The sovereign will, we say, is the source of law, and indeed of the nation itself. To identify with the popular sovereign is to understand the self in and through will. It is to read the self—quite literally the finite body—as a point of access to, and expression of, the nation, which confronts us as an ultimate value. This is never a matter of abstract reason or of the particularity of interest. Neither can account for our sense of the nation as a unique historical actor, nor of ourselves as participants in this political project that has both a privileged past and a necessary future.

The experience of the will is of the idea become flesh, or of the body as the expression of an idea. For the will, the body is a point of revelation of a meaning that simultaneously defines the self and is greater than the self. Thus, will is intimately connected to love. In love, the body appears neither as end nor as means, but an instantiation of meaning. Love locates the infinite in the particular; love expresses a faith in a world that embodies a transcendent meaning. This is why Plato can describe love as daimon, mediating between the gods and the merely mortal.[21] The world constructed by the will is miraculous; it is one in which every object can take on an infinite value. This is a world of faith, which liberal theory sees only as a threat to the order of reason. While liberal theory would cabin faith within the domain of the private, this cannot be true of the faith that holds together the public world of politics.

Religion, politics, and love all demand an understanding of the will that is simply unavailable in the liberal tradition. The reason at the center of liberalism rapidly becomes a demand that one's actions and one's demands be reasonable.[22] Reasonable means moderate and

---

[21] See Plato, *Symposium* 202E.

[22] One sees this movement quite literally in Rawls. In 1971, he claims that his work is "a part of a theory of rational decision" (*A Theory of Justice* at 16). Twenty years

reciprocal: one must offer fair terms of cooperation to others, which requires a willingness to abide by a common set of standards. A will in thrall to the infinite is not easily bound by the reasonable. Neither religious belief nor love is reasonable. Neither, in the end, are our political practices. They too are founded on faith. In all of these cases, we are claimed in ways that cannot be contained by the reasonable.

Politics, even the politics of a liberal state, remains a deeply erotic phenomenon. The state makes a claim upon us that we perceive as one of ultimate meaning. Quite literally, we can be conscripted by the state: it can demand of us that we sacrifice the self for the maintenance of the political community. To comprehend this experience, we need more than the philosopher's conception of reason, and more than the economist's conception of interest. Indeed, we will need more than the communitarian's idea of community: not just any community can demand sacrifice. We will have to trace the way in which the history of the popular sovereign has displaced, while borrowing from, the revelatory character of the Judeo-Christian God. We will have to examine as well the erotic character of the political.

To understand what is at stake for us in the current controversy over multiculturalism, we must confront some very *unliberal* experiences of the self and the polity. This is not a work for the faint-hearted liberal who lacks the ability to push him or herself beyond the polite boundaries of rational discourse, on the one hand, and the individualism of interest on the other. My aim is to bring us face to face with an idea of the politics of the will that presents an ultimate value and demands of us that we be willing to sacrifice. I want to bring liberalism back into touch with our forgotten ultimates, and in the process offer a thicker description of our own ethical and political practices. A liberal conception of interest must be set within a richer understanding of love, just as the liberal conception of politics as contract must be set within an understanding of politics as sacrifice. Love and sacrifice are the terms within which we conduct a meaningful life. Politics hardly exhausts the domain of love and sacrifice, but it does compete with other understandings of the self within love's domain.

---

later, he disavows this claim, saying now that his effort is only to provide "an account of reasonable principles of justice" (J. Rawls, *Political Liberalism* at 53n.7 [1993]).

Contemporary liberal theorists might respond that their position is political, not metaphysical, and that the liberalism of a political order hardly exhausts the set of values that individuals find compelling.[23] There are two problems with this position. First, liberal political theory is narrower than our liberal culture. Liberal theory is attractive because it emphasizes core elements of the liberal culture—for example, a commitment to reason and individual autonomy. While careful theory pushes no further than it believes it can justify, liberals generally push those same values much further. Liberal theory may try to avoid a comprehensive liberalism, but liberals do not. Second, liberal theorists are generally content not to explore the other values—that is, nonliberal values—for which they leave room. But these values are just as much a part of our political life as are liberal values. Failure to explore these other political values will leave us with a distorted image of the character of our commitment to the political.

I hope to plot the shape of the world of meaning that I find all around me.[24] To do so, I draw on a wide variety of sources—myth, literature, history, law, and political theory. Some may object that those sources include the thought of that most illiberal of political philosophers, Carl Schmitt. Schmitt's categories of friend and enemy, as well as his insistence on the autonomy of the political, are useful tools in exploring those aspects of political experience that are beyond the reach of liberalism. Liberal theorists have been so concerned with the problem of internal coercion—that is, the government's exercise of force against citizens—that they have failed to focus on the ways in which our politics remains deeply enmeshed in war and the threat of war.[25] Citizens understand themselves not just in terms of a legal order

[23] See J. Rawls, "Justice as Fairness: Political not Metaphysical," 14 *Philosophy and Public Affairs* 223 (1985); but compare S. Okun, "Reply," in *Is Multiculturalism Bad for Women?* 129–30 (J. Cohen et al., eds., 1999).

[24] Personally, I have little taste for the politics of faith and sacrifice that I believe to be constitutive of an American culture of popular sovereignty. My own beliefs in this regard, however, are as irrelevant to the analysis as my own religious beliefs are to understanding the nature of Christian or Jewish faith.

[25] Contemporary theorists who have appealed to Schmitt have tried to "tame" his friend-enemy distinction into a description of opposition within a democratic debate, that is, they have tried to deploy Schmitt within liberalism's preferred model of politics as speech. See, e.g., C. Mouffe, *The Democratic Paradox* (2000). My appropriation

of rights, but also as potential instruments of state violence against others—or targets of that violence from others. This is all the more evident today when many believe that it is our liberalism that has made us the political enemy of various terrorist groups around the world.

By bringing liberalism into contact with Schmitt, I mean not to undermine liberal practices, but rather to expand our horizon of understanding. Schmitt can be read as celebrating a violent politics, which he took to be a more authentic experience than ordinary political practices. I think our politics continues to demand sacrifice, and it is all too often violent. I don't, however, celebrate these aspects of our experience. Nevertheless, I do insist that we confront the character of our political faith. Our faith in popular sovereignty does not make us indifferent to the liberal content of the rule of law. Law and popular sovereignty exist in a reciprocal relationship. Our faith in the popular sovereign is to some extent a function of the law it speaks. Were the law to appear to us regularly to violate our deepest moral commitments, we could lose faith in the popular sovereign. Something like this was true for those radical abolitionists who declared the Constitution to be a "covenant with death and an agreement with hell."[26] On the other hand, our faith in popular sovereignty makes us broadly tolerant of a legal order that never quite meets our moral standards.

While the structure of Schmitt's theory of the political offers a useful set of concepts, the content of his theory is not similarly useful. He believed that sovereignty had to be based on some prepolitical conception of a people's substantive homogeneity. The recent rise in ethnic nationalism is surely a warning that there are still real dangers in this direction. But American political experience has been directly to the contrary. Here, the popular sovereign brings itself into existence in the distinctly political acts of revolution and constitutional construction. Our conception of popular sovereignty has had to be adequate to a nation of diverse immigrant groups and diverse faiths. For Americans, popular sovereignty is always linked to the rule of law. Indeed, apart from revolution, the only act of which the popular sovereign is capable

---

of Schmitt is more radical. Politics, I argue in chap. 6, is not just speech, but the action that succeeds speech.

[26] See William Lloyd Garrison, Resolution adopted by the Antislavery Society, Jan. 27, 1843.

is the making of law. Conversely, all law must show itself, directly or indirectly, as the speech of the popular sovereign. Without that, what purports to be law is only "action under the color of law"; it is unconstitutional. More than theory is at stake here, for if we allow liberalism to block our view of this political experience of popular sovereignty, we will not comprehend the nature of the law in what may be an emerging American Empire. Nor will we understand our deepest disagreements with our old European friends or our new enemies.[27]

WHAT IS TO COME

My project necessarily moves back and forth between the abstract and the concrete, between theoretical structure and cultural practice. This is an advantage the legal theorist has over the political philosopher: to study law is to study ideas as they are actually used to structure the polity and resolve controversies. The judicial opinion is always a set of ideas embedded in a particular context. Each shapes the other; each sets the conditions for the possibility of the other.[28] From the perspective of the legal scholar, much of political theory has about it a disturbing abstractness. The close connection between liberalism and liberal theory seems to unleash the theoretician to imagine ever more refined conceptions of political justice, as if the point of scholarship were to get the rules right. But, as I will argue in chapter 6, political life is much more than a set of rules: it is a practice of life and death. Life and death continue to hang over American political life, but they remain far out of sight in the work of contemporary political theory. They are, however, very much on view in constitutional law. To study constitutional jurisprudence is to come face to face with claims of national security, of compelling national interest, of the power of the state in both its external and internal dimensions.

I am aware that my argument is not easy to follow. Our liberalism is a cultural practice drawing on a vast amount of conceptual material—philosophical and theological—that is itself a part of a larger, Western

---

[27] See Kahn, "American Hegemony."

[28] See R. Dworkin, *Law's Empire* 225–28 (1986) (on legal interpretation as deploying both moral theory and contextualized "fit").

cultural practice. It is also a response to very specific historical conditions. I explore the historically contingent character of that which appears to be a priori truth for us: the autonomous character of the individual, the privileged place of reason, and a government that respects the distinction between the private and the public. These elements have a history as well as a conceptual shape. The broad character of the inquiry, its historical sweep, and its crossing of genres—history, law, religion, literature, and philosophy—are as likely to frustrate as to fascinate the reader. I hope that these diverse forms of inquiry all work to provide support for a few common themes. I have tried to hold the argument together by providing summaries at the start of each section, in the conclusion, and in the sketch of the argument that immediately follows.

Part I applies the methodological techniques of cultural study to our liberalism: its conceptual architecture must be mapped; a genealogy of its central categories must be developed.[29] Chapter 1 explores the conceptual architecture of liberalism by examining the debate between liberal theorists and their communitarian critics over the last generation. To understand the world within which liberalism is *a* possibility, we have to understand the conceptual architecture of liberalism *and* its critics. The multiculturalists have succeeded the communitarians in the role of critics. Together, communitarianism and liberalism took up two sides of a single antinomy of meaning, which understands the subject as simultaneously bound to and transcending context. Liberals systematically privilege one side of this antinomy; communitarians the other. The same antinomy is at issue today in the debate with the multiculturalists. Chapter 1 aims to show that this debate is not open to a resolution on its own terms; each side is irretrievably bound to the others. The antinomy, I argue, is rooted in the in the very structure of language.

Chapter 2 offers a genealogy of the practice of American liberalism. I explore the resources out of which American liberalism is constructed and demonstrate that these actually support two different forms of liberalism: a liberalism of faith and a liberalism of speech.

[29] I have discussed this methodology in detail in P. Kahn, *The Cultural Study of Law: Reconstructing the Legal Scholarship* 41–43 (1999).

These point in quite different directions: one privileges the private, the other the public; one privileges the particularism of faith, the other the universalism of reason. American legal and political culture has never resolved the deep tension between these forms. Our ambiguous attitude toward difference—shifting between tolerance and universalism—reflects this deeper ambiguity in our liberalism. This chapter also traces the way in which American liberalism has had to maintain an awkward relationship with an experience of our politics as a source of ultimate value. Liberalism has served as a kind of creed. Every creed derives its symbolic energy not from its specific content, but from the identification of the individual with the underlying social reality. As Americans, we are liberal. It is not because we are liberal that we are Americans.

The method of chapters 1 and 2 is designed to illuminate from within "the historical a priori"—a concept I borrow from Michel Foucault.[30] Bernard Williams gives voice to this same methodological ambition when he writes of an inquiry into freedom:

> [T]hese various conceptions or understandings of freedom, including the ones we need for ourselves, involve a complex historical deposit. . . . That contingent historical deposit, which makes freedom what it now is, cannot be contained in anything that could be called a definition. It is the same here as it is with other values: philosophy, or as we might say a priori anthropology, can construct a core or skeleton, or basic structure to the value, but both what it has variously become, and what we now need it to be, must be a function of actual history.[31]

When he speaks of "a priori anthropology" constructing a "core," he is referring to what I have termed "architectural inquiry." That, however, will not get us to the cultural phenomena of interest. For that, we have to take up what he calls "the contingent historical deposit," or what I have called "genealogy"—the methodological point is the same.

---

[30] See M. Foucault, *The Order of Things* xx–xxii (1970); *The Archaeology of Knowledge* 127 (A. Smith, trans., 1972).

[31] B. Williams, "From Freedom to Liberty: The Construction of a Political Value," 30 *Philosophy and Public Affairs* 3, 4 (2001).

Chapter 3 takes up the results of the inquiry into the historical a priori and asks whether they can form the basis for a stable and adequate conception of politics. It focuses on the role of reason in delineating the public order and the distinction of the private from the public. These critical elements of the liberal project are shown to fail: the discourse of reason becomes a discourse of the body; the political always seems to bridge the private and the public. The conceptual apparatus of liberalism is incommensurate with the experience of the political. Liberalism offers a theory of political order, but liberalism cannot understand the conditions of the political upon which it depends. In our political life, we affirm liberal values, but liberalism fails as a theory of politics.

Part II offers a positive account of self and politics, within which liberalism must find its place. The fundamental problem with the liberal conception of the soul is that it is far too thin an account of our own experience. Chapter 4 switches the psychological inquiry from a focus on reason to a focus on meaning—that is, meaning for us. Here, I explicitly develop an alternative theory of the will to replace the liberal conception of will as contract. This is the pivotal point of the book. Prior to this, my technique is essentially critical. From this point forward, I offer a positive account of the shape of our experience within this dimension of the will. Chapter 4 makes this transition by demonstrating that liberalism fails as a theory of politics because it substitutes contract for sacrifice.

Chapters 5 and 6 develop this richer account of ourselves and of our politics based on the idea of the will. They start not from the perspective of reason but from that of meaning. The question of meaning is inevitably a question of identity. Chapter 5 takes up the problem of individual identity, love, and chapter 6 that of collective identity, politics. Together, they develop a conception of the will as the psychological faculty that places us in a meaningful world.

Meaning, I argue, is never a matter of abstract ideas alone. Rather, it is experienced in and through the body. Meaning is not of the body, but it is certainly in the body. The body is "read" as the expression of an idea. The primary terms of this reading of ourselves involve love and politics, both of which are characterized by sacrifice. We know who we are when we know the concerns for which we are willing to sacrifice. These are all ideas beyond the capacity of liberalism to understand or even to recognize. Nevertheless, these have been the terms within which we have lived our political lives—even as we appealed to liberal values in structuring our law and institutions. The ambition of this part is not to offer an answer to the problem of cultural difference, but to illuminate from within the character of *our own* cultural difference. Even a liberal political order is still a political order. Our liberalism must be informed by a better understanding of our politics.

Having achieved a better understanding of ourselves as political—and not just liberal—actors, I turn again to the problems of cultural pluralism in the conclusion. Here, I argue two points. First, we are presently seeing a challenge to that political self-understanding, which put sovereignty before law. Second, it is too early to know whether that challenge will succeed.

The traditional forms of political participation in the sovereign through the logic of sacrifice have been substantially challenged, if not displaced, by a politics of rights. In the last decade, there has been a kind of human rights triumphalism, marked by the emergence of new transnational institutions that are not compatible with the idea of political sovereignty, upon which the modern nation-state rested. Whether one believes this development to be good or bad, its presence is undeniable. It is part of the general movement of globalization, its legal face.

These new political formations are reciprocally linked to new understandings of the self. The network has joined with the market in opening ever further possibilities of a fluid identity, on the one hand, and a cosmopolitan conception of the self, on the other. The political rhetoric of sovereignty and sacrifice, the idea that political identity offers a source of ultimate meaning, is a language that no longer speaks to the condition of many citizens. The rule of law does, but this is law severed from its connection to sovereignty. This emerging networked self is not sufficiently bound to any single conception of the content to respond to a claim for sacrifice. Rather, individual subjectivity appears as a project—increasingly one of global dimensions. Multiculturalism, as both a descriptive and normative concept within a broadly liberal culture, occupies this space made possible by a conception and a technology of the self that can be simultaneously global and local. Cultural pluralism as a threat to liberalism marks a deep division of attitudes toward this fluid conception of the self.

What remains wholly indeterminate, however, is whether this postmodern displacement of a politics of ultimate meaning will lead to the rise of other forms of ultimate meaning, to understand which we again need to consider the structure of eros and the will. Political forms may be more contingent than the erotic foundation upon which they build. Our increasingly depoliticized age has, for example, been marked by new investments of ultimate meanings in a child-centered ideal of the family, in fundamentalist faith, and in ethnic communities. None of these are consistent with the ideal of the liberal subject, but each may be compatible with a liberal rule of law. We are simultaneously living in an age marked by the free flow of information on the Internet and by fundamentalist faith. Contrary to the expectations of many liberals—contrary, as well, to the fears of many religious communities—the former has not undermined the latter.

It is much too early, however, to proclaim the triumph of a networked self that takes up its own subjectivity as a project carried out within a global order of law, markets, and information. The contemporary phenomenon of depoliticalization may itself be coming to an end, as we find ourselves returning to a more traditional politics of friends and enemies. Symbolically, this return was marked by the attack of September 11, 2001, and the American turn to war in response. The contemporary Western state—particularly the United States—may be simultaneously undergoing an internal depoliticization and an external repoliticization. This is not a question of the scope of the "coalition of the willing," but of a realignment of political identity that reflects—and indeed coopts—the new fluidity of the self represented by markets and networks. This new understanding of the networked self may be forced into a revitalized distinction between self and other. That very fluidity may come to define a Western subject in which we invest a politics of ultimate meaning: We are a people of the Internet. That too may be a powerful political idea, separating friends from enemies. The result will not be the death of politics, but it may very well be the end of the nation-state as we have understood it for the last two hundred years. Political meanings may remain no less vital even as the geography of the political may be shifting.

Finally a word on the scope of the inquiry. Just as it would be wrong to claim that this study illuminates universal attributes of the Western soul, it would be wrong to think the account is wholly particular to American practices and beliefs. American practices and beliefs are contingent, but they nevertheless occupy a conceptual space made possible by the broad reach of Western history, theory, and language. Much that is at stake here is similarly at stake in other modern Western states. Major themes here, however, may appear as minor themes elsewhere, and vice versa. Comparative work remains for future volumes.[32]

[32] See P. Kahn, "Comparative Constitutionalism in a New Key," 101 *U. Mich. L. Rev.* 2677 (2003).

PART I

■ ■ ■ ■

CULTURAL STUDY AND LIBERALISM

Liberalism has at least three different senses. First, it refers to a family of political theories. These extend across a wide range bounded by libertarianism, on one side, and social-welfare theories on the other. Second, liberalism refers to a partisan political practice. In this sense, we contrast liberals with conservatives. Opponents at this level may find their disagreements actually stem from their support of different liberal philosophies. Even conservative politicians may support a liberal political theory. Third, liberalism refers to a political culture that has neither the sophistication of a theory nor the partisanship of a political party. This is the sense in which we speak of American political culture—or, more generally, of the West—as liberal. Liberalism in this third sense characterizes values and institutions both private and public; this liberalism provides the context within which both liberal theory and liberal partisanship operate.[1]

There are reciprocal relations among all three levels. Liberal theory, for example, is an effort to understand an ongoing set of practices within a liberal society, just as partisan political battles can be efforts to realize ideals clarified by, or even derived from, liberal theory. Starting at any one level, an investigation of liberalism is likely to be pulled across the others as well. Nevertheless, my concern in this work is primarily with the third level: liberalism as a cultural phenomenon. By this I do not mean culture in the sense of popular culture, but in that broader sense in which our law, our political rhetoric, and our

[1] See R. Unger, *Knowledge and Politics* 6 (1975). ("Liberalism must be seen as all of a piece, not just as a set of doctrines about the opposition of power and wealth, but as a metaphysical conception of the mind and society.")

political philosophies all contribute to an expression of who we are and what we stand for. Literature and art, as well as popular culture, also operate here. My point of access to our liberal culture, however, is through law, history, philosophy, and religion. These are not the only possible points of access; they are only those with which I am most familiar.

In the first two chapters, I bring the methodological tools of culture study to the task of understanding our liberalism. In the first chapter, I trace the conceptual architecture of our liberalism. Liberalism occupies a position within a schema that organizes thought about the self and its relationship to the polity. The liberal position is deliberative or self-conscious; it is understood as the product of choices made within a horizon of alternative possibilities. Of course, many liberals believe these are the right choices, because they follow from a correct understanding of the nature of the self. These beliefs, however, are always contested. A liberal political culture stands opposed to the illiberal; the liberal's understanding of the autonomous character of self is held in opposition to an understanding of the self as embedded or constituted by relationships that are always already in place.[2]

Accordingly, to understand the architecture of liberal belief, we have to understand this broader context within which liberalism finds itself. Chapter 1 describes that architecture as a set of dichotomies: reason/unreason, autonomy/heteronomy, public/private. Liberalism provides a normative ordering within each pair by privileging the subject's capacity to separate self from context and to re-form the self on the basis of deliberative choice. The opponents of liberalism, on the other hand, privilege context over choice—that is, the already formed self over a critical capacity for reform. One way to expose this architectural structure is to turn briefly to the debate between the communitarians and liberals, which dominated the political theory of the 1980s and 1990s. This is a particularly appropriate starting point not only because it illustrates possible locations within this architectural structure, but also because it prefigures the contemporary debate between the liberal universalists and the cultural pluralists.

---

[2] See S. Holmes, *The Anatomy of Antiliberalism* (1993).

Chapter 2 traces the genealogy of American liberalism deep into the Christian past. That past extends well beyond the idea of religious liberty that emerges out of the sectarian wars of the Reformation. Liberalism carries forward the deeper idea that ultimate truth is to be found in a turning away from politics. That turning away of the soul—toward God—is the source of liberalism's radical egalitarianism. But if liberalism bears the imprint of Christ on the cross, it equally bears that of the church, which offers the first and most successful paradigm for linking institutional expression to an ideology. Christianity simultaneously turns away from this world and restructures this world as an expression of faith. A similar ambiguity of a turning away from, and a turning toward, the state provides competing elements of our faith in liberalism. In the New World, this double-inheritance from Christianity takes on a new form. Approached genealogically, American liberalism is seen to have as much to do with the Protestant experience of exile into the wilderness as with the liberal philosophers of the Enlightenment, whether John Locke or Immanuel Kant.

Chapter 3 completes the inquiry of part I by taking a more critical stance. Having elaborated the architecture and genealogy of liberal belief, I argue that there is a disequlibrium between those beliefs and the character of our political practices and beliefs. The fundamental categories of liberalism do not help us to understand the character of our own experience of political meaning. The consequence of this disequlibrium is not just the unresolvable debate between communitarians and liberals, but a similar sort of unsettling dialectic among all of liberalism's fundamental concepts: the private/public distinction, and the separation of reason from interest. Because liberalism and its critics are bound to each other as constitutive aspects of a single world, the problems of liberalism cannot be met simply by turning to its communitarian or multiculturalist critics. The positive work of reconstruction requires exploration of the development of a set of concepts that are not accountable to reason and beyond the range of most of the communitarian discourse: love, sacrifice, and will. These are the subjects of part II.

CHAPTER 1

■ ■ ■ ■

THE ARCHITECTURE OF
THE LIBERAL WORLD

Our ability to engage in moral deliberation suffers from the success
of liberalism. That success has left us with a moral language too im-
poverished to recognize what is at stake when we confront extreme
differences in cultural norms. This should not be surprising, since
the end of liberalism is to create a form of public discourse in which
these differences would have no significance. This is the ambition behind the effort to theorize from the perspective of Rawls's original
position. From the point of view of this imagined discourse, differences are literally of no interest; they cannot even be seen. But, of
course, they are exactly what is of most interest from the point of view
of an individual life.

Consider what cannot be said in the Rawlsian original position.
Excluded are any references to one's family, religion, or community—
or even to one's conception of oneself as a unique subject with specific
ambitions or a life plan.[3] Nothing can be said that could not be said
by everyone: "[S]ince the differences among the parties are unknown
to them, and everyone is equally rational and similarly situated, each
is convinced by the same arguments."[4] The scope of expression of this
"everyman" is bounded by undifferentiated physical need, on the one
hand, and by reason, on the other. Anyone who cannot strip himself
down to this position of bare rationality and undifferentiated need
is excluded; he is "unreasonable." Unreasonableness appears as nothing less than a form of prejudice. Worse, it is an intolerant privileging of the self, which is the source of all prejudice. Thus, "the veil of

---

[3] See J. Rawls, *A Theory of Justice* 137 (1971).
[4] *Ibid.* 139.

ignorance prevents the parties from invoking inappropriate reasons, given the aim of representing citizens as free and equal persons."[5] Representation here does not mean acting in consideration of interests. Rather, this is representation as synecdoche. The voice of the original position represents by virtue of being that of everyman. "[W]e can view the choice in the original position from the standpoint of one person selected at random."[6]

The person in the original position is everyone and anyone because he is no one in particular. He is nothing more than a capacity to express reason itself. Reasonableness, one might say, is a transcendental condition of the individual who is a citizen of the liberal state. A reasonable person is ready to imagine himself in the original position, from which he will rationally derive the basic conditions and structures of fair cooperation in the society.[7] The question, then, becomes which aspects of the individual self will be allowed back into the political community once the original position is left. The burden of justification arises at the moment of differentiation. This is also the moment at which the subject gains an identity beyond that common identity of pure practical reason. The reach of liberal tolerance is defined by the limits of justification at just this point.

Toleration, on this approach, is not the outcome of a discursive encounter among diverse individuals or groups.[8] Rather, the boundaries of toleration are already present before any differentiation is even recognized. The result, however, is that we never get beyond the starting point. Liberal theory becomes a closed circle of discourse among those already committed to liberalism—in Rawls's terms, among those who maintain comprehensive doctrines open to the demand of reasonableness.[9] Theory can help to elaborate the demands

[5] J. Rawls, *The Law of Peoples* 31 (1999).

[6] J. Rawls, *A Theory of Justice* 139.

[7] See J. Rawls, *Political Liberalism* 50 (1993) ("Reasonable persons . . . desire for its own sake a social world in which they, as free and equal, can cooperate with others on terms all can accept.")

[8] Compare, for example, J. Tully, *Strange Multiplicity: Constitutionalism in an Age of Diversity* (1995).

[9] See Rawls, *The Law of Peoples*, 54–57; see also S. Fish, "Mission Impossible: Settling the Just Bounds Between Church and State," 97 *Colum. L. Rev.* 2255 (1997).

and obligations that liberals should recognize in their mutual dealings, but it has literally nothing to say to those whose beliefs are illiberal. Awareness of radical difference may prompt the inquiry, yet the inquiry itself never seems to get to the point of recognition of just those differences.

This closed character of liberal tolerance is present not just in the voice of the Rawlsian original position, but more surprisingly in contemporary multicultural critics of liberalism. The three most important defenders of multiculturalism against traditional liberalism—all Canadian—are Charles Taylor, William Kymlicka, and James Tully.[10] Taylor and Kymlicka insist that the only cultural minorities that merit political recognition and legal protection are those that extend and protect liberal values of autonomy and equality within their own communities.[11] Both would allow the polity to advance a particular conception—or conceptions—of the good, to privilege certain cultural practices over others, and to extend unequal treatment to diverse groups. Both seek to protect cultural goods from the potential homogenizing effects of liberal egalitarianism. Taylor does so in the name of a communitarian critique of liberalism; Kymlicka in the name of liberalism's commitment to individual self-realization. Both believe that individual identity is constituted in and through communal discourse and that the political order neither can nor should be neutral with respect to the communities it encompasses. Both argue that group recognition comes with a parallel demand for individual respect. That is, the cost of political recognition for a culture or group is toleration of its internal dissenters and, thus, an openness to change. That one reaches this position as a communitarian and the other as a liberal tells us a good deal about the reciprocal character of these categories.

("All of liberalism's efforts to accommodate or [to] tame illiberal forces fail, either by underestimating and trivializing the illiberal impulse, or by mirroring it.")

[10] W. Kymlicka, *Multicultural Citizenship: A Liberal Theory of Minority Rights* (1995); C. Taylor, "The Politics of Recognition," in C. Taylor et al., *Multiculturalism: Examining the Politics of Recognition* 25 (A. Gutmann, ed., 1994); Tully, *Strange Multiplicity.*

[11] W. Kymlicka, *Liberalism, Community and Culture* 182–205 (1989); Taylor, *Multiculturalism* at 59–61.

Taylor speaks of the minimal conditions of individual justice that must be met even by a community that pursues a culturally specific good: these are rights of the minority to reasonable treatment and recognition of their own distinct pursuit of a good different from that of the majority.[12] A thin, or minimalist, liberalism must be the background political condition against which communitarian claims operate. Kymlicka finds the justification for recognition of cultural diversity in the claim that only within a societal culture can individuals realize life projects of their own. Liberalism's own commitment to individual self-realization, accordingly, demands recognition and protection of group claims. Because culture is protected for the sake of individual development, a culture that fails to advance individual freedom has no prima facie claim upon us.[13] But what if the problem of difference arises not as a conflict among liberal societies, but with respect to liberal values themselves?

Tully promises much more. Focusing on the relationship of the majority community to Native American communities, he rejects the claim that liberal majority can set the conditions of a group's entry into a multicultural engagement. All subgroups, he argues, must enter a constitutional process on equal footing, guaranteed by norms of mutual recognition and consent.[14] But when pressed, Tully argues that these same norms of recognition and consent must apply within groups as well, that is, to the relationship between the group and its members.[15] At that point, he has become a kind of "superliberal," arguing for the normative priority of individual consent over group identity. He now has the problem of building political order out of these conditions of mutual recognition and consent among individuals. That, however, is just the liberal program he sought to escape.

[12] Taylor, *Multiculturalism*, 59.

[13] Kymlicka, *Multicultural Citizenship*, note 152. Both Taylor and Kymlicka often write as if the paradigmatic problem of multiculturalism is presented by the French-speaking *community* of Quebec.

[14] To these, Tully adds a third norm of "continuity." But continuity, he suggests, can be understood as the product of the first two norms: "The *mutually recognized* cultural identities of the parties continue through the constitutional negotiations and associations agreed to unless they explicitly *consent* to amend them." Tully, *Strange Multiplicity* 124–25 (emphasis added).

[15] *Ibid*. at 165–66.

None of these theorists is comfortable with the possibility of a non-liberal culture. None wants directly to address issues of power and authority outside of the framework offered by a liberal theory of rights. None, we might say, escapes his Canadian roots. The ambition of contemporary moral and political inquiry, however, must be to orient action and thought when differences are beyond the capacity of reasoned discourse to overcome. Normative deliberation today must be a reflection on the sources of meaning in a deeply divided world. As long as those differences are not even recognized, theory will be only an elaboration of the liberal values already present in our own tradition.

The belief that differences in values can be overcome through discourse is itself only a restatement of the liberal faith in a dialogical model of reason as though talking together will inevitably move us toward a set of common propositions.[16] Ethical inquiry, however, is not science; it occurs across a field of difference that is not properly understood as grounded in mistake or ignorance.[17] Normative differences can remain even after each party fully understands the other.[18] Achieving an "unbeatable" argument, or reaching a synthetic proposition upon which all will unite, may simply not be possible. Rather, the approach must be to deepen our understanding of ourselves.

We can begin to make progress toward such a reorientation by returning to the debate between liberals and communitarians, which formed the immediate background to the current concern with multiculturalism. Exploring that debate illuminates the conceptual structure within which liberalism operates. Communitarians and liberals are bound to each other as two sides of a single antinomy. That same

[16] See S. Benhabib, "Liberal Dialogue versus a Critical Theory of Discourse Legitimation," in *Liberalism and the Moral Life* 143 (N. Rosenblum, ed., 1989).

[17] Compare Rawls, who locates the sources of "reasonable disagreement" in the "burdens of judgment." His inquiry into these "burdens" begins with the question "What, then, goes wrong?" J. Rawls, *Political Liberalism* 55 (1993).

[18] The idea that reasonable disagreement cannot be overcome by discourse is central to Charles Larmore's conception of modernity. He nevertheless believes that political liberalism can be constructed from a common commitment to equal respect among those who disagree. C. Larmore, *The Morals of Modernity* (1996). On the persistence of the problem of normative disagreement and Larmore's failure to overcome this, see M. Moore, *Foundations of Liberalism* 129–38 (1993).

antinomy reappears in the contemporary debate over multiculturalism, and explains why even liberalism's critics cannot escape the pull
of liberal values.

LIBERALS AND COMMUNITARIANS: AN ENDLESS DEBATE

When communitarians accused liberals of failing to offer a substan-
tively rich conception of the subject, and of undermining communities
within which identity formation is a mutually reinforcing project, they
were pointing to the failure of a discourse of rights adequately to describe the reach of our normative experience.[19] The opponents of liberalism wanted to begin moral inquiry from the point of view of a subject who already has an actual identity within multiple communities:
family, town, church, workplace, nation. They could see no reason to
grant a normative or epistemic priority to an abstract conception of a
subject who would deploy reason in order to find basic rules to guide
his or her interactions with similarly abstract subjects. The critics of
liberalism argued that normative theory need not begin behind
Rawls's "veil of ignorance" or with any other effort to obtain "the
view from nowhere."[20] It begins there because of an intellectual tradition that puts forward the autonomous subject as the central ideal—
the foundational norm—of the moral order.

To exercise choice as an autonomous, rational agent requires at least
an imagined withdrawal from every relationship within which the subject finds him or herself. Existing relationships become authentic only
when, and if, they are reaffirmed through choice. Life becomes a project made and unmade through the exercise of choice. Choice is valuable just to the degree that it produces an "examined" life. Thus, the
autonomous individual frees the self from the unexamined irrationality of tradition.[21] Context is evaluated by the autonomous chooser,

---

[19] See M. Sandel, *Democracy's Discontent: America in Search of a Public Philosophy* 201–49 (1996); P. Gabel, "The Phenomenology of Rights—Consciousness and the
Fact of the Withdrawn Selves," 62 *Tex. L. Rev.* 1563, 1566–67 (1984) (criticizing
traditional legal rights discourse from a Critical Legal Studies perspective); M. Ignatieff, *The Needs of Strangers* 74–75 (1984).

[20] See T. Nagel, *The View from Nowhere* (1986).

[21] See I. Kant, "What is Enlightenment" (L. Beck, trans., [1784] 1959).

and the source of that normative scrutiny is reason. Reason, of course, cannot determine the content of every choice. But where reason ends, we say the choice makes no difference to the moral quality of the agent. Conversely, the moral character of the will extends no further than the reach of reason. Accordingly, Kant thought that all that is of moral worth is the quality of the will.[22]

The communitarians feared that this conception of the individual subject as the active agent of rational choice was a kind of false start for moral theory. It may even have been a mistaken turn in Western culture. We need not begin ethical inquiry with the question, what should I do? as if the future were a kind of blank slate to be filled in by reason's directions. Indeed, this moral blank slate corresponds to the epistemic blank slate of the British Empiricists. Both slates assume a kind of pure subject: the viewer of the slate, the agent of the will.

The communitarians reject the primacy of rational autonomy in the domain of moral theory; they are skeptical of the ambition to deploy reason to manage matters of belief, faith, or value. We do not have to approach moral deliberation, they tell us, as if we constantly confront an open future to be determined by an act of individual will. The normative domain includes as much a regard for the past as for the future; it involves narrative as well as reason, realizing the already existing truth of the self as much as exercising the faculty of choice.[23] The communitarians reject the blank-slate model. They ask not, what should I do? But, for whom am I responsible? Individuals never appear for themselves alone, but are always already tied to others—family, friends, fellow citizens, or coworkers.[24] The corresponding epistemic move was to deny the Lockean model of sensation on a blank slate and to begin the explanation of knowledge from within the language that we already use to order all our experience.[25] Morally and

---

[22] I. Kant, *Groundwork of the Metaphysics of Morals* 16 (L. Beck, trans., [1785] 1959).

[23] See, e.g., C. Taylor, *The Ethics of Authenticity* 5–29 (1992).

[24] See M. Minow, *Not Only for Myself: Identity, Politics and the Law* 19–22 (1997); C. Gilligan, *In a Different Voice: Psychological Theory and Women's Development* (1982).

[25] Wittgenstein's later work became a critical bridging point between the epistemic and the practical inquiries. See L. Wittgenstein, *Philosophical Investigations* (G. E. Anscombe, trans., 1967); C. Mouffe, *The Democratic Paradox* 65–73 (2000); R. Flath-

epistemically, the individual is not the beginning of experience but a product of distinct forms of community self-understanding. We know the whole before we know the part—even if that part is the self. We find ourselves already in a world, and there is no self apart from that world. Each of us is located in a community—actually multiple communities—that are substantially constitutive of who we are. Only from within these particular communities, with their unique circumstances—both empirical and normative—do we confront demands from others and, in turn, make demands upon them. We do not interact with representations of "everyman," but with family members, co-workers, friends, fellow citizens, and co-religionists.

On this view, the conditions imposed on moral deliberation are not those of pure reason, but those of attached individuals: love, friendship, trust, and support. Without parents, friends, and fellow citizens, one should decline to enter the original position. Concrete difference, not abstract equality, is the starting point of moral behavior. That which is most morally praiseworthy in the individual is not the product of reasonable choice, but of the community's power to move us in ways that are beyond reason. Parents' actions on behalf of their children, just as citizens' actions on behalf of their state, are based on virtues other than justice: for example, courage, duty, love. We are not attached to others on the basis of choice. Indeed, if we reason about these attachments as if they were objects of choice, we are likely to fail to be true to ourselves.[26] Consider, for example, if we were to subject the experience of love to the condition that it must survive a theoretical inquiry into the appropriate norms of commitment to others.

The liberal can concede the descriptive claim made by the communitarian: we do find ourselves already to be members of particular communities with distinct obligations to others. Yet, each of us is capable of abstracting from the particulars of our actual lives, of imagining a subject prior to such attachments, and of pursuing an inquiry into norms from this abstract perspective. People are not so bound to con-

---

man, *Willful Liberalism: Voluntarism and Individuality in Political Theory and Practice* 51–60 (1992).

[26] See H. Frankfurter, *The Reasons of Love* (2004); B. Williams, "Persons, Character and Morality," in *Moral Luck* 1, 18 (1981).

text that they can only imagine themselves interacting with subjects who are already part of their own communities. I am always within and without my present context.[27] If one can imagine such a "contextless" interaction, one can take up the question of justice before any particular community or context is irretrievably fixed. Indeed, because one can always take up the question, no such fixed position is possible. Moral claims are, in this respect, similar to epistemic claims: we may believe certain things about the world, but that hardly qualifies as a reason not to test those beliefs against independently grounded standards for true belief. Justice serves that function with respect to normative beliefs.

Liberals worry that communitarians lack the ability to talk in a normatively compelling manner about their communities and the values those communities support. The communitarians can appeal to no counterpart to the universal norms—justice and liberty—of a liberal order. They have no noncontextualized standard that allows them to distinguish between good and bad communities.[28] What starts as a normative inquiry seems to end with a disquieting appeal to fact: we are subjects situated in particular communities from which we inevitably draw our values. True, say the liberals, but this is hardly an adequate account of our moral life. We have values about our values, and at the top of the hierarchy of values is justice. To understand our own conception of justice, we have to confront this capacity for detachment from any particular context. Detachment is as much a part of who we are as attachment.

Neither context nor abstraction—personal attachment or reason's detachment—makes a stronger claim to be the foundation of our moral life. An emphasis on context may lead to a belief in a "false necessity," but equally an emphasis on abstraction may lead to a false

---

[27] See R. Unger, *Passion: An Essay on Personality* (1984).

[28] Efforts to assess "social capital," for example, cannot easily distinguish between just and unjust sources of such capital. See, e.g., L. McClain and J. Fleming, "Some Questions for Civil Society-Revivalists," 75 *Chi.-Kent L. Rev.* 301 (2000); C. Boggs, "Social Capital as Political Fantasy," in *Social Capital: Critical Perspectives on Community and "Bowling Alone"* 183, 189 (S. McLean, D. Schultz, M. Steger, eds., 2002). ("Putnam never gets around to making ideological or political distinctions of any sort, so we are provided with no means of determining the particular *content* or direction of [social capital], or even identifying variable types of [social capital].")

sense of unbounded choice.[29] If the former creates a danger of moral complacency, the latter creates the danger of hubris. We see these twin dangers in both individuals and states. For nations, the danger of complacency can take the form of a xenophobic, conservative nationalism, while the danger of hubris can be seen in the zeal of revolutionary or authoritarian ideologies. In a parallel fashion, individuals can turn toward a strict maintenance of traditions or toward a radical reconstruction of the self. Of course, things need not go to extremes in either individuals or states. An emphasis on context may make more prominent the norms of commitment—for example, love and forgiveness—while an emphasis on choice may make more prominent the norm of justice. Balance may be difficult in theory, but a kind of practical balance may be a necessary condition of political or individual stability.[30]

The problem of combining freedom and necessity has been a traditional puzzle of metaphysics; it is no less a problem of political and moral theory. We respond to both freedom of choice and commitment to others as ultimate values. We live a life in which the freedom of the self is constantly confronted by the need to constrain that freedom for the sake of others, whether family, friends, or fellow members of a common political community. Individuals and communities need both love and justice. We cannot say one is more important that the other.

Each perspective tries to coopt the other by showing its own compatibility with what appears to be its opposite. Precisely because the opposing norms make such strong claims, this move to include the opposite is a felt necessity of theory. Thus, liberals say they are not against community. Liberalism, after all, started as a way of protecting religious communities from the authority of the state. Community has the same normative force as any other source of a conception of the good. This force is derived from the fact of individual choice. Individuals are free to choose to be communitarians within the constraints of a liberal conception of justice.[31] Of course, we might still argue about

---

[29] See R. Unger, *False Necessity: Anti-Necessitarianism Social Theory in the Service of Radical Democracy* (1987); and C. Taylor, *The Ethics of Authenticity* 51–53 (1991).

[30] For an example of the idea of balancing these norms in legal theory, see R. Post, "The Social Foundations of Privacy: Community and Self in the Common Law of Tort," in *Constitutional Domains* 51–88 (1995).

[31] See, e.g., Y. Tamir, *Liberal Nationalism* (1993).

the breadth of those constraints. Yet, every conception of liberalism recognizes the possibility of rich religious and familial communities.

One can say the same sort of thing from the communitarian point of view. Communitarians are not against individual autonomy and free choice wherever they appear. The values for which a community stands, and which are inculcated in its members, can be liberal values. A community can be a liberal community.[32] We can reach liberal values through a particular historical community, just as we can reach particular communities through liberal individuals' free choices.[33]

Liberals and communitarians begin at opposite ends of this two-termed, normative experience, but neither can seek to dismiss the values of the other as simply "false." Liberals appeal to the character of our *moral* discourse; communitarians appeal to the fact that it is *our* moral discourse. Each feels the need to assign normative priority to one term over the other. In doing so, each attempts to trace both normative phenomena to a single source. Either the particular community is viewed from the perspective of liberalism or liberalism is viewed from the perspective of the particular community.

THE UNHAPPY SYNTHESIS

The most significant development in contemporary political theory has been the effort to marry liberalism's claim for autonomous choice with narratives of the development of values within particular Western communities. This shift from the logic of the original position to the actual history of liberal communities describes Rawls's later work, as well as that of Habermas and Ackerman over the last twenty years.[34] It is central to Dworkin's mature jurisprudence as well.[35] Indeed, this

[32] See, e.g., M. Walzer, "Comment" in Taylor, *Multiculturalism* 99, 102.

[33] Henry Jaffa notes a similar phenomenon in American history: what appear as "self-evident" truths in the Declaration of Independence have become historically validated propositions of the founding fathers in the Gettysburg Address. H. Jaffa, *Crisis of the House Divided* 227 (1959); but cf. G. Fletcher, *Our Secret Constitution: How Lincoln Redefined American Democracy* (2001).

[34] See A. Ferrara, *Justice and Judgment: The Rise and the Prospect of the Judgment Model in Contemporary Political Philosophy* (1999).

[35] See R. Dworkin, *Law's Empire* (1986); *Freedom's Law: The Moral Reading of the American Constitution* (1996).

is the point at which constitutional law—always tied to particular community practices—intersects with political theory, which is why there has been so much interest, among contemporary constitutional theorists, in the "republican revival."[36] Nevertheless, what may be possible as a matter of institutional interpretation—reading the Constitution as an articulation of liberal norms—may be much harder as a matter of coherent theory.

For liberals, the very idea of *a* liberal community is problematic. Precisely because liberalism is committed to the principle that every individual—as rational and willing—is of equal moral worth, justification of a privileged position for some individuals over others is a chronic problem. Citizenship, however, is just such a privileging of some over others. The liberal subject is universal; he or she is not defined by membership in a particular community. Liberalism warns not only against the false necessity of seeing one's present self as the limit of one's possibilities, it also warns against the false limit of seeing geographic proximity as a measure of one's concern for the lives and well-being of others.[37] The open future of the liberal subject corresponds to an open geographical reach of the liberal community.

The bonds of our particular community may indeed support a liberal attitude of respect for the autonomy of others within the community. Yet the distinction between citizen and noncitizen is the fundamental inequality of political life. This inequality is defined both geographically and historically. The dual sources of this political inequality are represented explicitly in the dual sources of citizenship at birth: bloodline and geography, or *ius sanguinis* and *ius soli*. These derive from Roman law, not liberal theory. Liberalism adds the idea of the "naturalized" citizen who obtains through consent what otherwise works without reference to choice. But except under extraordinary conditions—for example, emigration to the New World—this liberal contribution never adds much to the constitution of citizenship.[38] Ac-

---

[36] See, e.g., "Symposium, The Republican Civic Tradition," 97 *Yale L.J.* 1493 (1988).

[37] Kant was led to speak of moral obligations toward other "rational" agents, regardless of whether they were human. See, e.g., *Foundations of the Metaphysics of Morals*, 56. ("It follows inconstestably that every rational being must be able to regard himself as an end in himself.")

[38] New-World colonization was characterized by a population displacement, which allowed it to invert the ordinary priorities of blood and soil.

tual communities severely restrict the opportunities for naturalization, privileging those who have no claim of right but for the accident of their births. Our political communities, even our liberal communities, are overwhelmingly founded on "blood and soil."[39]

This means that the internal morality of the liberal community is "at war" with the normative conditions of the community's existence. The very fact of the community becomes a problem to itself. A liberal political community seems always to be in a crisis of theory over the grounds of its own legitimacy. For this reason, the law with respect to the "rights" of aliens, immigrants, and refugees always reads like an exercise in "bad faith."[40] This reality of the nation-state is a constant source of cognitive dissonance for the liberal theorist.[41] If we are serious about our liberalism, we are led ever outward toward a global extension of transnational forms of government.

Liberals, accordingly, tend to embrace an aspiration for a system of comprehensive global governance under universal principles of justice. Contemporary liberal theorists are quick to see positive signs of globalization and to believe such developments will inevitably lead to a normative shift away from the modern nation-state with its concomitant idea of citizenship. We are all to be cosmopolitan citizens of the world linked together through transnational markets, a universal law of human rights, and global institutions of public governance.[42] Universal markets may be first in time, but they lead to universal law and universal governance.

The movement of liberalism from the particular to the universal can be traced in the development of a law of human rights out of a history

[39] This does not mean there is no difference between national socialism and liberal democracies. It does mean that both are first of all organizations of *political* communities. See G. Agamben, *Homo Sacer: Sovereign Power and Bare Life* 129 (D. Heller-Reazen, trans., 1998).

[40] There is a constant return to the claim of a "plenary" congressional power over aliens, by which is meant a power beyond the ordinary constraints of judicial enforcement of law. See, e.g., *Kleindienst v. Mandel*, 408 U.S. 753, 766–70 (1972).

[41] See, e.g., O. Fiss, *A Community of Equals: The Constitutional Protection of New Americans* (1999).

[42] See A. Slaughter, "Judicial Globalization," 40 *Va. J. Int'l. L.* 1103 (2000); "Governing the Global Economy through Government Networks," in *The Role of Law in International Politics: Essays in International Relations Law* 177 (Michael Byers, ed., 2000); M. Nussbaum, "Patriotism and Cosmopolitanism," in *For Love of Country: Debating the Limits of Patriotism* (1996).

of constitutional bills of rights. If rights are founded on an idea of the autonomous, rational subject, then there should be a convergence of the law of rights in all modern states. If so, it makes little difference whether we speak of a universal law of human rights or multiple sources of constitutional rights. The content of the rights should be the same. This reciprocal relationship between the transnational and the national describes the development of the European law of rights.[43] It also describes the trend toward constitutional incorporation of international human rights law, as well as the contemporary support for the exercise of universal jurisdiction by domestic courts.[44] In all of this, we see the liberal ideal of a single order of law enforced by a single set of institutions, all organized around the same normative ideal of the autonomous subject guided by reason.

Just as the geographical scope of the liberal community expands, the relevant past for the liberal is not a particularized history. Rather, it is the imaginary past of the original position. This is the moment of entry into the social contract. The original position, of course, is not past at all, just as it has no particular geographical place. It is a timeless source of legitimacy, which is cast as the possession of everyman. The actual past appears, if at all, only as a threat: the "dead hand" of the past. To those who take their liberalism seriously, there is no more reason to look to the founding fathers than to the voices of the leadership of the French Revolution or of the Glorious Revolution. What they said, not their position within a particular community, is the determinant of respect.[45] For the liberal, our actual political life always has the character of original sin—inescapable, yet still sin.

The communitarians' problems with the compromise represented by the liberal community are just the opposite. They believe that liber-

[43] See A. Sweet, "Constitutional Dialogues in the European Community," in *The European Courts and National Courts—Doctrine and Jurisprudence: Legal Change in its Social Context* 305 (Slaughter et al., eds., 1998).

[44] See e.g., J. Levitt, "Constitutionalization of Human Rights in Argentina: Problem or Promise?" 37 *Colum. J. Transnat'l. L.* 281 (1999); R. Slye, "International Law, Human Rights Beneficiaries, and South Africa: Some Thoughts on the Utility of International Human Rights Law" 2 *Chi. J. Int'l. L.* 59 (2001). But cf. P. Kahn, "American Hegemony and International Law—Speaking Law to Power: Popular Sovereignty, Human Rights, and the New International Order," 1 *Chi. J. Int'l. L.* 1 (2000).

[45] See, Nussbaum, *For Love of Country*.

alism, even if historically grounded, threatens the necessary conditions of any particular community. Thus, while the critics of liberalism have often focused on liberalism's disconcerting abstraction, communitarians have also argued the opposite: that the problem of liberalism lies not in its abstract character, but in the very concrete characters that a liberal order produces. The problem now is not liberalism, but liberals.[46]

Confronting the liberal's demand that we respect each individual as an autonomous source of choice, the communitarian fears that we may find such a subject lacks any definite character to which we can attach dignity. We have difficulty respecting a subject who makes choices without commitment. Such a subject will lack a particular identity even to herself. One cannot be "true" to oneself, if the self has no content to be true to. Without a capacity for self-respect, we are in no position to demand respect from others. There is a fear that liberalism will leave individuals adrift and thus subject to the pull of immediate satisfactions that have neither depth nor constancy.[47] Without depth of character, the individual who frees the self from the immediacy of desire is likely to be the victim of abstract theory.[48]

The communitarian fears that there is an inevitable movement from political to comprehensive liberalism. You cannot place only part of your faith in reason. Comprehensive liberalism rests on a comprehensive pursuit of reason such that belief in scientific progress, political self-rule, and self-creation become aspects of a single project. A partial liberalism comes to be seen as a kind of internal contradiction, as difficult to maintain as belief in God in an age committed to scientific explanation. In this sense, there may be no return from the original position.[49] Belief in the original position, the communitarian fears, can

[46] See, e.g., M. Glendon, *Rights Talk: The Impoverishment of Political Discourse* (1991); A. Etzioni, *Rights and the Common Good: The Communitarian Perspective* (1995).

[47] See C. Taylor, *The Ethics of Authenticity* 4 (1992).

[48] The great fictional invocation of this theme is in Dostoevsky's *Crime and Punishment* (D. Magarshack, trans., [1866] 1977), which juxtaposes the life of "random" theory with that of random sexuality—of Raskolnikov and Svidrigailor—as equally failed models of identity under modern conditions.

[49] See S. Okun, "Reply," in Cohen *Is Multiculturalism Good for Women?* 129–30 (1999).

blind one to the actual commitments within which one finds oneself. Thus, a liberal morality founded on rational choice shows itself practically in the decline of those civic institutions that had provided a substantive content for self and community.[50] Lacking romanticism's faith in a unique, internal source of the self, liberalism may produce a crisis of anomie.[51]

This fear of liberalism's possible effects shows itself with a kind of symbolic concentration in the debate over easy and open access to the Internet. Cyberspace appears to many as endless possibility without substantive direction. It symbolizes an open-ended future within which individuals, usually imagined as children, can fall into sin, usually imagined as pornography. Others see the Internet as symbolic of unending progress in the construction of the self. It is literally a free market of ideas, and thus the ultimate means of individual freedom and self-realization in a liberal culture. If we are all connected to each other on a global basis, then each of us is an endless possibility of self-creation; or, each of us is nothing at all—always possibility, never actually anything.[52]

The debate over the Internet is so powerful because it symbolizes these deeply entrenched hopes and fears. It is the contemporary site of a cultural war that has been going on since the Age of Revolution, when politics was first detached from religion. If politics could be remade on the basis of deliberation and choice, then so could the individual citizen.[53] Not accidentally, in the course of the French Revolution, with its radical invocation of reason, we see both an attack on the church and the emergence of a vigorous pornographic imagination.

[50] See R. Putnam, *Bowling Alone: The Collapse and Revival of American Community* (2000).

[51] Of course, some liberal theoriticians have directed their work at this communitarian critique. See, e.g., N. Rosenblum, *Another Liberalism: Romanticism and the Reconstruction of Liberal Thought* (1987). Even Rosenblum, however, recognizes that her views are not characteristic of traditional liberalism, which "has vigorously warded off everything affective, personal, and expressive." *Ibid.*, 4.

[52] O. Fiss, "In Search of a New Paradigm," 104 *Yale. L.J.* 1613, 1617 (1995). ("The new technologies may turn us not into citizens but consumers, shopping for our favorite speech like we shop for our favorite ice cream.")

[53] See G. Wood, *Radicalism of the American Revolution* (1992); see also U. Preuss, *Constitutional Revolution: The Link Between Constitutionalism and Progress* 15 (D. Schneider, trans., 1995) (noting that Marxism too believes that a new individual will follow from a new organization of the political and economic order).

The Internet again shows us the linkage of reason and the pornographic imagination. The fear remains that the liberalism of reason will inevitably produce the imagination of the Marquis de Sade. This is not altogether a misplaced fear. The restlessness of reason denies the body the symbolic resources of love—romantic or communal.[54] The final product in the endless chain of self-reflective possibilities may look more like *The Philosophy of the Boudoir* than the *Critique of Pure Reason*.

In the end, the synthetic approach fails to meet the communitarians' objections because their real problems are not with the foundations of liberalism, whether abstract or historical, but with liberal values. Communitarians understand the individual not as an autonomous agent of choice but as an historically situated member of a community. A community of liberal individuals for them is not the answer to their concerns, but a nightmare vision of the practical consequences of poor normative theory.[55]

Nor is the synthetic vision adequate to the liberal for whom the power of the claim of justice comes from its foundation in a universal discourse of reason. Demoting reason to just another source of belief alongside religion, nationalism, or irrational popular enthusiasms undermines the liberal claim to put practical reasoning on a secure foundation. Liberalism is not a lucky historical accident for a privileged community but the endpoint of the progressive development of moral deliberation. That, at least, is its fundamental claim, without which it is not really liberalism at all.[56]

THE ANTINOMIES OF DISCOURSE

The debate between liberals and communitarians presents an unavoidable and unresolvable antinomy between a capacity for abstraction and a practice of contextualization. This antinomy is rooted in the

---

[54] See chap. 5.

[55] See, e.g., A. MacIntyre, "The Privatization of the Good," in *The Liberalism-Communitarian Debate* 12 (C. Delaney, ed., 1994) ("My accusation was not only that liberal theory involves a fundamental indeterminateness in respect of moral rules . . . it was that as such theory is lived out in practice, this indeterminance and this impoverishment are exemplified in social reality.")

[56] See J. Hampton, "Should Political Philosophy Be Done Without Metaphysics?" *ibid.* 151, 184.

very nature of discourse. It is already present in the ability to form the simplest element of discourse: the proposition. The same structural antinomy is found in the fully accomplished discourse that is narrative. It reappears again at the level of theoretical self-reflection. If the antinomy is a function of discourse itself, no resolution will ever be reached. For just this reason, efforts by liberals and communitarians to absorb the other always fail; they end up merely replicating the antinomy. The debate between the universalists and the multiculturalists must take just this same form. Thus a liberal theoretician like Kymlicka will try to show that liberalism properly understood already includes recognition of multiculturalism, while a multiculturalist theoretician like Tully defends a position that includes strong liberal norms.[57] Each effort at synthesis will offend both sides to the dispute for the reasons I have described. Inevitably each side is simultaneously bound to, but unhappy with, the other. Confronting an unresolvable antinomy in our conceptual resources, the only way forward is to deepen the framework of understanding. Synthesis is our lot, for this antinomy is inescapable.

Propositions: The I and the Me

Every proposition can itself become the object of new proposition. Once said, the proposition inevitably has a double-character: it conveys a representational content and it can itself be the object of a representation. Hearing a proposition—"John is here"—I can both repeat it in order to convey the same meaning or I can make it the object of a new proposition: "He said, 'John is here.' " No language can ever be specified in a finite number of propositions, because every proposition spawns an indefinite number of further propositions.[58] This capacity for a reflexive turn constitutes a language, as opposed to a code.

The same double-character is true of any sentence offered in the first person. Speech can always turn inward, that is, the speech act can become the object of a new act of speech. When applied to the first-person proposition, this is more than a claim that a representation can

[57] See note 10, above.

[58] The Jewish prohibition on naming God can be understood as a way of limiting this propositional move toward critical distance. The religious Jew never gets beyond a nonpropositional enthrallment before the fact of God's speech.

always become the object of a new re-presentation, as if one were to construct a set of mirrors that created an infinite series of reflections. The reflexive turn—the "second sentence"—is not a trivial repetition. Between presentation and re-presentation operates the subject. The reflexive turn exposes that subject. We see this in fiction: a narrative written in the third person always simultaneously constructs a new subject who is the narrator. The same separation and construction occur in the first person. In the "new" representation, the subject of the first proposition becomes an object of critical reflection. Because the speaker can always take his own speech as an object of discourse, the subject always appears to him or herself as an endless possibility reaching out beyond the present self. What it is to be me becomes a problem for the I.[59]

There is a necessary instability in the subject that is built into the very structure of the proposition in which the self first becomes aware of itself as a subject. The subject establishes itself in a proposition: "I am x." But I am always also that subject who will appear at the next moment of critical examination in which that proposition is the object of a new sentence: "Is this x really me?" I am unavoidably both subject and object of this discourse. I cannot speak as the subject without also becoming the object of my own next proposition. There is an endless transition from the subjective to the objective case. This is a kind of transcendental instability in the subject that corresponds to Kant's transcendental unity. Kant emphasized the conceptual conditions that make unity possible, but those same conditions make plurality possible. The subject is always one in many; unity is no more an essential conceptual category of the subject than is plurality.

I cannot say "I" without also saying "me"; I cannot say "me" without already creating a new "I."[60] In its most basic form, this was the method of Cartesian doubt. I am the person writing this sentence. But I am also the person observing the writing—that is, the person who takes the act of my writing as an object of contemplation. And, I am the person observing the observer. There is no stopping the movement

---

[59] See S. Zizek, *Tarrying with the Negative: Kant, Hegel, and the Critique of Ideology* 9–44 (1993).

[60] See G. Mead, *On Social Psychology* 230–40 (A. Strauss, ed., 1964).

of the subject to the position of object in a new proposition of critical self-reflection. No I is ever so attached to a particular proposition that it loses this capacity for critical reflection and reconstruction.[61] Doubt ends with physical, not theoretical, exhaustion. The Platonic dialogue, which takes just this form of critical self-reflection, ends with exhaustion, not a logical conclusion.[62]

Liberalism emphasizes the subject and communitarianism the object of this endlessly proliferating set of propositions. This is a distinction as basic as that between I and me. Liberalism always imagines the next moment as a kind of a second-order discourse taking as object the present subject's propositional truths. The subject can always take itself up anew as the object of a self-conscious act of deliberative critique and reconstruction. Because the liberal subject can never be stabilized in the present, it recedes indefinitely into the future. That subject can be approached only asymptotically.

Since the future is entirely open, the liberal subject is represented figuratively in a myth of origins: the original position.[63] The subject of the original position lacks a further capacity for self-reflection. Allowed to express only universal truths, the I and the me collapse into each other. There are no differentiated subjects because no one can have any thoughts not equally present to all others. The original position in the end looks not unlike the world of Platonic Ideas, despite the contemporary appeal to the language of social contract. It is the point at which language again becomes code, because propositional meaning is now complete in itself. It is as if our consciousness were imprinted with the moral law, and we were without a further capacity for doubt.

Communitarians locate themselves on the other side of the double-character of the proposition. They locate themselves in the set of first-order propositions that have always already been spoken. They see no

[61] To imagine speech without the capacity of doubt is to imagine speech without a subject who must be acknowledged as the speaker. Something like this is true of computer-generated speech. It may also be true of the speech of animals like dolphins.

[62] This is most vividly portrayed in the *Symposium*, in which all the speakers, except Socrates, eventually succumb to drink and sleep.

[63] Alternatively, it can be represented in a myth of a fully perfected future. The centrality of the idea of progress builds on this projection of an ideal self into an indefinite future; that ideal gives the direction and measure of progress. Thus, Habermas's ideal

reason to take up the invitation to Cartesian doubt, finding themselves already to have a fully defined self. Indeed, they are inclined to move in just the opposite way from the liberals, recognizing that there is no proposition that is not a communication to an other, potential or actual. The content of the proposition is always for someone. Without the possibility of being heard, there would be no proposition at all.[64] Thus, the communitarian argues that before we are alone, we are together. The withdrawal of the I is always subsequent to the creation of the me. And there is no me, without a you.

For the communitarians, the self is not possibility but actuality. It need not be constructed in a myth of origins, or projected into an indefinite future. It is compellingly present in the sum total of propositions already spoken, which together constitute the me. The fact that I can continue speaking does not mean that I must.

Of course, even if the communitarians are right about the dialogical foundation of language and the priority of the "me and you" over the I, nothing follows as a normative proposition. Pointing out that the other is a transcendental condition of speech and even of the construction of an original subject tells us nothing at all about whether we should value and pursue the critical capacity of the I. Recognizing that there is no subject without parents, for example, hardly tells us how we should view our parents. One can still leave home. In Taylor's terms, the normative dispute between communitarians and liberals is not settled by even an ontologically correct description of priorities.[65] Moreover, contra Taylor, the capacity to withdraw, to establish a critical distance from the me, is no less an ontological fact about the character of our subjectivity than is our embeddedness. For us, there is no me without an I, even as it is true that there is no me without a you.

But if there is no way to resolve our normative debate by finding a truth of the self in metaphysics, neither is it the case that the opposition between liberals and communitarians is a necessary consequence of the distinction between the I and the me. The critical capacity that defines the I need not take the form of the liberal's commitment to an

---

speech conditions point toward a self to be realized in an indefinite future. See J. Habermas, *The Theory of Communicative Action*, vol. 1 (T. McCarthy, trans., 1984).

[64] See e.g., C. Taylor, *The Ethics of Authenticity* 33 (1991).

[65] See C. Taylor, "Cross-purposes."

unending deployment of reason; the content of the me need not be linked to the social circumstances of community. We could, for example, understand the commitment to an "authentic" assertion of the will—I must will the essence of my own existence—as filling the space of the I. Similarly, we could imagine the bounded character of the me to be defined by the givenness of desire rather than by community. Or, for that matter, by the presence of the sacred. The antinomy is a product of the reflective capacity that is constitutive of language. The content of the antinomy is a function of history. The forms of critical self-reflection are no less a function of circumstance than are the forms of the contextualized me. To understand why the I takes the form of a rational, autonomous self, and why the me is located in conceptions of community and narrative, we must turn from architectural to genealogical inquiry, the subject of chapter 2.

Narrative and Interpretation

Contemporary communitarians sometimes argue as though they believe they can secure their position in this debate by appealing to narrative. This is a misstep for the antinomic nature of the proposition reappears in narrative. Narrative can be thought of, in the first instance, as the speech of a community: a narrative only exists for a community of readers or listeners. Just as narrative requires community, so a community needs narrative to make sense of its coming to be within a particular place and time. The narrative explains borders and history. We understand this to be a function of myth but it remains true of historical narratives. The movement from myth to history reflects changing conceptions of the truth—that is, of the object that the narrative relates—not of the function that truth serves. Through narrative, I learn of myself and the others with whom I find myself living as part of a group. Narrative gives me a past and constrains the future. Destiny is the way in which the future appears when it is tied to a particular past. In all of these ways, communitarians, as well as multiculturalists, find support in reminding us of the place of narrative in the construction of self and society. The appeal to narrative is the contemporary form in which the perspective that emphasizes the content of our speech—the already spoken—appears.

Without narrative, there would be no self as a particular subject participating in communities of different geographical and historical scope: for example, family, church, nation. Yet every subject has the capacity to offer a new interpretation of an inherited narrative. It is always possible to take the narrative as the object of a new discursive inquiry. Each narrative can be interrogated; each can be reinterpreted. A text is no more stable than a proposition.

Inevitably, there is a splintering along the lines of the same antinomy that we saw with respect to the proposition. Some communities—or some members of some communities—emphasize the unchanged repetition of the narrative. We can refer to them as "fundamentalist." They emphasize the sacred character of the text and adopt a variety of mechanisms to protect it from change: ritualized repetitions, creation of a priesthood, or doctrines of heresy. Outside of specifically religious communities, we often find the same impulse toward fundamentalism with respect to social texts—for example, the character of familial relations or community traditions. Politics too has its fundamentalists who may combine an appropriation of central texts—for instance, the Constitution—with embedded traditions. Others, however, emphasize the text as a source of endless interpretation. On the latter view, one must define for oneself a relationship to the text. Neither are the two positions mutually exclusive. The Talmud, for example, preserves and celebrates an interpretive tradition right alongside the preservation of a sacred text.

In law, this antinomy fuels the conflict in forms of constitutional interpretation: some emphasize formalism and the objectivity of text, others the interpretive commentary that the judiciary has established through countless rulings.[66] Some argue for conservation of the text with its inherited meanings; others argue for interpretations responsive to changing conditions. The same dispute occurs over the virtues of the common law: Is its virtue located in its value as a stable precedent or in its capacity to evolve?

Even in the face of communal efforts to suppress innovation, any individual can ask whether an inherited narrative is true. The question

---

[66] See P. Kahn, *The Reign of Law: Marbury v. Madison and the Construction of America* 220–21 (1997); S. Levinson, *Constitutional Faith* (1988).

of truth functions not so much as the origin of an effort to establish a set of conditions of epistemic validity, but as the moment of separation for the subject. Because I can ask whether it is true, I always have a capacity to create a distance between self and text, which means between self and the community that sustains this narrative. The question of truth is the epistemic equivalent of the question of justice. With respect to any social practice, I can ask, Is it just? Classically, the two questions were the same: Is it true that this is just? That we distinguish truth from justice reflects an intellectual inheritance separating fact from value. But when we deal with a community's narrative, this separation is likely to fail: the truth of the narrative bears on values and identity.

Asking the question of truth puts at issue the character of the relationship a subject should establish with a text. Ordinarily, we think of truth as a function of the relationship between a text—that is, a representation—and that which it purports to represent. But the question of truth is first of all an opening up of a gap between the subject and the text that has become the object of her scrutiny. For this reason, every religious community necessarily faces the problem of doubt, just as every political community confronts the possibility of revolution. This doubt can appear as a moment of freedom—religious or political—even as it is experienced as a failure of faith. It can appear as liberation or loss.

The sense of a failure of faith marks only one extreme in a range of attitudes toward the inherited narrative, which the question of truth makes possible. The moment of self-reflection directed at the inherited narrative can just as easily lead to a questioning of whether the understanding of a text is adequate to the experience of truth within the community. Not just a failure of faith, but the fullness of faith can launch the interpretative enterprise. This sense of disjunction between the fullness of faith and an inherited text can sustain a constant effort to reinterpret and re-present the narrative.[67] Reform always competes with revolution.

---

[67] See R. Cover, "The Supreme Court, 1982 Term—Foreword: Nomos and Narrative," 97 *Harv. L. Rev.* 4, 9 (1983); P. Kahn, "Interpretation and Authority in State Constitutionalism," 106 *Harv. L. Rev.* 1147 (1993).

The moment of separation of the self from the narrative text does not tell us, then, in which direction the reflective self will move, whether toward a rejection of or a fuller affirmation of the community's narrative. The possibility of separation creates the conditions for an interpretive debate that is without end. Every new product of interpretation becomes only another text that poses the same issues to the subject. No interpretation has, in itself, the power to protect a narrative from further interpretive rewriting. A peremptory truth claim does assert a power to secure the narrative from new interpretations, but that power always comes from outside, not from within, the interpretive debate.[68] For example, judges can end—at least temporarily—an interpretive debate over the meaning of a legal rule; they can tell us "what the law is." Not, however, because they have access to the one true interpretation. Their power is independent of the quality of their insight. The truth of their interpretation lies only in its finality. The same can be said of juries, when they establish the "truth" among contested narratives of the facts. The jury is not necessarily better than others at discerning the "real facts." The jury's power is nevertheless that of establishing the "truth of the case." Authority may claim to be based on truth, but in matters of interpretation, truth is a function of authority.

Narratives can be written broadly or narrowly; they can cover a longer or a shorter period of time. I can tell the story of my nation, my state, my community, or my family, or, conversely, of Western civilization, or mankind. These histories, like all other narratives, are constantly open to revision. If the rewriting is sufficiently radical, we might say a new subject—a new historical personage—has emerged. Our political narrative, for example, may shift such that instead of the nation, we now see the relevant subject as the Atlantic community, just as there was a shift from the narrative of Englishmen to one of the American people, or from citizens of different states (e.g., Virginians) to citizens of the nation. Our political narratives may splinter such that we now see the relevant actors to have been women or ethnic groups, rather than a single people.

---

[68] A current example of the effort to deploy power to end legal debate is the effort to label certain international-law rules *jus cogens*. See, e.g., E. Kornicker Uhlmann,

These multiple, proliferating narratives always threaten simply to fall apart in their reciprocal tensions and contradictions. Liberalism brings to this threat of proliferation a faith in the unity of the subject as author—that unity always transcends the plurality of contents. Confident in that unity, liberalism does not fear interpretive diversity. More precisely, the only interpretations it fears are those that would assert a claim of authority to end the debate. It models politics on an endless pursuit of truth—hence its focus on procedure—but is wary of any claim to have found that truth. Politics, as well as moral life, can be unceasing dialogue and disagreement. A well-functioning polity secures the necessary conditions for this debate. Communitarians, on the other hand, can find unity only in the affirmation of the content of the narrative itself. They fear the dissolution of the common narrative; they can appeal only to authority to maintain the stability of the whole. For them, the communal narrative has a "weight" that accrues to it from the support of many different authoritative sources: for example, schools, courts, politicians, and even popular culture. A community would undo itself were it systematically to undermine each such source of authority.

We can think of the liberal and the communitarian as both located in the present moment, each trying to use a narrative form to explain the political order. The communitarian emphasizes narrative as historical account; the liberal emphasizes the novel as the form of narrative. Each, we might say, is trying to write the polity into existence, but one pens a novel and the other a history. Of course, this is only metaphor as the liberal historian and the communitarian novelist cross genres in familiar ways.[69] Nevertheless, the communitarian wants to emphasize the givenness of a community's narrative as historical fact. The liberal, on the other hand, emphasizes the freedom of the author.

When we look forward to the endless range of discursive possibilities both for the self and the community, we are drawn by the theoreti-

---

"State Community Interests, Jus Cogens and Protection of the Global Environment: Developing Criteria for Peremptory Norms," 11 *Geo. Int'l. Envtl. L. Rev.* 101 (1998).

[69] Dworkin's chain-novel metaphor, for example, falls inbetween these two positions. See R. Dworkin, *Law's Empire* 228–32 (1986). Benedict Anderson's work on the role of the novel in establishing the postcolonial nation is also an interesting combi-

cal force of liberalism. Because of this openness toward the future, liberalism always appears with a kind of philosophic optimism. It is committed to the idea that the subject is free to create him or herself, free always to start that process of self-creation all over again.[70] Modern liberalism is the political morality of this endlessly proliferating, critical subject. Its conception of moral failing, accordingly, is to stop the discourse, to refuse to speak—in particular, to refuse to allow the possibility of a critical inquiry that takes as its object the subject's current truths.[71] This is the enduring morality of the Enlightenment.

Liberals, one might say, create a political doctrine on the basis of a literary form: the novel. Liberal theorists create the original position as a rhetorical trope based upon an experience of an endlessly open future. They write the imaginary discourse of the legitimate state.[72] This effort to recompose the national narrative corresponds to the capacity to withdraw to a second-order position, that is, to become the observer of the self. That experience is as immediate as a shift in emphasis within a proposition from the object to the subject.

Liberalism would enter into a crisis of identity were it to look forward and find no compelling reason to create one self rather than another.[73] The postmodern novel, in which the authorial voice disappears, is not an adequate basis for a political community. We need not only open possibilities, but reasons to choose. The postmodern questions whether we are entitled to have such reasons.

The only choices liberalism can confidently support are those that would not undermine this idea of a free subject. Liberalism, thus,

---

nation of roles. See B. Anderson, *Imagined Communities: Reflections on the Origins and Spread of Nationalism* (1991).

[70] R. Unger, *False Necessity: Anti-Necessitarian Social Theory in the Service of Radical Democracy* (1987).

[71] Habermas's ideal of "dialogical ethics" is the clearest example of this point.

[72] The best example of liberalism as a literary form, that is, as the "fictional life of reason" is B. Ackerman, *Social Justice and the Liberal State* (1980). He grounds liberalism in a fictional discourse of spaceships and mana.

[73] We think of this as the liberal crises of the postmodern era, but this complaint against liberalism was already present in both de Maistre's critique of, and Burke's attack on, the French Revolution. See J. de Maistre, *Against Rousseau: "On the State of Nature" and "On the Sovereignty of the People"* (R. Lebrun, trans. and ed., 1996); E. Burke, *Reflections on the Revolution in France* (C. O'Brien, ed., 1986).

becomes a doctrine of negative liberty, deeply skeptical about claims of positive liberty.[74] The founding virtue of the liberal ideal of the rule of law becomes freedom of speech: law is to secure the endless possibility of a proliferating discourse. Believing that we speak ourselves into existence, the first aim of the liberal state is to protect the freedom to imagine oneself otherwise. Politics and art would be indistinguishable in the fully liberal state.[75] The communitarians correctly question whether an actual polity can survive founded only on negative liberty and the premise of endless possibility.

The communitarian hopes to constrain the possible by appeal to the actual. The community already has a narrative; it need not wait for the liberal novelist. Yet in truth the communitarian has no more capacity than the liberal to terminate this endless process of interpretation. We can face the past with the same existential malaise that we find when we confront a future that makes no substantive demand upon us. The very idea of "our" past can disappear. Communitarians have no way of establishing a priority or rank among the endless plurality of communities that make claims upon us. We can find ourselves no more attached to the American Revolution than to ancient Mesopotamia. Even if we are settled on which communities, we can always ask, which narrative? Every history is subject to critique, and reinterpretation.

Historical narratives, no less than novels, proliferate endlessly. As narratives proliferate, there is no way to stop the splintering of the community. That is, there is no way to stop it from within the framework of the narrative and interpretation. Limitations are set by power. To understand power, we need a theory of politics. Neither the liberals nor communitarians succeed because each seeks to understand politics as a form of discourse. The antinomic character of discourse continually replicates itself in the endless debate between liberalism and its critics.

In sum, neither the liberals nor the communitarians offer an adequate theory of politics. Politics is a matter of choices made under

---

[74] See I. Berlin, *The Crooked Timber of Humanity* 238–61 (1992).

[75] See Post, *Constitutional Domains* 268–290 (discussing public discourse and rejecting limits imposed by Meikeljohn on that discourse).

compelling circumstances. A theory of politics must explain the possibility of sacrifice of self and others. The fictional discourse of liberalism continues endlessly. Political action always occurs before that debate is over simply because the debate is never over. Pursued rigorously, debate undermines the conditions of action, for action is always upon the particular while the discourse always moves toward the universal. Political choice marks the moment that discourse stops and the action follows:[76] liberalism fails just at the moment when politics begins.[77]

The communitarians, no less than liberals, confuse politics with talk—not the imagined discourse of the ideal position, but the found-discourses of our ordinary communities. But not every community is a political community, and not every narrative can provide a ground for political sacrifice. The state is not just another locus and product of narrative. It has the power to claim the life of its citizens. It is certainly a peculiar narrative that ends with the destruction of the speaker: communitarianism too fails just as politics begins.

CONCLUSION: POLITICAL THEORY OR THE EXPERIENCE OF THE POLITICAL?

Approached from the perspective of theory, liberals will win this debate with the communitarians. Calling it a "debate" is already to cast the dispute in terms favorable to liberalism. Liberalism takes the theoretical stance—the subject as a free inquirer operating under the norm of reason—as the source of its own normative order. Its origins lie in the possibility that theory can itself serve as a political practice. In this sense, liberalism is the normative practice of modernity; it claims to be the heir of the Enlightenment. The communitarians' insistence on commitment to particular others is not comprehensible in the abstract. In the abstract, commitment looks like constraint—an arbitrary claim

[76] Consider, for example, Thucydides' account of the Spartan decision to go to war. Thucydides, *History of the Peloponnesian War* 108 (R. Warner, trans., 1972), and the Mytilenian Debate, *ibid.* 222–23.

[77] The discourse of politics is not that of the original position, but that of rhetoric. Political rhetoric, however, will always fail to meet the standards of discursive rationality that are the foundation of liberal discourse. See chap. 6 on political rhetoric.

upon the freedom of the self. Theorizing a moment before my birth, I cannot imagine that I will be so committed to other individuals that I would be willing to sacrifice my life for them.

Liberalism, not accidentally, models the political community as a kind of enlarged university. Conversely, multiculturalism often appears as a threat to the university's ideal conception of itself. As we saw above, multiculturalists who appeal to a model of an embedded discourse will end up invoking liberal norms. They cannot abandon these norms without undermining their understanding of their own theoretical activity. Thus, the multiculturalist who wants to remove that threat may find that he or she has made a place for the critical subject of liberalism within the conditions of his or her own commitment to a project of cultural maintenance. How far that subject will take the process of separation and critique cannot be known in advance.

Despite the strength of liberal theory, there is no liberal cure for the problems of liberalism. There is no reformulation of its foundational commitments to reasoned discourse, to individual decision making, and to equal respect for the dignity of each individual by which the liberal will convince the recalcitrant communitarian. Everything seems perfectly obvious to each. To those who start moral deliberation from a foundation of revealed truth, whether historical or divine, rather than discursive deliberation, who see a priority of the community, whether familial, political, or cultural, over the individual, and who live in a continuity of history rather than in the open moment of individual decision, there is nothing liberalism can say that will convince them.[78] Nor is there anything that the communitarian or multiculturalist can say to those who begin their deliberations from the potential rather than actual, the I rather than me, reason rather than commitment. Each has grasped a necessary truth, and from the perspective of that truth sees the other as threat.

Even if liberalism, in its battle with communitarianism, has the theoretical advantages that come with system and abstraction, it nevertheless does not map our normative experience very well. That experience

[78] Reason has been contested at least since Callicles did battle with Socrates in the name of the passions and individual self-interest in Plato's *Gorgias*. Contemporary forms of the Calliclean challenge invoke Nietzsche and speak of power, rather than desire, but here too there is a rejection of the rational, universal ambitions of the liberal dialogue.

always includes the me as well as the I, the inherited narrative as well as the new interpretation. This is why liberal theorists are always trying to redescribe that ideal conversation from which liberalism flows. They hope finally to offer a description of first principles—of the situation before the first content of an actual narrative is formed—that will be compelling to every person who reads it. Their ambition reflects that of Hobbes, who wrote, "When I shall have set down my own reading orderly, and perspicuously, the pains left another, will be only to consider, if he also find not the same in himself."[79] Liberal theorists no more offer the universal truth of the self than did Hobbes.

Hobbes looks into himself and finds a fear of death. Death is the worst fate, he believes, because it is the end of every possibility: the point at which autonomous choice ceases. The task of politics is to put off death, that of political theory is to describe the political arrangements that will successfully accomplish this end. This belief, however, is hardly self-evident; it is by no means a product of merely observing the phenomena of political life. Western political life has involved sacrifice just as much as security.

Hobbes's account fails at just the point that most needs explanation in comprehending the distinctively political domain of meaning: sacrifice. For sacrifice is not experienced as mere negation. Hobbes cannot comprehend sacrifice at all. Indeed, he argues that the one thing that the sovereign cannot demand of the subject is his or her life.[80] That demand is illegitimate precisely because it contradicts what Hobbes took to be the individual's ambition in joining the social contract: the preservation of life. Whenever the sovereign demands life, the contract is violated, and there is a return to the state of nature.

The state, however, does not exist merely as an institution for the guarantee of individual rights—including the right to life. It makes a claim to the loyalty of the citizen. Political loyalty differs from contract in just that respect that eludes Hobbes: it asserts a power to demand individual sacrifice for the state.[81] Similarly, the state asserts a power

[79] Hobbes, *Leviathan* 83 (C.B. Macpherson, ed., [1651] 1968).

[80] Ibid. 268–70. My critique of Hobbes on this point generally follows that of Walzer. See M. Walzer, *Obligations: Essays on Disobedience, War and Citizenship* 80–88 (1970).

[81] See Agamben, *Homo Sacer*; Plato, "Crito," in *The Last Days of Socrates* 76, 78–92 (H. Tredennick and H. Tarrant, trans., 1993).

to punish betrayal as treason. Treason is not a matter of a contractual failure of performance; its punishment is not a matter of calculating damages. These claims for loyalty and against betrayal are not experienced as illegitimate by most citizens, most of the time. When they are, it is usually a sign that the state is in crisis.[82]

An adequate description of political life must acknowledge those normative phenomena that rarely appear within that branch of political theory beginning with Hobbes and continuing right through Rawls. The political community is experienced through a kind of love. Political identity is linked to a willingness to sacrifice: not contract, but love; not safety, but sacrifice. These are critical elements of political experience, yet they fail to appear when we begin with the Hobbesian state of nature or the Rawlsian veil of ignorance.

Hobbes is the first modern theoretician of the constitutional moment; that is, of a point from which political order is to be constructed anew on the basis of the insights of "political science." This moment is frequently reenacted in the revolutionary politics that begins in the seventeenth century and continues today. The drive toward scientific form leads Hobbes and his liberal successors to focus on individuals who must be reconfigured into new political relationships that are specified in the social contract. Understanding politics as an object to be constructed invited the liberal response. But politics, as we find it, is not a made object.[83] It is a way of life—a cultural, not a logical, phenomenon. To the degree differences among these rich normative communities can be theorized about, without simply suppressing difference under a single abstract standard, the inquiry may look more like aesthetics than liberal political philosophy. Meaning has the same problematic character from the perspective of theory as does beauty: neither can be detached from the circumstances of its instantiation.[84]

---

[82] See Fletcher, *Our Secret Constitution* 75–89.

[83] The perception of politics as an object to be made characterizes a postrevolutionary era of constitutional construction. See B. Ackerman, *The Future of Liberal Revolution* (1992) (on post-1989 revolutions); P. Kahn, *Legitimacy and History: Self-Government in American Constitutional Theory* 9–31 (1992) (discussing American constitutional construction).

[84] Or consider just how difficult it is really to understand the meaning maintained between two lovers.

While the communitarians may lose the theoretical dispute to the liberals, their understanding of an embedded self who finds him or herself in relationships that neither can nor should be modeled on contract is more right than wrong. For the most part, we are all still citizens of particular states, despite the theoretician's praise of liberal cosmopolitanism. Where the communitarians have failed, as have their multicultural successors, is in developing the conceptual tools necessary to understand the character of the political community as opposed to other forms of community. Appealing to narrative, the social construction of reality, or the constitutive character of dialogue is not enough. Modern communitarians better understand the nature of commitment than liberals, but they have no better understanding of politics. For this we need to take up the character of love and sacrifice, of rhetoric and power, and causal forms of explanation beyond that which Aristotle called efficient causation. These are the topics of part II of this inquiry. Before we get there, we must turn from the architectural to the genealogical inquiry.

CHAPTER 2

■ ■ ■ ■

A BRIEF GENEALOGY OF AMERICAN LIBERALISM

Liberalism feels the contradictory pull of a need to accept diversity and a need to affirm universal values. In the last chapter, I argued that this tension cannot be resolved because it is built into the very nature of discourse. Not surprisingly, therefore, the same arguments that motivated the debate between liberals and communitarians are again appearing in the contemporary arguments between the supporters of universal human rights and the defenders of cultural diversity. If there is no measure of truth by which to choose one side over the other, we can address this tension only from within what, at the end of the last chapter, I called the "circumstances of instantiation." We must look at the way in which a culture actually understands and negotiates this contradiction. To do this requires a turn from the abstract structure of discourse to the historical a priori within which we find ourselves.[1] The origins of our liberalism represent a particular confluence of political practice, religious faith, and philosophical belief. Out of this mix of resources, an American political culture of liberalism arose. That culture inevitably recognizes both sides of the dilemma: it must affirm the liberal value of individual freedom under the guidance of reason, while acknowledging the plurality of communities within which we find ourselves. We can trace two strands of our liberal culture—a liberalism of speech and a liberalism of faith—responding to these different starting points.

While the inquiry of this chapter is historical, it is not a narrative of a single line of development. A useful genealogy of a cultural practice must explore both "deep history" and contingent practices. The former has a framing function: it sets the limits of the possible in a

---

[1] See the introduction at 23.

way that no longer appears contingent. Christianity may have once been a contingent event, but today it defines basic elements of Western culture. The same can be said of the Enlightenment turn from faith to reason. On the other hand, the particular forms of American belief and practice arise out of choices that appear to us still as decisions that could have been otherwise. The American narrative of exile, exploration, and self-government remains a story of self-creation.

One model for this form of inquiry, combining an exploration of deep sources with the particular forms of their contingent realization, is Charles Taylor's *Sources of the Self.*[2] Taylor too believes that contemporary liberal theory lacks the capacity to speak of the normative context within which a liberal practice operates. Recovery of that context requires historical inquiry not just because the norms are richer than any theoretical expression can convey, but because individuals and groups understand themselves by placing themselves in these historical traditions. In chapter 1, I argued that this is not the only way they understand themselves, but it is surely the place from which each of us begins. In this non-normative sense, the me precedes the I.

The argument of this chapter begins with a distinction that is prominent, but unresolved, in American constitutional thought: that between a liberalism of faith and a liberalism of speech. This observation of the two forms of our liberalism serves as an opening onto two different strands of our Christian inheritance, which motivate very different attitudes toward the private and the public. This opposition is then traced in the concrete shape it takes in the construction of the founding narrative of American political culture.

LIBERALISM: PRACTICAL OR MORAL?

Liberalism is a cluster of ideas, but fundamental to every account of liberalism is the idea of tolerance.[3] Liberalism builds a political and moral order in the face of difference. Rather than eliminate differences,

---

[2] C. Taylor, *Sources of the Self: The Making of Modern Identity* (1989).

[3] Kymlicka notes that "there is a large and growing debate amongst liberals about whether autonomy or tolerance is the fundamental value within liberal theory." Kymlicka, *Multicultural Citizenship* 154 (1955); see also C. Kukathas, "Are There Any Cultural Rights?" 20 *Political Theory* 105–39 (1992), and "Cultural Rights Again: A Rejoinder to Kymlicka," ibid. at 674–80.

it attempts to find a form of association that can achieve unity despite difference. Liberal inquiry begins from the perception that the elimination of difference would be both impractical and immoral: impractical, because the effort would lead only to increased conflict undermining political peace and stability; immoral, because tolerance of difference follows from a normatively compelling understanding of the nature of the individual. Liberal tolerance is both a political practice and a moral demand.

The Liberalism of Faith and the Liberalism of Speech

These practical and moral sources of liberalism often work together, but in fact they rest on different foundations. There is a liberalism of religious tolerance and a liberalism of philosophical justification—a liberalism of faith and a liberalism of speech.[4] The former constrains the state in order to preserve a domain, or domains, of ultimate meaning beyond the state. Proceeding from the experience of religious faith, it asks under what political conditions citizens can be secure in their diverse religious practices and beliefs. Without that security, the state itself will be threatened by religious resistance. The latter takes no position on the locus or existence of ultimate meanings. Instead, it places its faith in reason itself. This approach builds a conception of legitimate political order from the ground up. Paradigmatically, it imagines a prepolitical moment at which potential citizens come together and establish the terms of their political interaction through a mutually agreed upon discourse. Political order gains its meaning not from something beyond politics—religion—but from an internal, discursive practice among citizens. Of course, not just any discursively constructed political order qualifies as liberal. The liberal politico-philosophical project imagines a prepolitical moment at the origin of the legitimate state authority, but it does so aware of the

---

[4] This distinction broadly connects to that Rawls draws between liberalism as a modus vivendi and liberalism as a political conception based on an "overlapping consensus." J. Rawls, *Political Liberalism* 146–50 (1993). Rawls, however, develops the distinction from below, that is, from the perspective of the participants in a political order, while I develop it from above, that is, from the perspective of the Supreme Court, which must rely on an understanding of the sources and character of our liberalism in adjudicating actual cases.

actual diversity of citizen belief and practice.[5] There must, in short, be a substantial overlap between the liberalism of faith and that of speech.

Taylor writes that "the legal code and its practices provide a window into broader movements of culture."[6] This is just what we find with respect to the two forms of liberalism. Thus we can express this difference in the idiom of American constitutional law by asking whether free exercise of religion or freedom of speech is the foundation of our liberal political order. Do we value the liberal state because it protects a private space for religious faith or because it is the product of a rational act of community self-construction, because of the good it makes possible or the justice it achieves? In the liberal state, we value both the rule of law and self-government. The former points to the protection of the private and the meanings achieved by the individual within that private space; the latter points to the public character of an enterprise of mutual deliberation, joint responsibility, and civic commitment.

There is a substantial difference between reaching the idea of liberal tolerance through a search for the conditions under which religious practice can flourish, and reaching that idea through a mutual commitment to self-government under the guidance of reason. God has everything to do with the former and nothing to do with the latter. Religion, on the first view, does not operate as a direct source of governmental authority, but it does establish necessary conditions of valid authority. This approach produces an essentially negative attitude toward government, emphasizing the need for limits on the power of the state. This is the liberalism of "negative liberty."[7] On the second view, legitimate authority arises from self-government. Liberal self-government arises from a common commitment to a regime of reason. The commitment to tolerance, on this view, arises out of an inquiry into the

---

[5] Rawls writes that "justice as fairness tries to construct a conception of justice that takes deep and unresolvable differences on matters of fundamental significance as a permanent condition of human life." J. Rawls, "Kantian Constructivism in Moral Theory," 77 J. Phil. 515, 542 (1980).

[6] Taylor, Sources of the Self 13.

[7] On positive and negative liberty, see I. Berlin, "Two Concepts of Liberty," in Four Essays on Liberty 118 (1969), discussed below in chap. 3.

conditions of free thought: the diversity of argument, not of faith, establishes the reach of tolerance.[8]

The liberal state of speech may not meet the conditions set by the liberal state of religious tolerance, and vice versa. The liberalism of faith begins from the fact of a diversity of religious beliefs; the liberalism of speech begins from a common intuition of the norm of justice. God and justice are not the same. A liberal state can aim for agreement on the nature of justice, but not on the nature of God.

Traditional, Christian faith in God was not particularly connected to speech. We think, for example, of silent prayer or of silent witnessing. Some Christian sects still take a vow of silence. The liturgy was spoken in Latin, a language not even understood by most of the community of the faithful. Speech in Christianity was associated with confession. Confession is a kind of preparatory act, an opening of the soul to faith. Not the speech, but the faith that follows speech, had ultimate meaning. Speech could not generate its own meanings, because speech was itself inadequate to the substance of the relationship to the divine.[9] The speech that sustains religious meaning is divine revelation, not the human act of mutual discursive engagement.

No longer confident that God is the foundation of meaning, the modern liberal turns to speech. The liberalism of speech imagines a moment of pure speech that organizes the state. It can imagine this as a hypothetical moment of origin or as an aspirational ideal. The key proposition is that each speaker will only enter into a political relationship in which all the others respect her as a speaking, that is, reason-giving, subject. Discursive equality is the beginning of the liberal state.[10] In the Rawlsian version, at the moment individuals enter the

---

[8] The different perspective on the origins of the liberal state might, for example, produce different evaluations of the legitimacy of a law prohibiting blasphemy. See R. Post, "Cultural Heterogeneity and Law: Pornography, Blasphemy and the First Amendment," in *Constitutional Domains: Democracy, Community, Management* 59–116 (1995).

[9] Compare the Jewish tradition, which placed its origins in a covenant and a legal text. But see R. Schwartz, *The Curse of Cain: The Violent Legacy of Monotheism* (1997) (on multiple variations on text).

[10] Ackerman offers as a first principle of liberal discourse that "the power holder must respond [to a challenge] not by suppressing the questions but by giving a reason

social contract, all that they have is the capacity to speak to each other and an open expectation about the future. Speaking purely, these imagined individuals speak for all future generations.

That these two sources of liberalism—faith and speech—substantially overlap in our own self-conception of a "constitutional democracy" is clear from their joint presence in the First Amendment. Early American history includes both the experience of religious communities seeking freedom from state interference and the appeal to an Enlightenment ideal of rational self-rule. Because they overlap, there has been no need seriously to address their differences. Nevertheless, both the conundrums and the hopes of American liberalism emerge out of the troubled relationship between these two different conceptions. By privileging faith over politics, the first form of liberalism always keeps open the possibility that an intolerant faith—an unreasonable faith—will assert a claim for recognition.[11] Yet the hope of the liberalism of speech is to find in reason limits on the range of that which must be tolerated. We seem to have to choose between tolerating a faith that will not tolerate reason or tolerating a reason that will not tolerate faith.

In this less religious age, culture is replacing God. Multiculturalism appropriates the traditional arguments for the liberalism of faith. Culture, like religion, is understood to make an ultimate claim upon the individual: a claim that cannot be understood simply in terms of rational deliberation and free choice. Instead, culture rests on something akin to faith. From this perspective, the virtue of the liberal state is that it preserves the conditions under which cultural diversity can be pursued. If individual meaning and personal virtues are to be found primarily in culture, then the state's first obligation is to protect the cultures that groups bring to the state.[12]

---

that explains why he is more entitled to the resource than the questioner is." B. Ackerman, *Social Justice in the Liberal State* 4 (1980). Those reasons must be "neutral" as between speaker and questioner. Ibid. at 11.

[11] Rawls recognizes this danger from a liberal toleration that rests only upon a modus vivendi among diverse groups. J. Rawls, "The Idea of an Overlapping Consensus," *Oxford Journal of Legal Studies* 1, 11 (1987).

[12] See, e.g., Kymlicka, *Multicultural Citizenship* 76–77 (1995) (on the idea of a "societal culture").

The liberalism of speech will pose the same threat to minority cultures that it has posed to minority religious groups: it will treat them as just another group of speakers in the political marketplace. Just as the liberalism of speech tends to understand religion as irrational speech, it tends to see the claims of culture as a dangerous source of irrationality. On this view, politics draws to itself the modern values of reason, progress, and deliberative self-construction. Claims for culture, on the other hand, are seen as potentially regressive forces if allowed to enter the public sphere.

These conflicting forms of liberalism are readily accessible in American constitutional law. In recent years, religion has lost its privileged place at the foundation of the state, while speech has become ever more central to the Supreme Court's conception of a democratic community under law. The religion clauses of the Constitution have been reinterpreted within the paradigm of the liberalism of speech. Free speech has come to dominate the Court's idea of the liberal state.[13] This jurisprudential loss for religion may actually reflect a growing political activism by religious groups. If religious groups can compete in the political domain, then perhaps their claims should be treated the same as those of other political groups. Equally possible, however, is that political activism by the religious has been encouraged by the Court's efforts to treat faith as a matter of speech.

The Demise of Free-Exercise Jurisprudence

Modern free-exercise jurisprudence began with a ruling that quickly came to be seen as a mistake, that in *Minersville School District v. Gobitis*.[14] There, the Court held that Seventh-Day Adventists could be required to participate in the public school ritual of saluting the flag. The Court saw a confrontation between two forms of ritual behavior: The secular religion of the state opposed yet another version of fundamentalist Protestantism that had broken away from the mainstream

---

[13] The reaction to this view is quintessentially expressed in a recent proposal in the Virginia state legislature to mount a placard in every public school announcing "in God we trust" and to require students to recite the Pledge of Allegiance. M. Hardy and J. E. Shapiro, "The Last Session: Policy Takes Backseat to Partisanship in 2001," *Richmond Times Dispatch*, Feb. 25, 2001.

[14] 310 U.S. 586 (1940).

denominations. (Of course there will rarely, if ever, be a conflict between the demands of the state and those of mainstream religious practices.) In this confrontation, the Court sides with the rituals of civic religion: "A society which is dedicated to the preservation of these ultimate values of civilization may in self-protection utilize the educational process for inculcating those almost unconscious feelings which bind men together in a comprehending loyalty."[15] The Court rejects the liberalism of faith, which understands the state as a means to protect religious experience. The Court is not particularly wary of a form of political coercion that rests on the belief that the state itself can assume a religious—that is, an "ultimate"—value.

Refusing to yield in the face of the decision, the religious group became the victim of widespread attacks for its opposition to the rituals of patriotism.[16] This willingness to sacrifice for religious faith undermined the state's victory, exposing it as an act of force rather than an expression of principle.[17] Rapidly, the Court changed its view, holding now that coerced patriotism is a kind of counterfeit patriotism in *West Virginia State Board Of Education v. Barnette*.[18] Real patriotism must be built on speech. Patriotic speech is not the "compulsory unification of opinion," but the activity of the classroom itself, where speech is the enlightened voice of reason.[19] Patriotic speech is, accordingly, the free speech of reason, which compels not through coercion but through the force of persuasion alone.

More is at stake here than a reversal with respect to the relationship of a small Christian sect to the state. There is a larger shift from the claims of a liberalism of faith to those of a liberalism of speech. When asked to affirm the liberalism of faith in *Gobitis*, the Court ruled against the religious resisters. By 1940, the liberal state in the shadow of the church was no longer a vision of the state commensurate with the experience of the nation-state as constitutive of citizen identity.

---

[15] 310 U.S. 600.

[16] S. Peters, *Judging Jehovah's Witnesses: Religious Persecution and the Dawn of the Rights Revolution* (2000); V. Rotnem and F. Folsom Jr., "Recent Restrictions Upon Religious Liberty," 36 *Am. Pol. Sci. Rev.* 1053 (1942) (describing violence against the Jehovah's Witnesses after *Gobitis*).

[17] On the political power of sacrifice, see discussion at 80–81 below.

[18] 319 U.S. 624 (1943).

[19] *Ibid.* 641.

The rituals of sacrifice had shifted from the religious domain to the political battlefield, and the latter needs its sustaining faith just as much as the former. The *Gobitis* opinion is full of the language of ultimate values—"an interest inferior to none," "treasured common life," "ultimate foundation"—all of which are now attributed to the state. Religion, on the other hand, is described as belief in "the supernatural." The problem, however, is to find a doctrinal form adequate to the experience of the state as the center of meaning.

Thus, in reversing its *Gobitis* decision, the Court does not appeal to the liberalism of faith. Instead, the Court finds the source of value for the state in the liberalism of speech. It now offers a positive vision of the state as the product of the discourse of public reason. This is the state that was the object of patriotic veneration in *Gobitis*. Repression in the classroom is wrong because it is self-defeating. It is self-defeating by definition, if the foundation of the state is free discourse. Worse, it is a kind of sin against our secular faith in the capacity of reason to bind us together.

Barnette translates religious faith into just another form of speech to be tested in the forum of reason, which is the classroom as metaphor for the state itself. Religion now appears as only another source of potential error or of private prejudice that the enlightened speech of the classroom is to confront. The ritual act of patriotism is not the pledge, but the debate. This is the liberalism of speech, which believes that public discourse is both the source of political order and the means of sustaining that order. The faith upon which the state is built is not a faith in the supernatural, but a faith in the citizen's capacity to exercise reason.

Because *Barnette* never directly confronts religion, it does not reach the issue of religious resistance to the state's speech. What happens when the religious refuse to enter into the rational debate that is at the center of the liberalism of speech? What if they never enter the domain within which reason's persuasive power is to do its patriotic work? This issue is posed directly in *Wisconsin v. Yoder.*[20] There, the Amish object to a state compulsory education requirement insofar as it requires students to attend school beyond the eighth grade. The Court

[20] 406 U.S. 205 (1972).

accepts the argument that exposure to the speech of reason can of itself be detrimental to religious faith and practice: "enforcement of the State's requirement of compulsory formal education after the eighth grade would gravely endanger if not destroy the free exercise of respondents' religious beliefs."[21] The Amish, accordingly, are protected from the secularizing effects of the liberalism of speech. Faith before reason, the Court decides.

Yoder relied on the earlier case of *Sherbert v. Verner,* which held that unemployment benefits could not be denied to a Seventh-Day Adventist who declines to take a job requiring work on Saturdays.[22] A constitutional infirmity arises, the Court held, whenever an individual is forced to "to choose between following the precepts of her religion and forfeiting benefits, on the one hand, and abandoning one of the precepts of her religion in order to accept work, on the other hand."[23] Government cannot put the individual to such a choice, because it is critical to the legitimacy of the state that it preserve the conditions of free exercise of religion. Together *Sherbert* and *Yoder* sketch a picture of the liberalism of faith. Thus, *Yoder* worries that the very conditions of the liberalism of speech may conflict with the liberalism of faith. In the face of such a conflict, the state must side with the liberalism of faith.

Over the next two decades, the Court generally stuck to this position.[24] The Court did not abandon the liberalism of speech set forth so clearly in *Barnette*; rather, it preserved an exceptional space for the liberalism of faith. The exceptions allow some continuity with the longer practice of the liberalism of faith, even as the central ideology of the nation moved toward the liberalism of speech. The peripheral Christian groups at issue in these cases were not about to join the forum of reasonable political debate that provides the judicially perceived ground of legitimacy for the modern state. The alternative for these groups would be a kind of symbolic martyrdom, just as occurred

[21] *Ibid.* 219.

[22] 374 U.S. 398 (1963).

[23] *Ibid.* 404.

[24] See *Thomas v. Review Board of the Indiana Employment Security Division,* 450 U.S. 707 (1981); *Hobbie v. Unemployment Appeals Commission of Florida,* 480 U.S. 136 (1987).

after *Gobitis*. Allowing exemptions, accordingly, is the course of charity as well as a reasonable accommodation.

When the Court does rule against religious claims to free exercise, it does so not to affirm the liberalism of speech and the secular religion of the state, but rather to affirm the requirements of a modern, bureaucratic welfare state. The tension between bureaucratic rationality and faith becomes too great when the religious attack those government institutions that bear the symbolic weight of the administrative state: taxes and social security.[25] The religious owe the state minimal cooperation with the conditions of administration; they do not owe it their faith, or even their participation in a common political discourse.

All of this changes abruptly in 1990, when the Court decides *Employment Division v. Smith*.[26] Several individuals had been denied state unemployment benefits after being discharged from a private drug rehabilitation organization because they had used peyote for sacramental purposes within the Native American Church. The Oregon Supreme Court held that such a religious use of peyote was protected by the Free-Exercise clause. The Supreme Court reversed, holding that the individuals could be denied unemployment benefits because of their violation of a state criminal statute.

The *Smith* Court rereads the line of cases based on the liberalism of faith, seeing all of them now as free-speech cases. They are recast in the mold of *Barnette*: what is protected is not religion, but speech that happens to be informed with a religious content. When the demand that the religious make cannot be reformulated as a claim to speak, there is no ground for extending to it any judicial recognition.[27] If *Barnette* is only about speech, then *Gobitis* is about religion, and the two do not necessarily make contact. Thus, the Court recovers *Gobitis* as a correct statement of the subordination of religious practice to state ends. Correct not because the Court again recognizes a compet-

---

[25] See *U.S. v. Lee*, 455 U.S. 252 (1982) (upholding mandatory participation in the social security system); *Bowen v. Roy*, 476 U.S. 693 (1986) (rejecting challenge to use of social security numbers as means of identifying applicants for government welfare programs.). See also *Goldman v. Weinberger*, 475 U.S. 503 (1986) (rejecting a free-exercise challenge to military uniform).

[26] 494 U.S. 872 (1990).

[27] To reach this point, *Sherbert* has to be limited to its facts, since *Smith* is a *Sherbert*-like case.

ing civic religion of ultimate values, but because it subordinates the liberalism of faith to that of speech. State policies are legitimated not by the space they leave religion, but by their production through a democratic process in which all may speak.

The reformulation of the foundation of the state in the liberalism of speech is particularly evident at the end of the *Smith* opinion, when the Court sends the religiously motivated back to the political process: "It may fairly be said that leaving accommodation to the political process will place at a relative disadvantage those religious practices that are not widely engaged in; but that unavoidable consequence of democratic government must be preferred to a system in which each conscience is law unto itself or in which judges weigh the social importance of all laws against the centrality of all religious beliefs."[28] This judicial weighing process, however, is just what the liberalism of faith required. It was not too much to ask; rather it was the necessary condition of a liberal state that lived in the shadow of the church. Judges had to do more than protect the purity of the process by which laws were made: they had to measure the product itself.

To tell the religious that they must fend for themselves through political discourse is to say that they have no privileged position. Like every other citizen, they are seen only as actual or potential speakers. Their speech must compete with that of others. The Court will defend their right to speak, but it will not recognize a value of religion apart from that of speech. There is no longer any need for a separate Free-Exercise clause.[29]

The last fifty years of First Amendment jurisprudence have been a search for the liberal soul of the polity. We cannot expect to find systematic political theory coming from the Court, but we can trace the influences and deployment of the two streams of thought that have

[28] 494 U.S. at 890.

[29] This shift from the liberalism of faith to that of speech is equally reflected in the Court's recent Establishment clause jurisprudence. In *Rosenberger v. Rector and Visitors of University of Virginia*, 515 U.S. 819 (1995), a student religious organization made a claim to state funds available to other student publications. Seeing the religious as only another group of speakers, the Court could imagine no ground for distinguishing them from others with a communicative content to convey. Any such distinction would amount to "viewpoint discrimination"—the cardinal sin of the liberalism of speech.

been central elements of the liberal tradition. We find a Court struggling with the two forms of liberalism—of faith and of speech, negative and positive—and trying to understand the values of the modern state within the terms provided by these models. The present ascendency of the liberalism of speech should not be seen as a kind of final victory. Both forms of liberalism are deeply embedded in our political culture. It was, therefore, no surprise to see Congress respond to the *Smith* decision by passing the Religious Freedom Restoration Act, which sought a return to the liberalism of faith of the earlier case law. The effort was struck down by the Court, but the Court does not have the power to end this debate.[30]

CHRISTIANITY, MARTYRDOM, AND THE STATE

The liberalism of faith rests in substantial part upon a perception that intolerance would be politically self-defeating. If we ask why intolerance has been thought to be politically impractical in the modern West, the answer points toward Christianity. After all, in much of the world intolerance has been a successful political practice. Even in the West, there was often a link between political power and religious faith. Socrates, we recall, was executed for failing to believe in the gods of Athens. No one objected that there should be a separation of church and state, only that the charge was not true. But in a Christian world, the idea of separation is a part of the framework within which politics is conceived. This doesn't mean that separation was always a fact, but it was a conceptual possibility.

Believing that the end of the world was literally at hand, the earliest Christians had no interest in the state. They did not seek to take over the state but to leave the state—spiritually, if not geographically. The relationship of Christianity to state power is captured in the image of Christ on the cross. From the perspective of the state, Christ is rendered powerless. He is destroyed, made nothing at all. The believer, however, reverses this equation, and sees a triumph of faith over politics. This is expressed directly in the image of the cross: Christ is executed by the state, but conquers the entire domain of politics through his resurrection. This is the end of politics, not a victory within poli-

---

[30] *City of Boerne v. Flores* 521 U.S. 507 (1997).

tics. Neither Islam nor Judaism shares this image of a negation of politics through transcendence. Abraham and Muhammad, the founders of their faiths, exercise a kind of political rule within re-formed communities that are to endure temporally by expressing a divine order. These are religions of law, not of love.[31]

To the believer, Christ demonstrates the ultimate emptiness of political power and the insubstantiality of the state. Paul announces to new believers: "You also died to the law through the body of Christ."[32] The believer's response to the appearance of Christ is not—at least not at first—the bringing of the state to Christ, but a radical turning away from the things of this world. Christ's experience on the cross becomes paradigmatic for subsequent Christian martyrs, who together give shape to a tradition of otherworldly resistance to the state.[33]

Political power is measured by its geographic reach and its temporal endurance. A political community has geographical borders, a unified past, and a common future. There is no abstract political power, but only the power to act within and against particular communities. Within that geographical-temporal space, political power makes a unique claim to control the body itself. Thus, political power is ultimately a power over life and death. It is most vividly displayed at moments of conscription and criminal punishment. Apart from the capacity to coerce, an individual's possession of political power is ordinarily a function of wealth and fame, or class, status, and role. Most of all, political power reproduces itself, that is, present power can be traced to past power.

Christianity announces that all of these are nothing: history is about to end, geographical borders are irrelevant to the community of the faithful; fame, wealth, role, and status count for nothing in the kingdom of heaven; family and class determine nothing; and there is no earthly power that can overcome death. The power of faith cannot be inherited, transferred, or sold. To the Christian, it makes no difference who your parents are or which position in society you occupy. Christianity first appears as a religion of the poor, the outcast, and women:

[31] See P. Kahn, *Law and Love: The Trials of King Lear* (1996).

[32] Rom., 7:4, New International. Version; see also King James Version, "Wherefore, my brethren, ye also are become dead to the law by the body of Christ."

[33] See P. Brown, *The Body and Society: Men, Women and Sexual Renunciation in Early Christianity* 73–75 (1988).

those without political power. The fundamental metaphor of Christianity is, accordingly, rebirth—to be born again in the community of the church, which is the body of Christ. The church is without temporal or geographic boundaries.

The expectation of the Christian about his or her relationship to the state cannot be more than the message of Christ on the cross, which is a message of sacrifice, martyrdom, and redemption. The martyr denies the state power, while yielding to its violence. The martyr confronts the state in a contest of power, putting forth his or her own understanding of the meaning to be attached to death. A political execution read as an act of martyrdom proclaims the weakness, not the strength, of the state. This is not a kind of quietism in the face of the state, but a faith imbued with an idea of resistance from the very beginning.

The early Christians prove their faith by resisting the state and suffering death in response to that resistance. Later Christians go through a similar rite of political passage, which often leads to exile instead of death. Exile, too, is an expression of resistance and sacrifice: it is a kind of suffering at the hands of the state, imposed on those who will not renounce their religious beliefs. Both the martyr and the exile understand their behavior as following the example of Christ's sacrifice. To those who believe that the state of the soul determines the conditions of eternal life, politics can neither promise nor threaten much. Politics is of this world; what is truly important is beyond.

This idea of resistance and sacrifice survives into the modern era as a paradigm of the relationship between religious belief and the demands of the state. It fuels a religious—and moral—wariness of the state. In response to political demands contrary to religious belief, the Christian will suffer martyrdom or exile rather than concede authority to the state. Resistance to the state is built into the fundamental tenets of Christianity. From there, it has been generalized as a fundamental tenet of the Western—and particularly American—understandings of the relationship of the individual to the state. At the center of that moral experience is the image of the "conscientious objector," who proves his moral virtue through the denial of the state's power.[34]

---

[34] See generally M. Walzer, *Obligations: Essays on Disobedience, War and Citizenship* 120–45 (1970).

In the West, politics and morality can never merge completely.[35] We tend to be political realists, at the same time that we are moral absolutists. Politics cannot usurp morality; it cannot declare moral resistance treason. Neither, however, can morality usurp politics; it cannot declare moral norms to be law. Conscientious objection remains a moral possibility that stands outside of every political value. The conscientious objector bears witness; he does not organize a political party. The ambition for a comprehensive theory that can stand beyond this incommensurability—for example, theories of natural law—is understandable, but unfulfillable. In the United States, resistance to claims of natural law is as old as the practice of constitutional interpretation itself.[36]

The early Christian community appears as a sort of inverse image of the state. It is universal, not bounded by geographical borders. The universality of the Christian community is founded on its complete absence of political ambition. Not seeking to conquer, it attempts to unite all in an image of power forsaken. It has no history and no future, apart from the breaking into ordinary time of the divine presence. Christ's appearance and his promised return create a sacred narrative apart from the ordinary succession of events within which political power rises and falls. The Christian communities that emerge as societies of brothers or of sisters are indifferent to the ordinary values of the political community—that is, to power in the form of wealth, fame, or family connections. Indeed, these are often communities of celibates, giving up any idea that the intergenerational maintenance of the community has value.

This idea that the church and the state exist in separate dimensions has a troubled life as each sphere tries to coopt the other to its own purposes. Because the church is concerned with the salvation of all, it cannot be indifferent to political actions that it believes may cause ruler or ruled to exist in a state of sin. And because religious motivation and belief are so extraordinarily compelling, political rulers cannot be indifferent to the support that they could potentially obtain

---

[35] See B. Williams, "Politics and Moral Character," in *Public and Private Morality* 55 (S. Hampshire, ed., 1998); M. Walzer, "Political Action: the Problem of Dirty Hands" 2 *Phil. Pub. Aff.* 160 (1973).

[36] See *Calder v. Bull*, 3 U.S. 386, 399 (1798) (Iredell, J., concurring).

from the church. To attack the church risked civil war, but to coopt the church held out a promise of greater security: These two opposing forces provide the motivations through which we can read much of European history. This is a history of a struggle among separation, hegemony, and cooptation. We are hardly done with this struggle today, as we witness a renewed political activism of religious groups as well as efforts by government to deploy religious institutions to further the social-welfare policies of the state.

This is a paradoxical history—a history that was not even supposed to be, according to the fundamental tenets of Christian belief. Anticipating the imminent end of time and the Second Coming of Christ, all of history appeared as a kind of baffling ontological pause in which we lead our lives. It is a history that has always taken an ironic stance toward itself, because the state is always denied the one thing that power desires most: an ultimate authority over the individual.

Hegel writes of the master-slave relationship as the origin of political history. The slave is not willing to die; he is a failed martyr. He grants others the power to script the meaning of his life. The Western state actually exists, however, under the very real threat of Christian martyrdom: a threat to expose the state and its claim to power as nothing at all. In the end, sacrifice is always stronger than murder. The martyr wields a power to defeat his murderer, which cannot be answered on the field of battle. This may seem like an antiquated idea, but we need only think of the continuing place for the politics of human rights or the nonviolent resistance of the civil rights movement.[37]

More broadly, we see in this history the origin of the Western idea that ultimate meanings are to be found in a turning away from the public order and toward a private struggle with one's own soul.[38] There is a deep distrust of the state in the Western tradition—both a sense that involvement with politics threatens us with moral corruption and a sense that politics must always be tested against an uncorrupted moral vision. American political parties draw on this tradition

[37] See M. L. King Jr., "Letter from Birmingham Jail" (Apr. 16, 1963); for recent examples, consider tactics of Greenpeace and of the velvet revolutions of Eastern Europe. See J. Schell, *The Unconquerable World: Power, Nonviolence and the Will of the People* (2003).

[38] See Taylor, *The Sources of the Self*, chap. 7.

when they campaign for office by "running against government." Politics always appears as a moral threat and, therefore, is always in need of moral revitalization from outside.

The early battles between faith and politics, and then between church and state, were not fights in which a liberal program played a role. These were not disputes between a religious consciousness, on one side, and a liberal, secular consciousness, on the other. Nevertheless, they set the stage for thinking about the relationship between religion and state. They created an enduring memory of the relationship between political authority and religious belief as one marked by separation, as well as a sense of danger to both sides when that which should be separated comes in contact. The ideas of separation and resistance, of the monkish retreat to a life in prayer, and of potential martyrdom continued as sources of critique within Christianity, even as the church pursued its own political ambitions. This is a unique resource of the West. Separation of church and state enters the Western imagination not as an expression of a philosophically justified, secular politics, but as an aspect of religious belief. It includes not simply an idea that the state poses a danger to religion, but equally the opposite idea that religion poses a threat to the state because it reveals the insubstantiality of the concerns of the state and the limits on the state's power over the individual. The state's power is ultimately the power to threaten life, but Christianity begins with a sacrificial act that undermines that threat by announcing life to be death, and true life to lie beyond death.[39]

Even as the West becomes the place of Christian empires, the ancient image of the Christian martyr remains an important resource. The threat of martyrdom is always a dangerous power that the religious can wield against the state. It is the means by which the religious claim an indefeasible power: if defeat means martyrdom, then the state's victory is always precarious. The history of the West is full of such

[39] Plato makes a parallel claim in the *Phaedo*, which announces philosophy to be a practice of dying. For Plato too the state loses power when it confronts the philosopher willing to sacrifice the self. This suggests that Christianity was already responding to and deepening a Western tradition. But the Christianity of Saint Paul suggests a general social norm of what had been exceptional in Plato's vision of Athens. See Brown, *The Body and Society* 8–10.

examples of the martyred saint, who claims victory even as he or she suffers at the hands of the state.[40]

Liberalism has traditionally been understood to have had its birth as a secular response to the religious wars of the Reformation. Those wars created a perception that the alternative to tolerance of religious diversity is a kind of fight to the death among those willing to sacrifice themselves for their faith. This understanding is not wrong, but it is incomplete. The liberal solution to the problem of religious competition does not come from nowhere. The idea of separation that founds the idea of liberal tolerance is in fact a much older idea. Its origins reach deep within the substantive character of fundamental Christian belief. It comes from the Christian idea that religion is fundamentally a turning of the soul toward God, and thus a turning away from the things of this world. All of the varieties of Christian sects make a direct claim on the founding experience of Christ. All carry forward the same language of martyrdom. All of them can appeal to the images of sacrifice and separation.

CHRISTIANITY, SOVEREIGNTY, AND THE STATE

The continuing threat of martyrdom is only one part of the movement of Christianity from a millennial expectation to a long-term confrontation with the state. The history of Christianity is a history of adaptation to the frustration of its most fundamental belief: the world does not come to an end. Christ does not return in the lifetime of the disciples or even in the millennia since then. Christianity must reconcile itself not just to the political history of the state, but to its own history as well. The church is the institutional expression of a religion that was to have no historical presence because it announced the end of time. Christianity accomplishes this reconciliation of the timeless and the temporal so well that the church becomes the model for the development of the European state. When Henry VIII rejects the pope and puts himself at the head of a politico-religious community, he is only

[40] Consider Sir Thomas More, who was reputed to have said to his executioner, kissing him, "[t]hou wilt give me this day a greater benefit than ever any mortal man can be able to give me." P. Ackroyd, *The Life of Thomas More* 406 (1999); see also, R. Warren, *John Brown: The Making of a Martyr* (1929).

making particularly visible a process that all Western states pursued: an identification of the community of faith with the political community. We find ourselves deeply within this tradition, for example, when we speak of the American civic religion. Liberal values play a role within this civic religion. We saw this above in the interplay of the secular faith of *Gobitis* with the liberalism of *Barnette*. Yet, these liberal values do not even begin to explain the experience of ultimate meaning that the individual finds in his or her identity as a citizen. We need another form of discourse—one beyond the capacities of liberalism—to understand the political claim of even the liberal state. To begin, we need to turn again to Christianity.

The church demonstrates the possibility of creating a political order on the basis of an experience of a transcendent or ultimate meaning. To outsiders, the church may appear to operate as an ordinary political power, but insiders understand it in a symbolic dimension. Of course, at times the church has exercised a political power of coercion. We can ask, how many divisions does the pope command? Yet to believers the point of the church is to give historical life to a truth that always appears beyond and above any particular institutional expression. The church's authority flows from its capacity to present that meaning to its own members. Institutions, ritual, and doctrine are all ways of translating the immediacy of the experience of transcendent faith into finite historical forms. The relationship between the particulars of church practice and doctrine, on the one hand, and the transcendent meaning that founds the church, on the other, is surprisingly immediate. Within the church, one is never far from God. This is even more true in the various Protestant sects that come into being objecting to forms of institutional mediation between the believer and his or her God.

The church's authority is coextensive with belief in the meaning it offers. Ideally, ruler and ruled are united not through threat or coercion, but on the basis of shared belief. Only in part is this belief a matter of doctrine. Doctrine, like ritual, is never exhaustive of the experience of transcendent meaning. It is an effort to put into words that which is experienced as beyond language. Christianity offers the West its most important model of the political power of an ideology.[41]

---

[41] See C. Geertz, "Ideology as a Cultural System," in *The Interpretation of Cultures: Selected Essays* 193–233 (1973).

An ideology, however, should not be confused with a doctrine. Doctrine is the effort to express in systematic form ideological belief, but it is never commensurate with that belief. Systematic theology—no matter how elaborate—is not the same as Christian faith. Thus, the church demonstrates that the power of coercion is as nothing compared to the power of shared belief. But it also shows that this ideological power is not captured in doctrine alone. The endless debates over doctrine, both religious and political, are sustained by a prior commitment—a faith—that doctrine expresses a singular truth of ultimate significance.

While the church holds forth the divine as its own foundation, it is never itself a complete expression of the divine. Only in Christ is there a complete convergence of the divine and its historical expression. This coincidence of the infinite and the finite is expressed in the concept of the "sovereign." The sovereign is always located at the point at which the divine enters history, that is, the point at which it takes a concrete shape. In this sense, the sovereign is always miraculous.[42]

In its symbolic dimension, the paradigmatic, modern Western political organization—the nation-state—is built on this model: The state is to maintain the historical presence of an experience of ultimate meaning. It brings what is out of time into time. For the individual, participation in the life of the nation gives a dimension of depth to this experience—that is, an experience of a fundamental meaning that transcends the ordinary. As with the church, the transcendent meaning of the state is close to the surface of its institutions, practices, and doctrines. The state claims to be a manifestation of the sovereignty of the nation. Sovereignty is the point of intersection of the symbolic character of church and of state, of religion and politics. Shared belief in an ultimate meaning—sovereignty—secures for the state, as for the church, the power of faith.

In the modern period, the popular sovereign steps into this position of an inexhaustible source of ultimate meaning: the sacred source behind and beyond any particular political expression, whether doctrinal or institutional. There may be competing understandings of the basis of national sovereignty—for example, civic or ethnic national-

---

[42] See chap. 6 below.

ism—but regardless of these differences, the state is the historical and institutional expression of a meaning that always transcends its institutional expression. The institutions of political order gain their symbolic meaning as expressions of the sovereign, yet they never capture completely the fullness of sovereignty. Political life is not exhausted in either the forms of contract or coercion. It is never exhausted in the present; it maintains a sacred past and opens up the possibility of a national destiny.

As with the appearance of Christ, there are founding political moments at which the finite character of politics and particular political actors intersects with the fullness of sovereign meaning. In the modern age, revolution is the paradigm of such an intersection; it steps into the place previously occuied by coronation. Revolution always claims to be action by the popular sovereign; it is, for that reason, miraculous.[43] The origins of the modern Western state are not in the social contract, but in communities of political faith. The state is the contemporary institutional form within which that faith takes a geographical and temporal shape. State borders that fail to match the borders of a community of faith—that is, that fail to cohere with a recognition of national sovereignty—generally fail or there develops a matching conception of sovereignty. The shifting of borders in Eastern Europe in the last decade represents just such an effort to match political institutions to popular conceptions of the sovereign.

The church demonstrates the possible power of a politics founded on belief. There are no natural limits to such a community of faith. Its geographical reach is as broad as its ideological message is acceptable. Its temporal endurance is as long as the beliefs are sustained. The church also demonstrates the potential weakness of a belief-based political order. Power founded on ideological belief can be no more secure than the beliefs themselves. When belief fails, the collapse of the political order can be swift indeed. Moreover, the content of belief provides a ground of critique of those who would exercise power as the representative of those beliefs. Thus, while offering the promise of unlimited extension, the ideological foundation also limits power from within. A claim of religious authority is always vulnerable to

[43] See, e.g., C. Bowen, *The Miracle at Philadelphia* (1966).

critique by new "prophets" who claim to speak the truth of religious belief. A king who purports to rule on the basis of divine right is vulnerable to the criticism that he has fallen from God's favor; a king who purports to rule as representative of the will of the nation is vulnerable to the critique that he is unrepresentative. A democratic polity will invest a tremendous amount of power in the person or persons believed to represent the people. But just this fact means that the representative is always subject to the criticism that he or she is not performing in a representative fashion.

Like every other formation of power that depends on an ideology, the church is vulnerable to internal critique. Precisely for that reason it develops defensive doctrines, including most obviously the use of esoteric language and ritual, which make members particularly dependent on a priestly class. These defensive doctrines also include the effort to make authority itself an element of faith, as in the doctrine of papal infallibility, priestly intermediation, and the practice of confession and repentance. Not surprisingly, when the internal critique arises in the Reformation, these defensive doctrines are the immediate targets of reform. The pope is infallible only as long as members of the church believe him to be. He is no more, and no less, infallible than that succession of absolute monarchs who follow him in European history, some of whom went to their death claiming infallibility. Of more relevance today, he has the same infallibility as a supreme court, which is infallible only as long as there is a faith that its voice is that of law's rule. When we see the individuals behind the robes, the claim of infallibility is hard to sustain.[44] In the same way, the development of an esoteric doctrine and ritual of constitutional law simultaneously makes ordinary citizens dependent on the "priestly class" of lawyers and judges, and in turn makes those functionaries vulnerable to attack for their failure to meet the demands of citizens. The Court may be the most respected institution of government in America, but lawyers are simultaneously among the least respected of professionals.

If the first contribution of the early battles of faith and politics supports the idea of separate spheres, and thus a liberalism in the shadow of the church, the second contribution points in exactly the opposite

---

[44] See P. Kahn, *The Reign of Law* 105–33 (1997).

direction—that is, to the deeply intertwined character of Western religious experience and political practice. Political organization takes as its model that combination of belief and institutional structure achieved by the church. Separation as a form of practical management of the conflict between spheres is not reflected at the level of conceptual organization. There, we find a massive migration of religious conceptions into the order of politics. At the center of this migration is the political adaptation of the concept of sovereignty.[45]

The sovereign God of the biblical tradition creates order ex nihilo: He wills an ordered cosmos into existence. The sovereignty of Christ is the physical or finite instantiation of the entire, divinely created cosmos. He is the material form of the logos: simultaneously universal and particular. Similarly, the political sovereign comes to be understood as the font of political order, creating a legal order through nothing more than the expression of its will. When John Austin declares law to be the command of the sovereign, he may believe that he is offering a secular jurisprudence set off from theories of natural law.[46] In fact, he is borrowing the oldest paradigm for the explanation of the origin of order in the Judeo-Christian tradition.

In premodern Europe, the king's will was the sovereign source of law. The kings of Europe took on the symbolic character of the body of Christ: they too had overcome death in their own bodies. And just as the body of Christ is the body of the church, so the body of the King is the mystical corpus of the state.[47] The political story of the rise of the modern West is, in large part, that of the transformation of the conceptual apparatus of the sovereign as the monarch to the sovereign as the people. The will of people becomes the source of legal order; the popular sovereign—not the monarch's body—is the mystical corpus of

[45] See C. Schmitt, *Political Theology: Four Chapters on the Concept of Sovereignty* 36 (G. Schwab, trans., 1985). ("All significant concepts of the modern theory of the state are secularlized theological concepts not only because of their historical development—in which they were transferred from theology to the theory of the state, whereby, for example, the omnipotent God became the omnipotent lawgiver—but also because of their systemic structure.")

[46] See J. Austin, *The Province of Jurisprudence Determined* (H.L.A. Hart, ed., 1954).

[47] See E. Kantorowitz, *The King's Two Bodies: A Study of Mediaeval Political Theology* (1957); F. Maitland, "The Crown as Corporation," 17 *Law Quarterly Review*, 131–46 (1901).

the state. It too conquers the death of the finite body. Only the locus of sovereignty, not its symbolic character, changes.

By the modern era, the people have become the new absolute. The people as a single subject are the source of ultimate meanings in and for the Western state. Revolution and constitutional construction mark the assertion of a power of the popular sovereign to destroy order by withdrawing the sovereign will and to create order by speaking it into existence. The state is founded on nothing more than this sovereign act of will, which comes from nowhere, and has no measure apart from the people's self-expression. The created order of the state is "good" as long as the people look upon their creation and pronounce it to be good. When they find it otherwise, their violent act of self-destruction can be as "terrible" as that of God when he rendered judgment on Sodom. Ethno-nationalism becomes such a powerful force in the modern era because it answers the question of who the popular sovereign is. Civic nationalism counters with a different answer to this question. Yet both take for granted the ultimate character of the popular sovereign.

Rousseau tells us that the sovereign people are infallible; they are also deathless, and—at any given moment—combine the universal and the particular.[48] Just as those exercising power within the church claim authority only as expression of the Sovereign, all legitimate political power in the nation-state is now conceived as a representation of the sovereign people. The sole warrant for political power is a claim to represent the people. The people have become the new god and their state founds the new world order.

The modern nation-state has definitively established itself when government asserts that it is entitled to demand of every citizen that he or she sacrifice the self for the continued existence of the state. This demand appears legitimate because individual identity has been reconceived as membership in the popular sovereign. We are all citizens and comrades. Ultimate meanings coincide with ultimate demands. The reverse side of this is that entire populations, as political communities, can become the target of attack. This understanding is

---

[48] See J. Rousseau, *The Social Contract* 45 (C. Sherover, trans. and ed., [1762] 1974).

the background condition of individual life within the modern state. It is what links the eighteenth-century revolutionary discovery of an ultimate meaning in popular sovereignty to the policy of mutual assured destruction in the twentieth century, and to the bioterrorism of the twenty-first. It continues despite the repeated efforts by international humanitarian law to protect noncombatants from the suffering of war. If we are today reluctant to accept this claim upon ourselves as citizens, or even reject it out of hand, then we may be entering a new era of postmodern politics.[49] In fact, contemporary politics is caught between a nostalgic romance for the nation-state as it has provided a source of ultimate meaning over the past two hundred years and an acknowledgment of a global form of bureaucratic administration that has increasingly displaced national meanings.[50] It is simply impossible to say which of these forces will dominate over the next one hundred years.

Modern politics became a distinctive form of religious experience in the West when popular sovereignty was experienced as a claim of ultimate meaning for the individual citizen. The domain of sacrifice shifted from that of religious resistance to that of political patriotism. Modern stories of sacrifice are less likely to be of religious resistance to the state than of individuals whose faith in the "truth" of the state— the popular sovereign—fuels an ultimate resistance against those who make "false" claims to represent the people. For Americans, Lincoln becomes the great image of the martyr—a politicized Christ. Martin Luther King, Jr., too is celebrated not for his adherence to a religious claim to truth in resistance to the state, but as a sacrificial patriot in the Lincolnesque tradition.[51] He too represents the sovereignty of the people against the false claims of representation by those in authority.

---

[49] See conclusion, below. No one should believe that we are in such an era until the continued maintenance of nuclear weapons is seen as profoundly incompatible with the legitimate role of the state. See E. Scarry, "War and the Social Contract: Nuclear Policy, Distribution, and the Right to Bear Arms," 139 *U. Pa. L. Rev.* 1257 (1991); see also Schell, *The Unconquerable World.*

[50] On the character of this conflict in modern Europe, see L. Siedentop, *Democracy in Europe* (2001).

[51] One aspect of the shock of the Holocaust is the failure of the political murder of the Jews to register as a triumphal sacrificial act of religious faith against the state. It is seen only in political terms of power and powerlessness. The political language of

The twentieth century can only be judged a secular age if we take a narrow view of religion. If we understand religious experience as the discovery of ultimate meaning, then the century was marked by the magnitude of its faith, and even by the extreme character of the sacrificial demand made by political communities of ultimate belief. Western nation-states became grand institutional structures for the sacrifice of their citizens to the idea of the necessity of the state's continued existence. Only under such an idea can we begin to make sense of the millions sacrificed on the battlefields of Europe, let alone the extension of the battlefield to the entire territory of the state. The modern state coopts the act of sacrifice to its own ultimate end, which is only the continued existence of the popular sovereign.[52]

If the modern state is understood as the product of the popular sovereign speaking itself into existence, the question that necessarily arises is, what does the popular sovereign say? Political liberalism and popular sovereignty intersect at just this point. The philosophical effort to found liberalism in a rationally compelling discourse is just the effort to "put words in the mouth" of the popular sovereign. The ideal discourse, the discourse behind the veil of ignorance, is the speech of the popular sovereign because it is the speech of no one in particular and therefore of everyone. This is the equivalent of eighteenth-century deism, which filled in the creative word of God—the logos of Genesis—with the scientifically discerned laws of nature. God's creative speech followed a text discovered by Sir Isaac Newton. Similarly, the speech of the popular sovereign today is to follow a text discovered by John Rawls—or some other modern political theorist. How could the divine source speak anything other than the truth of reason?

The modern liberalism of speech inhabits this political state of ultimate meanings. Paradoxically, liberalism is a political morality for a limitless state.[53] This was already suggested in the move from the discourse of ultimates in *Gobitis* to the liberalism of speech in *Barnette*.

---

sacrifice is redirected into a narrative of the birth of Israel, not a recovery of an ultimate truth for Germany.

[52] See chap. 6 below, on maintenance of sovereignty as the final cause of the nation-state.

[53] This is no more of a paradox than Christianity's morality of love within a limitless claim to power.

It is the replication of the two sides of our Christian inheritance: separation and empire. Failure to recognize the quasi-religious character of the modern nation-state as the context within which liberalism operates is the single largest failure of liberal political theorists. Reading them, one would never know that the modern nation-state has been the site of endless passion and of sacrifice for ultimate meanings. For them, the people appear only as a decision-making device—majority rule—in a world stripped of ultimate meanings. To the liberal theorists, the passion of politics appears always as a dangerous outbreak of archaic forms of belief and practice.[54] History must, therefore, be a story of progress away from the very conditions that generate history. Indeed, the ideal theory of the state is to help us to escape history. While Marx may have believed that the goal toward which history is moving is the disappearance of the state, today's theorists believe that the ideal state is the end of history.[55]

The first contribution of Christianity suggests the need for a limited state in light of the demands of religious belief. The second contribution points in just the opposite direction: to a state that makes ultimate demands upon the individual. The idea of politics as a limited domain directed primarily at creating a space for the safe pursuit of religious practice confronts the idea of the state as itself the constitutive source of citizen identity. This double-heritage—of a limited and of an unlimited state—continues today. Ultimately, the problem of cultural pluralism has to be located within this double-conception of the liberal state.

In one direction, liberalism traces its origins to the separation of religion and state; in the other direction, liberalism understands itself as situated within a state that is itself a successor to the church. This is the odd spectacle of bourgeois life in the modern West. On the one hand, the bourgeois demand the cultivation of civil society, under-

[54] See B. Honig, *Political Theory and the Development of Politics* 2 (1993). ("Most political theorists are hostile to the disruption of politics. . . . They assume that the task of political theory is to resolve institutional questions, to get politics right, over and done with.")

[55] See F. Fukuyama, *The End of History and the Last Man* (1992). Contemporary international law, dominated by a paradigm of human rights, also tends to view the modern nation-state as a pathological form. See P. Kahn, "American Hegemony and International Law—Speaking Law to Power: Popular Sovereignty, Human Rights, and the New Int'l. Order," *1 Chi. J. Int'l. L.* 1, 5–6 (2000).

standing this as the domain in which each individual is free to pursue his or her own interests and values. Liberalism protects the spontaneous self-regulation of civil society by erecting a series of barriers—legal rights—to state interference. On the other hand, the bourgeois inhabits the modern nation-state, which always threatens to make an ultimate claim upon the individual. No matter how large or important the private domain becomes, the modern nation-state always claims the authority to transgress the border of the private and to devote all of the available resources—physical, material, and personal—to the state's vital interests. The bourgeois is also the citizen, and the citizen exists his entire life with the understanding that he and his property may be conscripted, that is, literally made into an instrument of the state.[56]

This is the paradox of the liberal state that is also the absolute state. Liberalism is caught along this divide. Liberals cannot settle whether liberalism requires a recognition that the sources of meaning are always outside of politics or a recognition of politics itself as the source of meaning. That is, it cannot decide whether the state is end or means. This is the modern appearance of the paradox of Christianity, which has pursued both the quietism of separation for private faith and the institutional forms of political power for two thousand years. We cannot easily escape the genealogy of our own imaginations.

One might be tempted to argue that this situation is the modern version of the Hobbesian world, in which the cost of private security and civil society is a willingness to defend the state against both internal and external threats. Hobbes, after all, is seen as the common source for a philosophical defense of political liberalism and of state absolutism. The modern problem, on this view, is that in the field of international relations we continue to live in a state of nature. This

---

[56] See, e.g., *Toyosaburo Korematsu v. United States*, 323 U.S. 214, 219–20 (1944) ("Compulsory exclusion of large groups of citizens from their homes, except under circumstances of direct emergency and peril, is inconsistent with our basic governmental institutions. But when under conditions of modern warfare our shores are threatened by hostile forces, the power to protect must be commensurate with the threatened danger."); *Schenk v. United States*, 249 U.S. 47, 52 (1919). ("When a nation is at war many things which might be said in time of peace are such a hindrance to its efforts that their utterance will not be endured so long as men fight. . . no Court could regard them as protected by any constitutional right.")

requires us to be ready to mobilize the full resources of the state in its defense. Nevertheless, the value of the state derives from the civil society it makes possible, not from the acts of sacrifice it may occasionally demand.

This, however, is only a weak apology for the maintenance of the modern, sacrificial state. The wars and confrontations of the last two centuries have been made possible by the political imagination of citizens. That imagination extends well beyond protecting the bourgeois, civil order from external threat. The citizen sees the sovereign—now the people—as an expression of his or her own ultimate meaning, and sees in the act of sacrifice an affirmation of this transcendent meaning. The modern era has not been a period in which politics has been merely a means to maintenance of civil society; rather, politics has itself been a source of absolute meaning. For some two centuries, the politics of the West has been the scene of revolution and civil war, of nationalism and ideological confrontation.

THE EARLY AMERICAN EXPERIENCE

The early American experience occurs just at the point of emergence of the bourgeois world. It captures, in substantial part, the ambiguities of that world: one in which religion, politics, and civil society compete against each other to define the meaning of the individual's life. The colonies were the domain of the private, and the private man is the "new man." But the colonists, and we who continue to read their experience, could not offer a single characterization of this new man: he is simultaneously religious and economic, a person of faith and of reason.[57] The North American colonies were equally religious and financial ventures.[58] Already, early Americans did not know whether their freedom from the state was the freedom to pursue religious truth or economic well-being. Moreover, they did not know whether these aspects of their identity—their personal interests—were to be put aside

---

[57] See generally J. Butler, *Becoming America: The Revolution Before 1776* (2000).

[58] Compare Spanish colonies that did not carry either of these meanings of religious exile or private markets. They were expressions of public authority organized on a mercantile basis for the benefit of the state, as well as institutions for proselytizing the Catholic faith. See generally C. Gibson, *Spain in America* (1966).

when participating in self-government, or to be pursued through a representative system. Of course, only in the domain of theory must firm lines be drawn. Experience does not come neatly separated. Men muddled forward under all of these ideas. They hoped that religious belief would be rewarded with material success, but they also worried about the inevitable temptations of a world of material success. They hoped that reason and religion would point in the same direction, but each perspective worried about the limits of the other.

The founding narrative of many of the American colonies was one of religious exile. Martyrdom, I have argued, includes both the ideas of sacrifice and exile. The colonists understood themselves as sacrificing the security and comfort of the established order, accepting a dangerous crossing and then life in the wilderness. To do so was to place faith in God's providence; it was to see oneself as part of a continuing Christian narrative of exile into the wilderness.[59] Yet, the New World was also understood, from the very beginning, to promise new sources of wealth. The colonies were a place where fortunes could be made. With wealth came new forms of power that could stand up to the traditional claims of class and status. To this ambiguity in the meaning of departure into the wilderness we have to add the experience of self-government within these colonial communities. American liberalism continues to reflect these historical roots: a conception of the private covering both faith and markets, and a conception of public life as participation in self-government.

The Atlantic crossing symbolized a separation from the traditional forms of power that were supported by the conjunction of political authority, religious belief, and family wealth. By the time of the Revolution, the new world order was understood to be effectively beyond the reach of a state authority that was inevitably corrupted: first, by the influence of religion; second, by economic interests that managed

---

[59] See P. Miller, *Errand into the Wilderness* 11 (1956). ("The [Massachusetts] Bay Company was not a battered remnant of suffering Separatists thrown upon a rocky shore; it was an organized task force of Christians, executing a flank attack on the corruptions of Christendom. These Puritans did not flee to America; they went there to work out that complete reformation which was not yet accomplished in England . . . but which would quickly be accomplished if only the saints back there had a working model to guide them.")

to coopt the state for the pursuit of their own private ends; and third, by the very attractions of political power itself. These were represented by the problems of an official church, state-granted monopolies, and political cronyism. Eliminating these political failings became the program of early American politics.

Unable freely to practice their religion at home, the colonists chose exile to a place farther from the reach of the coercive authority of the state. The early colonies embody stories of religious resistance, of the adherence to ultimate meanings against the authority of the state. This is the fundamental theme of the Puritan emigration, of Penn's foundation of the Pennsylvania colony, and of Lord Baltimore's creation of an early Catholic community in Maryland. The colonies attract dissenting Protestants from all over Europe: French Huguenots, Scottish Presbyterians, German Lutherans, as well as Baptists, Amish, and Mennonites. The story of martyrdom, as a story of religious intransigence before the demands of the state, continues within colonial life in the well-preserved stories of Ann Hutchinson and Roger Williams, and in the rise of the Anabaptists and the persecution of the Quakers. Later still, we see the adoption of these themes by the Mormons as they pursue their own trek into the wilderness. Any practice of intolerance by political authorities always threatens to invoke a religious response of sacrifice and exile. Exile is itself a geographical representation of the disestablishment of a political community. The exile of the saints stands for the idea that truth is more important than power, that every existing political formation is subject to critique on the basis of an ultimate truth.[60]

The easy transfer of this theme of exile from the British authorities to the colonial authorities is characteristic of Protestantism: the proliferation of sects is an unavoidable feature of this faith. By displacing the church hierarchy and holding forth an unmediated relationship between the believer and God, Protestantism creates a doctrinally unstable situation. In a religion founded on a direct relationship to a text, interpretations will inevitably proliferate. This proliferation has no "natural" stopping point. Every believer can claim his or her own

[60] See M. Walzer, *Revolution of the Saints: A Study in the Origin of Radical Politics* (1965).

interpretation of truth; each interpretation can offer a foundation for a new community of belief. This is a situation that invited the recurring revivalist movements, which would challenge established, that is, conventionalized, communities and beliefs.[61]

Protestantism denies any authority the power to judge among these interpretations or to prevent their appearance. Conflicting interpretations simply confront each other as conflicting claims to truth. Thus, every effort to create interpretive authority by linking political power to religious belief recreates the conditions that invoke the Christian response of sacrifice and exile. The very circumstances that led to the religious emigration to the New World inevitably reproduce themselves within the colonies, leading to a continuous proliferation of new communities of belief that separate themselves from their colonial progenitors.[62]

Different colonies have different amounts of success in constraining this movement toward proliferation. New England, with its decentralization of authority to the community level through Congregationalism, was more successful than those colonies—Virginia and the Carolinas, for example—in which there had been a centralized effort to establish the Anglican Church. Magnifying authority, they also magnified resistance. By the 1730s, evangelical movements were proliferating and were making deep inroads among the established churches.[63] The amount of disruption caused by this Great Awakening was di-

---

[61] See Butler, *Becoming America* 198–204.

[62] Robert Cover labeled this process of interpretive pluralism "jurisgenerative" and the opposite process of stabilizing meaning "jurispathic." See R. Cover, "The Supreme Court, 1982 Term—Foreword: Nomos and Narrative," 97 *Harv. L. Rev.* 4, 40 (1983). The jurispathic moment is necessary in any political community founded on an ideology—whether religious, historical, or sociological. We can imagine a community of scholars—or monks—endlessly debating interpretations of a text. Without some device to end that debate, speech never turns to action. The device by which authority is established may be nothing more than a vote. Voting is precisely a political device for ending debate by creating authority. But the jurispathic moment is directly challenged in the image of exile that the colonists bring with them.

[63] See H. Brogan, *The Penguin History of the United States of America* 91–92 (1990) (the Awakening's "emphasis on the importance of individual experience may be said to have democratized American religion. . . . Many congregations split into New Light (ranting) and Old Light (respectable) portions; and a gulf opened, which has not yet closed.")

rectly proportional to the extent of centralization of religious practice and political power.

The Evangelicals stand in the tradition of the colonial exiles, insisting on the absolute priority of faith over authority. The coincidence of a renewed outbreak of evangelical faith with the establishment of new state and national governments, at the start of the nineteenth century, led to an early constitutional focus on religious freedom. Government, it quickly appeared, must tolerate diverse religious practices because there is no ground for compromise of religious belief. Intolerance will inevitably lead to the sort of disruptive situation one found earlier in Virginia in which Baptists and Presbyterians entered and proselytized despite the threat of repression. A religious people, pursuing a Protestant faith with a tendency toward sectarian proliferation, could have no other government than one tolerant of free exercise. The willingness to suffer martyrdom stands as a threat to delegitimate any effort at religious suppression or intolerance.

Separation—first in the form of exile to the wilderness and then in the form of Revolution—was equally understood as economic opportunity. Both God and property were absorbed into the conception of the private with which we still operate. Private life in America includes both the church and the market. The colonies show us the conceptual ambiguity inherent in this concept of the private, but they show it to us as a matter of historical fact. Do we protect the private for the sake of religious faith and practice or in order to establish a market and opportunities for economic success?

The idea that wealth-generating activity can fill the meaning of the private steps into the place of a conception of the private that has a richer and longer history in religious experience. It, nevertheless, borrows much of the emotional energy of the private from that religious conception. Thus, the American conception of private economic activity bears little of the taint associated with it in classical Greek thought, where the domain of "economics" represented a sort of prerational activity linked to the interests of the body that men share with animals (and women).[64] Neither, however, does wealth bear the associations

---

[64] See Aristotle, *The Politics* 1. 1256a1–b39 (analogizing human acquisitiveness to an animal's collection of food).

of feudalism in which wealth and public authority are directly related to each other.

By the end of the colonial period, the emerging idea of the private market as a domain of personal virtue competes with a religious idea of the private.[65] The latter—the religious—includes attempts to denigrate this competing idea of the private as wealth-generation by associating it with passion and sin. The private as the satisfaction of desire appears now as "temptation," rather than "necessity," as in the Greek understanding. This denigration, however, is only the inverse side of the market-based effort to coopt the private virtues of religious faith to support its competing vision of the private. Together these constitute the normative configuration that we continue to face in understanding the competition between faith and markets as the basic elements of civil society. Is it the market or the church that offers the paradigmatic expression of the private? Best of all would be to believe that market success is a sign of religious virtue, but this synthesis is no more compelling than the actual divisions and competing normative claims that we find in the long history of confrontation between these conceptions.[66]

Even as the image of separation associated with the founding narrative of the colonies—that of exile—is a source of the liberal distinction between the private and the public, the early American experience of self-government gives a decidedly different cast to American liberalism. Because New England colonial communities are for the most part Congregationalist communities, they are self-governing communities from the start. Self-government may be a necessity in the wilderness, but here it was also a part of a religious practice that doctrinally resists claims of authority. Americans deliberately cultivated a form of private life that was simultaneously an expression of a common life: it was religious and it was democratic. The colonial New England "meeting hall," for example, was both the church and the center of town governance. Identifying public authority with the state from which the colonists exiled themselves, self-government could appear

[65] Franklin's *Poor Richard's Almanac*, for example, directs private virtue into market activity.

[66] See M. Weber, *The Protestant Ethic and the Spirit of Capitalism* (T. Parsons, trans., [1902] 1992).

as a form of private opposition to authority. Americans will need a new term for this conception of a community that stands opposed to public authority. That term will be "the popular sovereign" or simply "the people."[67] For this reason, Americans never quite adopt the distinctive European language of the private, that is, the language of a "civil society" that stands opposed to the state. The idea of civil society seems to concede too much authority to the public order. The same category confusion continues to this day. Thus, Americans are uncertain whether freedom of speech is a right designed to protect civil society or an element of public governance itself.[68] Is speech a public or a private act? The categories of liberalism—for example, the public and the private—seem always to fail the closer we get to the distinctive American experience.[69]

Self-government seems to straddle the private and the public. It is both *self* and *government*. The voice of political authority is to be the voice of the self. Theorizing the combination of these two is the task that defines modern Western political theory. But in America, the point is not just one of theoretical ambitions; it is also a matter of historical experience. These ambiguities in the concept of the self, accordingly, repeatedly show up as ambiguities in the idea of self-government. Is a system of pluralist representation a means of moving seamlessly from a private order of interests to a public order of coordination among those interests? Or, is self-government a deliberative process in which

[67] G. Wood, *The Creation of the American Republic 1776–87* at 306–43 (1972) (on "people out of doors").

[68] See, e.g., A. Meiklejohn, *Free Speech and its Relation to Self-Government* 26–27 (1948) ("The principle of freedom of speech springs from the necessities of the program of self-government. It is not a Law of Nature."); O. Fiss, "Free Speech and Social Structure," 71 *Iowa L. Rev.* 1405, 1417 (1986) ("the approach I am advocating is not concerned with the speaker's autonomy, . . . but with the quality of public debate."); S. Holmes, "Liberal Constraints on Private Power? Reflections on the Origins and Rationale of Access Regulation," in *Democracy and the Mass Media: A Collection of Essays* 21, 32–33, 47 (J. Lichtenberg, ed., 1990) (free speech cases should be decided not by "reference to . . . personal autonomy, or the right of self-expression," but instead by the First Amendment's "positive purpose of creating an informed public capable of self-government."); compare R. Post, "Meiklejohn's Mistake: Individual Autonomy and the Reform of Public Discourse," 64 *U. Colo. L. Rev.* 1109 (1993) (arguing against any role for the state in regulating speech).

[69] See chap. 3 below.

individuals must suppress their "less-than-rational" private interests and act only according to the "true" self of reason?

More importantly, self-government is experienced as a form of political resistance from the start. This idea of resistance dramatically powers the idea of self-government that is reconfigured as direct action by the people in the Revolution, and then carried through to the process of making a constitution. Americans experience in self-government an expression of a truth that is both private and communal, both personal and public, constitutive of the self at the same time that it is constitutive of the state.[70] "The people" remains a concept that cuts across the public and the private. The act of popular sovereignty is the ultimate act of public governance and also the ultimate expression of individual identity. This experience of self-government, which has its origin in the religious community of exile, eventually separates from any particular sectarian religious context. Nevertheless, it continues to maintain the intensity of the communal experience of common faith and practice.

Because the origins of the experience of self-government lie in religious practice, popular sovereignty has an ambiguous relationship to the Enlightenment project of rational construction of a constitutional structure. There is no question but that the great constitutional project is conceived as a project of rational deliberation, the success of which is thought to turn on the capacity of the people to put aside interests and take up reason.[71] Seen from this perspective, the problem of self-government is located within a political psychology of reason and interest; the former is objective and public, the latter is subjective and private. We should not, however, read this distinction too quickly in modern secular terms. The turn away from private interests, and the cultivation of public reason, were also elements of religious practice and faith in the eighteenth century. They remained so deep into the

---

[70] See H. Arendt, *On Revolution* 173–78 (1963).

[71] See *The Federalist No. 1* (A. Hamilton) (C. Rossiter, ed., 1961) (the United States is an experiment to decide "whether societies of men are really capable or not of establishing good government, from reflection and choice, or whether they are forever destined to depend for their political constitutions on accident and force."); P. Kahn, "Reason and Will in the Origins of American Constitutionalism," 98 *Yale L.J.*, 449, 455 (1989).

nineteenth. The minister was the most educated person in the community, claiming access to reason as well as revelation.

Not until the twentieth century does the problem of reason completely separate from that of perceiving the divine order of creation. Before that, reason and revelation were considered to be mutually supportive.[72] In both the religious and political domains, reason was thought to unify the whole community, while interests would lead to factions and divisions. Sin, understood as the pursuit of self-interested desire, was a problem for both the religious and the political community. Sin, religious or political, is a deliberate blindness to the truths that reason makes available to every person. A self-governing people requires individual virtue of its citizens; individual virtue requires religious belief and practice.[73] That which a religious character made it possible to pursue is a truth stripped of the taint of personal interest, and that truth is not something concealed from, or opposed to, reason. This linkage is given visible expression in the early American colleges, all of which linked religious faith and scientific inquiry.[74]

Nevertheless, the revolutionary experience suggests that these terms—reason and interest—are not adequate to an emerging political psychology. Beyond this division are the sovereign people, who stand in opposition to both government and to private factions.[75] The old concept of resistance remains, but more as an experience of plenary fullness expressed now in the conception of popular sovereignty. No institutional form is adequate to the experience of the people acting, but neither is any private form of life. Thus, the experience of the sovereign people is not wholly captured by reason or by interest. It opens another dimension of political psychology—that of faith. Belief

[72] See, e.g., F. Manual, *The Religion of Isaac Newton* (1974); R. Westfall, *Life of Isaac Newton* 110–44 (1993).

[73] See Washington's Farewell Address (Sept. 16, 1796), in 1 *Documents of American History* 173 (H. S. Commager, ed., 1973). ("Of all the dispositions and habits which lead to political prosperity, religion and morality are indispensable supports. . . . And let us with caution indulge the supposition that morality can be maintained without religion whatever may be conceded to the influence of refined education on minds of peculiar structure—reason and experience both forbid us to expect that national morality can prevail in exclusion of religious principle.")

[74] See P. Westmeyer, *A History of American Higher Education* v (1985).

[75] See Wood, *Creation of the American Republic* 531.

in the people and in the idea that the Revolution and the Constitution are the products of the sovereign people's action becomes the fundamental faith—the founding of myth—of our civic religion.[76] Again, the religious sources of the structure of American political experience are clear. Just as reason has the task of presenting and interpreting the divine truth made present through an inexplicable act of divine revelation, reason has the political task of elaborating the meaning of the sovereign people's revelatory act of establishing a revolutionary new beginning for political order. Revelation in both domains is not incompatible with reason, but reason never exhausts the full meaning of revelation.

There are, then, three lines of early American experience that contribute to the tradition of liberalism that emerges in this country. First, the experience of religious exile; second, the ambiguity of the concept of the private spanning both faith and wealth; third, self-government as a form of public reasoning and self-definition. Out of this mix emerges just that ambiguity in liberalism that I described above: a liberalism of private rights—specifically of religious tolerance, but also economic liberalism—that will become a permanent feature of American thought; and equally a liberalism of speech that creates and maintains self-government. Liberalism is a normative conception of governance that points toward the protection of the private from public authority, but also toward the problem of translating the experience of popular self-government into a stable institutional form. The first strand produces the liberalism of faith; the second, the liberalism of speech. Neither form, however, fully captures the distinctive experience of American political life as a matter of ultimate meaning. For this reason, *our* liberalism always seems to carry more weight—more significance—than its philosophical defenders can explain. It is inextricably linked to our faith in ourselves as a sovereign people.

This complex story of religious exile, economic opportunity, and popular self-government continues throughout the nineteenth century, informing the concept of the frontier. Like the earlier idea of Old World emigration, the frontier marks both a division between the pri-

[76] See P. Kahn, *The Reign of Law* 72–74 (1997); S. Levinson, *Constitutional Faith* 9–53 (1988).

vate and the public—crossing the frontier one enters a world beyond public authority—and a competing conception of the public as new communities emerge. The frontier offers the possibility of always moving beyond the power of the public authority of the state, of creating a real separation for a new community of belief. This is the narrative of the exodus of the Mormons, but of other sects as well—the Shakers, the Amish, the Amanas. For one hundred years after the Revolution, the frontier continues to offer an image of the wilderness within which religious truth can be realized.

But right alongside of this theme of religious exile across the frontier, there remains the theme of the frontier as offering the possibility of economic progress. Thus, the frontier appears as a space of unlimited opportunity, a space in which success is determined not by the accidents of personal history, but by one's own individual effort. The individual American can always start over on the other side of the frontier. This idea of starting over has the same ambiguity: it means rebirth within a Christian sect, but it also means a refounding of one's wealth-generating endeavors. In this sense, bankruptcy law is the secular equivalent of the Protestant experience of being born again.[77]

Finally, the frontier represents the space for the free exercise of political reason beyond the corruption of established society. America seems an endless experiment in self-government as new communities and new states again and again face the requirement of drafting charters and constitutions.[78] As long as there is a frontier, these experiments can continue without first invoking a revolutionary power to destroy the old order. The frontier, accordingly, offers an alternative to revolution.

If we try to imagine the position of government in this matrix of beliefs, we can see the origins of some distinctly modern themes. First, the theocratic ideal of some early colonial communities was exception-

[77] See V. Countryman, "A History of American Bankruptcy Law," 81 *Commercial L.J.* 226, 229 (1976); J. McCoid II, "Discharge: The Most Important Development in Bankruptcy History," 70 *Am. Bankruptcy L.J.* 163 (1996) (first English statute providing for a discharge was in 1705, 4 Anne, chap. 17); C. Tabb, "The History of the Bankruptcy Laws in the United States," 3 *Am. Bankruptcy Institute L. Rev.* 5 (1995).

[78] On state constitutionalism as reiterated attempts to achieve a liberal American constitutionalism, see P. Kahn, "Interpretation and Authority in State Constitutionalism," 106 *Harv. L. Rev.* 1147 (1993).

ally vulnerable to the Protestant inclination toward the proliferation of sects. Whenever a new interpretive truth arose, founding a new community of believers, the resistance of existing authorities would be seen as an image of the British regime that the early colonists had fled. Early American authorities would be accused of being as intolerant as their English predecessors, recreating the danger that is always present when state and religion coincide.[79] Because of this, American government tends toward an internal replication of the idea of separation that was the central theme of colonial foundations. Government separates itself from religion in order to preserve the conditions of private faith that earlier relied upon geographic separation. Free exercise is thought to require disestablishment. Thus, by the early part of the nineteenth century, every state had pursued disestablishment; all had adopted provisions on religious toleration.[80]

Second, public authority was also open to challenge from those who saw wealth as the measure of personal success, and economic opportunity as the meaning of the New World. Again, this theme transferred to early American life the experience of resistance to the authority of Britain. The colonists resisted efforts by English authorities to assert a power to tax. The same narratives of resistance were available to resist assertions of local, and eventually federal, authorities. The colonists created a world in which private property took on a kind of religious meaning; it shared with religion the symbolism of resistance to authority. Property and God are a linked pair in the American imagination from a very early point. Together they defined a domain of freedom that was the product of the experience of exile in the wilderness.

This does not mean that American government was born with a full-blown theory of laissez-faire capitalism. But it does mean that Americans easily adopted the Lockean idea that government comes

---

[79] This theme of American governments becoming mirror images of the corrupt regime in England continues not just through the Revolution, but right through the Republican challenge to the Federalists in the election of 1800, which was labeled the "Second American Revolution" by Jefferson and his supporters. See D. Sisson, *The American Revolution of 1800* (1974).

[80] See J. Witte Jr., "The Theology and Politics of the First Amendment Religion Clauses: A Bicentennial Essay," 40 *Emory L.J.* 489, 497 (1991).

into existence in order to protect private property. Property quickly came to mark the boundaries of legitimate authority: government must respect private property in its own dealings with individuals, and it must protect private property from trespass, theft, or destruction. Government, from this perspective, is feared as endlessly voracious, always wanting more: taxing private wealth, regulating market activities and land use, intruding into private contracts, and deploying force to extend its territorial domain. Government should be designed in such a way as to place some hindrances in the path of this voraciousness. America, one might say, begins with an antitax bias.[81]

Because this is America, in which religious communities of exile compete from the beginning with a new commercial order, there is an easy transfer of the themes of resistance to government from the religious idea of the private to the market idea of the private. Thus, men of property are to be a moderating influence on government. In and through their private life, they—like the clergy before them—are naturally public leaders. A profligate soul cannot succeed in commercial enterprise; a person who cannot be trusted in his economic dealings cannot be trusted in politics. The successful businessman will come to public service as a duty, not as an opportunity to further his private interests. Success in the market qualifies one for a political career because it has the same kind of character-forming effects as religious belief. If government is to pursue the public good, it must not become a means of private advancement. This requires leaders who have already become, either through faith or wealth, all that they desire to be. There is a deep distrust of the professional politician, but also of the "professionalization" of governmental positions, that is, a distrust of the idea that government employment can generate its own norms of behavior without violating liberal principles. We see in all of this a priority of the private over the public: the private is both the end of and the means for successful governance.

Just as the ideology of the religious formation of character transfers easily to that of property and business, so the same pattern of accusations of corruption transfer easily across domains. The possible link-

---

[81] See E. Morgan, *American Slavery, Freedom: The Ordeal of Colonial Virginia* 276–79 (1975).

age of public power and religious belief raises a fear of establishment that fuels a continuous insistence on protection of free exercise. Similarly, there is a fear that property interests will coopt government to their own ends. Instead of serving out of duty, the man of wealth will advance his private interests through his public responsibilities. Just as private faith must be separated from public authority, so must private property. Thus, alongside of the religion clauses, we find the Takings clause, the Contracts clause, and the Due Process clause. Government is subject to capture by both religious belief and commercial interests. And just as sin can be unknowing, so can the corruption of wealth. The well-meaning businessman can make of government an instrument for the advancement of his private interests, thinking all along that he is serving the public interest.[82]

Property and religion define the character of an American civil society that exists in an inevitable resistance to political authority. Government is resisted in the name of interests and faith from the beginning. American private life simultaneously values national—and even global—markets, and local communities that are thought to maintain distinct forms of life, culture, and belief. We are inevitably attracted to a romance of the local, at the same time that we live more and more of our life on a national and global scale. The classic, American political conservative is a liberal with respect to markets, but remains a kind of symbolic congregationalist with respect to localism. Both are opposed to an idea of public authority, which in its most threatening form tends to be projected upon the national government.

Just as the private appears as both the threat of corruption to the public and the source of virtue against a corrupt public authority, so the public appears as threat and promise. The religious background of the American colonial experience contributes to a tendency to identify all governmental authority with the fallen condition of mankind. Government is necessary because individuals are drawn to the temptations of the flesh, and away from the virtues that flow from the

---

[82] This is how many today read the capture of American constitutional law by an idea of laissez-faire capitalism, with its own idea of justice, at the end of the nineteenth century. See O. Fiss, *Troubled Beginnings of the Modern State 1888–1910* at 49 (1993).

experience of divine meaning or even the lesser virtues of objective rationality. Strong government is not a measure of success but of failure—moral and religious. As Madison says in the Federalist Papers, "[i]f men were angels, no government would be necessary."[83] But in an emerging commercial republic, this theme that government is rooted in the corruption of the body can never quite succeed, for it shares this position with that alternative form of corruption of the religious soul: property and markets. If men were angels, neither would commerce be necessary.

Against these themes of competition across diverse conceptions of the private and the public, we have to recognize a third theme: self-government as a source of ultimate meaning. The distinctly American political consciousness is born in the experience of revolution as an act of popular sovereignty. This can never be seen as corrupt; it is an inexhaustible source of meaning for the citizen and the state.[84] It confronts ordinary experience as absolutely other; it is our sacred history. American political experience becomes an endless interpretive debate over the meaning revealed by the popular sovereign. No other society organizes so much of its political life around a constitutional text. We substantially frame our national debates as disputes over the meaning of the Constitution—keeping consonant with that meaning appears to be our sacred trust.

Americans experienced the birth of popular sovereignty with all of the emotional fervor and ultimate significance that accompany religious revelation. They experienced revolution as a new beginning which made of them new men.[85] This was the "great awakening" that continues to inform the consciousness of the citizen long after the other Great Awakenings have faded from view. Like the religion of their fathers, this new civic religion is a sacrificial religion. Americans continue to celebrate the sacrifices of the founding fathers and of succeeding generations.

[83] *The Federalist No. 51*, at 322 (J. Madison).

[84] For two vivid exceptions to this claim, see C. Beard, *An Economic Interpretation of the Constitution of the United States* (1935); Justice Thurgood Marshall, "Reflections on the Bicentennial of the U.S. Constitution," 101 *Harv. L. Rev.* 1 (1987).

[85] See Arendt, *On Revolution* 195–215; G. Wood, *The Radicalism of the American Revolution* (1991).

In American political life, it was early noted that the law had become king, and that law was now a product of self-government.[86] No one individual embodied the truth of the state. Rather, that truth was fundamentally democratized such that each individual had the same relationship to the source of public meaning as every other. One participated in self-government by following the law—and, on occasion, helping to make or administer the law. But what is not emphasized enough is that the displacement of the king by law was also a displacement of religion by politics. The king functioned as a political link to a divine order. In America, the sacred authority of the law is rooted in popular sovereignty. There is no further source of meaning; nor is there any need for more. The state under the rule of law becomes the center of a new civic religion of popular sovereignty that offers generations of Americans a common core of belief and an ultimate meaning for which they are willing to sacrifice themselves.

Political activity had to translate the extraordinary experience of popular sovereignty into the idiom of the ordinary.[87] To this project of preserving the revolutionary inheritance, the founders brought their faith in reason, as well as their prerevolutionary experience of a liberalism of faith. It was reason that led to their arguments against Britain and for revolution; it would now be reason that designed the new state. The Constitutional Convention was conceived as a great exercise in applied political science—even though, on some points, that science had to compromise with interests.[88] So too, the ratification effort was understood as a mobilization of the deliberative capacities of the citizens.[89] Reason borrowed the revolutionary idea of stripping the self of merely private or factional concerns, and identifying wholly with the common good of the public enterprise. Republican governance under the province of reason takes on the virtues of selflessness and assigns to the private the taint of the body: desire, interest, and passion. Still today, we believe that the Constitution must speak with

[86] See T. Paine, *Common Sense*, in *Political Writings* 28 (B. Kuklich, ed., [1776] 1989).

[87] See B. Ackerman, *We the People: Foundations* 230–95 (1991) (on mediation between high and low politics).

[88] See P. Kahn, "Reason and Will in the Origins of American Constitutionalism," 98 *Yale L.J.* 449 (1989).

[89] See *Federalist No. 1* (A. Hamilton).

the voice of reason: our founding, sacred text cannot require irrationality of us.[90] For the content of reason, the founders could not help but draw on the tradition of rights, including the liberalism of faith, that was their inheritance under British law. The source of legitimacy had shifted from king-in-Parliament to the sovereign people, but the rule of law had long claimed to be the voice of reason.[91]

No country invests more in politics, nor is any more skeptical about politics. Politics is always both the source of ultimate meanings and the threat of a corrupt turning away from the true sources of ultimate meaning. It is our fundamental faith, and our image of sin. Every act that expresses political meaning is in danger of being revealed to be only the product of special interests. Indeed, this is our institutionalized form of political competition: each party claims the virtues of the public good and accuses the other of representing only special interests. Each claims to speak with the voice of reason, but is always threatened with the charge that this is a false voice masking the irrationality of interest.

Liberalism is more than a strand within this complex world view. It is a way of appealing simultaneously across all of these elements. It is a privileging of the private over the public, but without deciding between competing ideas of the private. It is a public morality for the state that always exists in opposition to civil society. Because we interpret the product of popular sovereignty through the device of reasoned discourse, liberalism is identified with reason itself. If it is the experience of reason, it expresses that which many hold to be most valuable in the constitution of the self. And, if that is so, the privileging of the private over the public is an order of values that liberalism itself always threatens to reverse. Finally, the tremendous emotional investment in liberalism as our public ideology reflects the ultimate meaning that we experience in the state itself. There is more at stake for us in liberalism than liberalism itself can grasp.[92]

---

[90] On reason and law, see P. Kahn, *The Cultural Study of Law* 7–30 (1999); but cf. R. Posner, *Problematics of Moral and Legal Theory* (1999).

[91] See Kahn, *Reign of Law* 153 (on continuity of reason in law across the Revolution).

[92] Charles Taylor has described this flaw in modern moral theory as a sort of "inarticulacy." Taylor, *Sources of the Self* 88–89.

CONCLUSION

American liberalism traces its origins to the beliefs of a deeply religious people who privileged faith over politics. But the opposition of the political and the religious tended from the eighteenth century on toward a somewhat different opposition of reason and faith. This opposition, however, is too often considered in the abstract, as if the modern state had become merely a product of rational deliberation. Here the relationship of *Gobitis* to *Barnette* can be extremely helpful. *Gobitis* sees a state that has itself become an object of ultimate value; *Barnette* adopts the language of the liberalism of speech to express that value. The secular religion of *Gobitis* informs the Enlightenment rationality of *Barnette*, and vice versa. We need to understand reason in context, and this context remains a politics of ultimate values and citizen identity.

To many who are deeply religious, the idea of a state that lives in the shadow of the church remains the appropriate approach to government authority. In our modern secular age, however, liberalism cannot be easily defended on the ground that it recognizes the subordination of politics to faith. The modern state is hardly willing to live in the shadow of the church. More importantly, the modern liberal state is not willing to cede the claim of ultimate meaning to the religious community. If anything, the twentieth century has been marked by the apotheosis of the state, including liberal states. Liberalism today must find its place within a state that has usurped from the church the function of providing an ultimate meaning to citizens.

Liberal political theory, however, has failed to pay attention to the quality of faith in a politics of popular sovereignty. To understand that, we need to recover a substantive concept of the will quite different from the will of the autonomous, rational chooser of the liberal tradition. We need, in short, to reexamine the liberal soul in order to locate the erotic foundation of politics—even of a liberal politics.

CHAPTER 3

■ ■ ■ ■

THE INSTABILITIES OF
LIBERALISM

Liberal political theorists might describe their enterprise as reason's response to its own limits.[1] Because men are moved by forces that are not subject to proof or disproof by reason, a political system has the task of establishing a rational order in the face of the continuing threat of irrationality. Early liberal theory spoke of the state of nature as the site of this chaos of conflicting interests. Today, we are more likely to project that chaos into the individual. The soul is a tangle of conflicting interests, desires, and passions. Still, liberalism turns to reason for a discipline of order.

While it may seem that reason starts off only as a means to an end— controlling the conflicts within the individual and the community— reason inevitably becomes an end in itself. This is the move from the liberalism of faith to the liberalism of speech, which I traced in the last chapter. The powerful attraction of liberalism today is grounded less in the faith that it allows us to practice than in its claim to be the product of reason. Reason allowed to turn in upon itself—the politics of pure reason—is the source of the liberal idea of justice. That is what our liberal political philosophers try to prove; it is what the broader political culture believes of itself.

We can, of course, disagree over the substantive content of justice. Within the broadly liberal tradition, there has been a deep division between utilitarian and deontological models of justice. Both models

---

[1] Speaking of the privileged place of his own time, Kant wrote: "Our age is, in special degree, the age of criticism and to criticism everything must submit. It is a call to reason to undertake anew the most difficult of all its tasks, namely that of self knowledge." Kant, *Critique of Pure Reason* 9 (N. Smith, trans., [1781] 1929).

agree, however, that the end of justice is to impose the order of reason on what would otherwise be the disorder of individual interests. We are, in this sense, all children of the Enlightenment. Americans can most easily get a sense of this if they consider how hard it is to believe that the Constitution requires some irrational action. Indeed, the perception of a gap between the constitutional order and rational action often marks the beginning of a constitutional crisis. The most famous example is that of the early New Deal, in which the Court held unconstitutional key elements of Roosevelt's plan for rational reconstruction of the economy.[2] We tend to believe that justice is a matter of reason, and that injustice arises from irrational interests. Because citizens of a liberal political culture believe their basic norms to be a product of reason itself, it is very hard for them to approach illiberal cultures with much sympathy. As I argued in chapter 1, even contemporary multiculturalists don't have much regard for the illiberal: they too are driven by the appeal of reason.

So far in this inquiry, I have argued that liberalism occupies a space made possible by the capacity of the subject for critical self-reflection and that this capacity for critique takes the form of an appeal to reason under the conditions of modernity. The critical terms that emerged from this inquiry are, first, reason itself, and second, the distinction between the private and the public. In this chapter, I continue the critical exploration of liberalism by investigating both the reach of reason and the integrity of the distinction between the private and the public. The distinctions of reason from interest and of the public from the private simply cannot be maintained either in theory or in practice. The effort to chart a public political practice of reason always collapses into its opposite. Politics is neither the practice of reason, nor the expression of interest; it is neither public, nor private. The categories of liberal thought are unstable because they are fundamentally inadequate to the task of explaining the experience of the political as an autonomous form of meaning.

---

[2] One theoretical expression of this same impulse toward constitutionalism as perfected rationality is Dworkin's theory of interpretation. See R. Dworkin, *Law's Empire* (1986). For an opposing view, see H. Monaghan, "Our Perfect Constitution," 56 *N.Y.U. L. Rev.* 353 (1981).

LIBERALISM, REASON, AND THE BODY

To begin, we must distinguish norms from meaning, staying within the rules from living a life experienced as one worth living.[3] A person can live a morally proper life, in the sense of living within all of the moral rules that she acknowledges or that others use to evaluate her behavior, yet still live a life that appears to her to be desperately without meaning. The same is true of the norms and rules of politics: obeying the rules does not necessarily correspond to a life of civic pride, patriotism, or national identification. One can, for example, be present as an alien—temporary or permanent—following the law with little understanding of, or care for, the political community. Citizens too can feel alienated from their own communities, even while complying with their norms.

There may be a moral norm that one treat others with respect; there is no moral norm that one enter into relationships of mutual love or friendship with others. One must obey the laws of the jurisdiction within which one resides; there is no similar norm that one experience citizenship as a matter of patriotic identification and self-fulfillment. Each of these oppositions marks a distinction between rules and identity. One wants not simply to be just, but to be someone.[4] No set of norms in itself can constitute a meaningful or complete life. In none of these examples would the problem be solved by reforming the rules, that is, by bringing contested rules more in line with the demands of reason. Indeed, violation of rules can itself be a rich source of identity—at least in fiction.[5] This is the position theorized by Nietzsche in

---

[3] Habermas makes a similar distinction between the moral and the ethical. See J. Habermas, *Between Facts and Norms: Contribution to a Discourse Theory of Law and Democracy* 159–62 (W. Rehg, trans., 1996). Taylor too insists that moral inquiry must take up the issue of meaning: "The problem of the meaning of life is . . . on our agenda, however much we may jibe at the phrase." C. Taylor, *Sources of the Self: The Making of Modern Identity* 18 (1989).

[4] See S. Wolf, "Moral Saints," 79 *J. Phil.* 419, 424 (1982). ("The way in which morality, unlike other possible goals, is apt to dominate is particularly disturbing, for it seems to require either the lack or the denial of the existence of an identifiable, personal self.")

[5] Consider, e.g., Shakespeare's Iago or Arthur Conan Doyle's Professor Moriarty. The uniquely evil individual is an even more prominent theme of modern films.

his attack on both the Christian roots and herd mentality of Western moral norms.[6]

To draw this distinction between norms and experience is not to suggest an opposition with which liberal theory is unfamiliar. Indeed, many would argue that the distinction is at the heart of liberalism. Liberal theorists understand moral and political norms as rules for the interaction of autonomous subjects, all of whom are free to find their meanings wherever they like. Or, indeed, free to fail to find any such meaning. A first principle of liberal theory is that neither the polity nor any other group or individual that can exercise coercive force should dictate to the individual the character or source of meaning in his or her life. For any particular individual, a meaningful life is presumably one rich in those things, acts, or relationships that he or she considers to be good. A virtue of a liberal polity is that satisfaction of its norms does not require the belief that compliance will lead to a meaningful life. Liberal norms are designed to be independent of any conception of the good that is rich enough to satisfy this longing for meaning. Thus, liberalism seeks to regulate behavior among individuals who do not agree on the sources of meaning in their lives. Liberalism requires, as a matter of political psychology, that individuals be able to take the same attitude toward their own conception of the good that they take toward that of others. That is, they cannot be so bound to it that its realization is the measure of every judgment and act. They must be able to treat themselves as they do others. In terms of the language I introduced in chapter 1, they must separate the I from the me.

Liberalism aims to establish a framework of just rules that operate as conditions within which individuals must make their own choices about meaning. It takes this approach precisely because it believes there is no possibility of reaching agreement, through rational discourse, on the sources and forms of meaning. Chapter 2 argued that our liberalism is broad enough to include a private life that locates the good in religious faith or in market success. These values speak to the question of who we are, rather than how we should act toward each

---

[6] F. Nietzsche, *On the Genealogy of Morals* (W. Kaufmann and R. Hollingdale, trans., [1887] 1967).

other. They are the products of diverse contexts, while a liberal order establishes just norms that are context-neutral. We may be able to trace the psychological and social causes of these diverse substantive beliefs; we cannot provide normative arguments for them. Reason is to work as a kind of filter on actions and claims motivated by diverse conceptions of the good.[7]

The paradigmatic institutional expressions of this liberal conception of the private are, first, the principle of religious free exercise—the state is to take no position on matters of religious belief; and second, the free market—the state cannot match material resources to desires. The state is to tolerate all religious variations, as long as they stay within the conditions of a liberal political order. Similarly, the state is to interfere in economic transactions only when it can identify a market failure. In both cases, the state's regulatory reach goes no further than responding to externalities. The state does not generally have the capacity to allocate either spiritual or material goods. The soul remains beyond politics whether it is enthralled to God or the market.[8] Of course, different liberal theories take different positions on the appropriate point at which these regulatory principles apply. All agree on the need to intervene to protect the young—to bring them to the point at which they can operate autonomously.[9] Some believe that a basic level of distributive justice is required prior to or independent of market transactions.[10] None, however, believe that the public order of the state should make judgments about the source or character of private meanings, whether spiritual or material.

Isaiah Berlin's essay, "Two Concepts of Liberty," illustrates just this distinction between rules and identity, and firmly locates liberalism in

[7] See, e.g., B. Ackerman, *Social Justice in the Liberal State* 4–8 (1980) (on liberal discourse as a filter or check).

[8] Indeed, as we saw in chap. 2, the liberalism of speech tends to collapse these sources, seeing religion as just another expression of interests coordinate to those of the market.

[9] See, e.g., A. Gutman, *Democratic Education* 44 (1987). ("a democratic state must aid children in developing the capacity to understand and to evaluate competing conceptions of the good life and the good society.")

[10] See J. Rawls, *A Theory of Justice* 274–84 (1971) (discussing background institutions necessary for distributive justice); B. Ackerman and A. Alstott, *The Stakeholder Society* (1999).

the former.[11] Berlin distinguishes negative from positive liberty. Negative liberty is the freedom to act without coercion by others; positive liberty is capacity to realize a substantive idea of the self. The former is that freedom pursued by a classically liberal political order. It aims to establish a protected zone, within which individuals are to make choices about where to invest themselves religiously, socially, politically, and economically. The trick of liberal political thought and governance has always been to create sufficient political authority to protect individuals from coercion without creating a source of illiberal coercion in the state itself. This is a politics in which no individual or institution has unchecked authority and in which individuals are protected by a strong doctrine of rights directed at both the state and other private persons. This ambition gives us the central structures of the liberal state: separation of powers in order to check governmental power; human rights to protect against the government; property rights and the criminal law to protect against other private persons. To this, modern liberalism adds democratic elections, but whether this is another check on the concentration of governmental power or a matter of individual right to participate in a structure of self-government is never quite clear.[12]

Positive liberty responds to a different concern—that of identity or meaning. When I describe myself as acting freely, this is not just a matter of the absence of constraints, but also of governing myself. A person without the means to sustain himself, for example, may be free under the law, but may not feel himself to be capable of acting to realize his "true" identity. Failures of self-government may also be the result of a failure in self-conception. A person who lacks a sense of herself may feel she has no positive liberty to realize.[13]

For Berlin, positive liberty's attack on the liberalism of negative liberty represents a rejection of the entire project of political moder-

---

[11] I. Berlin, "Two Concepts of Liberty," in *Four Essays on Liberty* 118 (1969).

[12] The problem, of course, is that voters can act on illiberal values. Populism, for example, has not been a particularly liberal political phenomenon. See W. Riker, *Liberalism Against Populism* 12–14 (1982).

[13] The modern welfare state straddles both negative and positive liberty. It maintains a strong doctrine of rights, but it also seeks to construct social safety nets that will assure each individual a basic capacity for self-realization.

nity, which began with the Enlightenment delineation of the distinction between politics and religion. But, of course, the proponents of positive liberty equally claim roots in the Enlightenment. Each side in this dispute sets forth its own title to "the empire of reason." Indeed, the claims for positive liberty build on the fundamental principle of the morality of the Enlightenment, according to which the subject is only free to the degree that he or she is self-governing. Self-government is not just a matter of having an unconstrained space in which to act, but also of acting on the basis of reasons that are one's own. To be one's own, they must be reasons that one gives oneself. Kant's view that action on the basis of desire is a form of control by forces that do not truly characterize the self is just such a theory of positive liberty. For Kant, the possibility of being a coherent subject over time requires a life governed by principles, because only principles have the requisite unity.

Positive liberty becomes illiberal when this aspiration to achieve a truth of the self moves from the domain of an individual morality to that of politics. Then, the theoretical task becomes that of identifying a "true" political subject: perhaps the nation conceived as an ethnic community, perhaps the class understood as the bearer of a particular ideology. A polity operating with an idea of positive liberty will force individuals to be "free." It can link coercion and freedom because it claims to recognize the truth of individual identity. Looking back at the first half of the twentieth century, Berlin saw the comprehensive character of modern political ideologies from social Darwinism to Marxism. Each offered a science of politics based upon a theory of the true nature of man. In asserting that reason could locate the point at which the truth of the self and of the polity coincide, all of these modern political ideologies stand within a two thousand-year-old western tradition of identifying the true self with reason's truth and deploying that truth in order to build a political order of positive liberty. Philosophers still would be kings.

Berlin rejects any such notion of a single truth of man. Yet his analysis masks the degree to which liberalism is itself a product of reason and thus stands in this same tradition. No less than its competitors, liberalism too believes that reason should control the political order. It too believes that the privileged place of reason establishes an identity between citizen and state. Modern liberalism is not merely a regime of rights, but of rights embedded in a self-governing state. The end of all of our experiments in liberal constitutionalism is self-government. This is more than an institutionalization of negative freedom.[14] The state's establishment of a regime of negative liberty is simultaneously an act of giving the law to oneself: that is, an act of positive liberty. This idea of "self-legislation" is critical to the modern, liberal political project.[15]

The ambition of the liberal political philosopher is to find that set of arguments that is so compelling that every individual, not corrupted by the illogic of interest, would necessarily affirm those reasons as his own. Each citizen sees himself in the sovereign's acts because each is a rational self. For just this reason, liberalism is a cosmopolitan political position with its own imperial ambitions.[16] Liberalism can perceive no legitimate opposition because it has preempted the entire domain of public values by making an exhaustive claim to reason. Outside of liberalism, there may be faith, but it is a faith corrupted by its rejection of reason.

We see this process quite literally in Rawls's conception of "public reason."[17] Public here describes the quality of the reasoning, transparent and equally compelling to all, as well as its product, the basic public order of the liberal state. Those who cannot engage in public reason are not entitled to participate in the construction of public norms. Yet, because the public norms are to be the product of reason, we can aspire to universal agreement on their content. Anyone who cannot raise him or herself to the level of public reason suffers, from

[14] De Tocqueville pointed out that the ancien regime was already moving toward recognition of rights constitutive of negative freedom. A. de Tocqueville, *Democracy in America* 3–9 (H. Mansfield and D. Winthrop, trans., [1835] 2000).

[15] See, e.g., R. Dworkin, *Law's Empire* 189 (1986) (citizen must understand himself as author of laws). Already, Hobbes's ambition was to justify sovereign power through appeal to an agency model under which the sovereign's actions can be described as those of the citizens. See T. Hobbes, *Leviathan* 227 (C. Macpherson, ed., [1651] 1968).

[16] See, e.g., A. Slaughter, "A Liberal Theory of International Law," 94 *A. S. I. L. Proc.* 240 (2000).

[17] J. Rawls, "The Idea of Public Reason Revisited," in *The Law of Peoples* 133 (1999). For a legal reflection of this idea of realizing the truth of the self in the paradigmatic acts of deliberation by others, see F. Michelman, "The Supreme Court, 1985 Term—Foreword: Traces of Self-Government," 100 *Harv. L. Rev.* 4 (1986).

the perspective of liberalism, a kind of political pathology. Such people are excluded from the body politic until their condition has been remedied—or conditions have been established such that they can safely participate in a limited way. Alternatively, we could say that those who exercise public reason effectively "speak" for those who do not: they say what all reasonable people would say, and thus what all of us should say.[18]

If liberalism shares the character of positive self-legislation, can it maintain the moderation that Berlin associates with negative liberty? Does it not carry forward an idea of identity or meaning. Berlin believes that the moderate reach of reason within liberalism is a function of the diversity of ends individuals pursue. If individuals have diverse ends that conflict among themselves, then citizens must be left a substantial domain of negative liberty in which they can make their own choices. This diversity of ends cannot be overcome by an appeal to reason or reason's truth. These goods, which are beyond the reach of reason, constitute the substance of the private domain.

Liberalism depends, then, upon the vitality of the private sphere. Contemporary theorists speak of the importance of "civil society"; earlier theorists spoke of religion or markets. Classic, Millian liberal theory actually built the idea of the public out of the private. Actions become subject to public regulation when they violate the private space of a third party: "[T]he only purpose for which power can be rightfully exercised over any member of a civilized community, against his will, is to prevent harm to others."[19] Because everyone equally privileges his or her own self as an agent, all should be able to agree on this minimal principle of noninterference. Reason, thus, finds a ground-norm out of which to build the public order of the liberal state—the minimal, "nightwatchman" state.

Liberalism's articulation of the division between the public and the private relies on a spatial metaphor to describe a conceptual distinction. The distinction has no necessary spatial extension. Markets, for

---

[18] Mill embraces the same point as an ethnographic fact: "Despotism is a legitimate mode of government in dealing with barbarians, provided the end be their improvement, and the means justified by actually effecting that end." J. Mill, *On Liberty* 81 (D. Bromwich and G. Kateb, eds., [1859] 2003).

[19] Ibid. 80.

example, might be classified as private, but can be global in extension. Not even the individual body defines an essentially or objectively private space. The male body is traditionally subject to military conscription; the female body traditionally served the public in its reproductive capacities.[20] The body bears the public quality of the state no less than the private quality of family and markets. Liberals have a skeptical attitude toward both forms of public "conscription" of the body.[21] But that is only to say that they maintain a normative understanding of the distinction of the private from the public; they are not simply describing objective facts.

The public/private distinction, then, is neither spatial nor material; it rests on a prior division of the reasonable and unreasonable. The issue is never, when does an act cross some natural boundary marking the private space of individual autonomy? Rather, the question is always, what constitutes a reasonable demand upon a subject? In determining the reasonable, the character of the actor and the context of behavior have a substantial effect. Thus, the reasonable demands of the state are different from the reasonable demands of an employer. Both are required to remain outside of a protected domain of the private, but the dimensions of the private are different for each. The same is true of neighbors arguing about competing uses of their property.[22] For the liberal project, the issue is, what can the state reasonably demand of the individual? To cross that boundary, to make an unreasonable demand, is to enter the domain of the private. This inquiry defines the dominant form of judicial reasoning in constitutional courts today: proportionality review, balancing claims of individual right against the

[20] For an interesting example of "conscription" of the female sexual body, see J. Dower, *Embracing Defeat: Japan in the Wake of World War II* 124–32 (1999) (on Japanese creation of brothels for the occupying American troops).

[21] See, e.g., R. Siegel, "Reasoning from the Body: A Historical Perspective on Abortion Regulation and Questions of Equal Protection," 44 *Stan. L. Rev.* 261, 276–77 (1992).

[22] Establishing property rights is a way of articulating what is "reasonable" under the circumstances. Bringing economic rationality to bear on this judgment was the founding insight of the law and economics movement. See R. Coase, "The Problem of Social Cost," 3 *J. L. & Econ.* 1 (1960); G. Calabresi and D. Malamud, "Property Rules, Liability Rules, and Inalienability: One View of the Cathedral," 88 *Harv. L. Rev.* 1089 (1972).

public interests of the state. This is an "all-things-considered" judgment of whether the state has remained within the bounds of reason.[23]

The end of this conversation among the reasonable, whether in law or theory, is a constitutional order that establishes the character and reach of the public domain. Where it ends, the private begins. Pursuit of this discourse of reason in Rawls's *Theory of Justice*, for example, leads to a dramatic shift in the line between the private and the public: my natural talents and abilities turn out not to be "my own" at all, but rather a public resource.[24] An historical example, equally dramatic, has been the shift in legal understanding of the married woman's possession of her own body.[25]

Arguments among competing conceptions of liberalism are arguments over the location of the border of the public and the private, that is, over the point at which there is a crossing from reason to unreason. Every conception of liberalism, however, is vulnerable to the argument that reason can go still further, that is, that it has conceded too broad a domain to the private. Liberalism's protection of private choice assumes a playing field already leveled by reason. That leveling occurs in two directions. First, choices made under circumstances of coercion or false belief are not deserving of respect. Second, choices that cause harm to an unwilling other are unreasonable. The problem, however, is that every actual choice can appear to violate both of these conditions. Every choice can be seen as a product of a particular context that is itself unchosen; every choice will have some harmful effect on an unwilling other. Reason can endlessly pursue both of these claims.[26]

Critical theory's most basic argument is that traditional liberalism has not allowed reason to go far enough: behind the categories of liberal thought are habits of belief that carry forward irrational, and thus unjust, assumptions about groups of individuals and kinds of

---

[23] See P. Kahn, "Comparative Constitutionalism in a New Key," 101 *U. Mich. L.R.* 2677 (2003).

[24] Rawls, *A Theory of Justice* 100–102.

[25] See R. Siegel, "The Rule of Love: Wife Beating as Prerogative and Privacy," 105 *Yale L. J.* 2117 (1996).

[26] See chap. 1 on the dialectical relationship of the I and the me, or freedom and context.

behavior.[27] The very distinction between the public and the private perpetuates gendered understandings of value that work to the disadvantage of women.[28] Similarly, doctrines of constitutional rights allegedly suppress the diversity of minority groups, as well as arguments for remedial obligations the state may have toward these groups.[29] Liberalism invites critical theory by taking its stand on reason. Thus, Roberto Unger can simultaneously attack the limits of reason as it operates in liberal theory and label himself a "superliberal."[30]

Liberalism's vulnerability to the claim that the work of reason is not yet done has increased with the decline in traditional religious practice, precisely because religion provided a fairly clear line beyond which the state was not to intrude. It was clear, however, not as a matter of logic, but of shared belief. After all, religious belief is quite vulnerable to attack from the perspective of reason. Religion can easily be seen as an irrational source of inequality, a structure of ideological coercion, or a limit on individual autonomy that has the effect of infantilizing believers.[31] Similar vulnerabilities are created today as reason penetrates other traditional domains of the private: for example, the family, the club, the market, and the ethnic or cultural community. The liberal understands reason to be silent on matters of individual taste, preference, or value. Yet an exercise of free choice that is not the product of deliberation and reason always threatens to appear as not a matter of choice at all. We can identify the "coercive" influences of ideology, peer pressure, advertising, habit, or social norms. We are never sure whether our tastes are our own or are a part of the context against which we must establish our identity.

This borderline of reason shifts as different issues come to seem matters of right or, conversely, as the asymmetries of power appear in

---

[27] See, e.g., R. Unger, *Democracy Realized: The Progressive Alternative* (1998).

[28] See, e.g., C. MacKinnon, *Feminism Unmodified* 93, 101–2 (1987); R. Copelon, "Unpacking Patriarchy: Reproduction, Sexuality, Originalism and Constitutional Change," in *A Less Than Perfect Union: Alternative Perspectives on the U.S. Constitution* 303 (J. Lobel, ed., 1988).

[29] See, e.g., M. Tushnet, "An Essay on Rights," 62 *Tex. L. Rev.* 1363 (1984).

[30] R. Unger, "The Critical Legal Studies Movement," 96 *Harv. L. Rev.* 561, 602 (1983).

[31] See, e.g., S. Freud, *The Future of an Illusion* (J. Strachey, ed. & trans., [1927] 1961).

different contexts. Today, for example, there are arguments over the redistribution of property as a means of providing equality of opportunity—that is, an equal capacity for choice—among autonomous subjects. Does a property regime constrain free self-determination or is it the expression of that freedom? A generation ago, there were arguments about whether moral injury constitutes an infringement of individual autonomy. Is my moral suffering from an awareness of homosexual activity different from my suffering from a lack of material resources?[32] It is the same issue appearing in different context: my bedroom is no more private in and of itself than is my property. In all of these disputes, the appeal to the "private" is only convincing insofar as it appears as an answer to the question what is reasonable? That, however, is never a matter of reason alone; it depends on a context of values and expectations.

Reason is never quite through with establishing the necessary conditions under which choice can be valued. As background beliefs become less stable, reason extends its imperial claims into what had previously appeared as protected domains of private choice and meaning. Family, for example, may once have been paradigmatic of the private, yet the penetration of family by law pursuing the standards of reason is characteristic of our liberal political order.[33] There are no natural barriers beyond which reason cannot penetrate. Reason alone cannot establish the point at which individual choice is the product of the subject's autonomy rather than the result of unjustified coercion.

Every action or decision can simultaneously be seen as a free act and as one that is contextually bound. This is the same dynamic as that separation of the I from the me described in chapter 1. If the

---

[32] See *Griswold v. Connecticut*, 381 U.S. 479, 522 (Black, J., dissenting) ("That formula [in *Lochner*] based on subjective considerations of 'natural justice,' is no less dangerous when used to enforce the Court's views about personal rights than those about economic rights."). For a dramatic example of the shifting understanding of the boundaries of the private defined by the reach of the reasonable, compare *Bowers v. Hardwick*, 478 U.S. 186 (1986) (upholding criminal sodomy statute), with *Lawrence v. Texas* 123 S.Ct. 2472 (2003) (overruling *Bowers*).

[33] See J. Goldstein et al., *Beyond the Best Interests of the Child* 49–52 (1973) (arguing that law sometimes fails to recognize its inability to order intimate relationships and must be carefully circumscribed).

claims to freedom are without limit, the possibilities of reason's exposure of the constraints of context are also without limit. A claim of
right is often only an assertion of such a border, marking a line beyond
which the public pursuit of reason should not go—not a boundary
beyond which it cannot go.[34] Liberalism turns out to be less a product
of reason than of the bounded character of the imagination. As those
boundaries have shifted over the last two hundred years, the breadth
of reason's claims has shifted.

If the border of the public/private moves too far in either direction—
too much reason or too much individual interest—liberalism collapses
into competing, modern conceptions of the political. In one direction,
it becomes totalitarian; in the other, it becomes libertarian. The libertarian allows the private person to absorb most of the public space of
reason; the totalitarian extends the ideological claim of reason deep
into private space. Liberals are distinguished from these modern competitors by their faith in the moderate reach of reason. Yet this middle
range is a product of experience rather than principle.[35]

Liberals have no way to speak of a middle range of normative values
that fall in between the claim of universal truth and the particularity of
choice. The position they occupy in fact is a position that they cannot
explain in theory. For that reason, moderation is always challenged
by those who believe reason can go further and those who believe it
has already gone too far.[36] Speech itself falls apart, becoming either
the articulation of universal reason or the expression of self-interest.

The contemporary debate between liberals and the defenders of cultural pluralism is a replay of modernism's larger problem of defining
the reach of reason. To the liberal, claims for a protected zone of cul-

[34] See W. Hohfeld, "Some Fundamental Conceptions as Applied in Judicial Reasoning," 23 *Yale L.J.* 16, 31–32 (1913).

[35] Of course, different liberalisms occupy different points "within" this middle. Historically, we saw substantial movement on the continuum with the enactment of the
New Deal and then the Great Society programs of social-welfare management of the
economy. Among political theorists, the willful liberalism of Flathman and the empire
of law of Dworkin are at very different points on the continuum. See R. Flathman,
Willful Liberalism (1992); Dworkin, *Law's Empire*.

[36] Paradigmatic of this conflict is the contrast of Unger, *Democracy Realized*, and
R. Nozick, *Anarchy, State and Utopia* (1974).

ture often look like yet another effort to raise a barrier to the extension of reason. Once again the boundary between the public and the private is being drawn at the wrong place, because there still remains ample room for the expression of public reason. The domain of cultural difference must be pushed back into a narrower domain of the private—for example, dress or cuisine. Any claim that culture has value apart from individual choice is rejected. If choice is what matters, then reason must scrutinize the conditions of choice to assure that it is a "free choice."[37] The choice of culture will be free when it is no more weighted than that of a cuisine. Exit options must be preserved; no choice can burden the continuing freedom of the subject. If this task appears impossible because every "free" choice occurs within some cultural context, then the liberal theoretician has no option but to argue for choice among multiple *liberal* cultures, that is, pluralism can only be valued if it is within a competition of liberal cultures.[38]

If context is always pregnant with coercion, there will inevitably be an effort to find a noncontextual foundation for free choice—that is, a foundation beyond the further claims of reason's critique. If tradition appears as the "unexamined" and relationships to others threaten the unconstrained I, that foundation will be located in the body itself. Only there can choice escape the relentless demand of reason that it justify itself. Thus, individual ends are explained by personal interests, which are, in turn, modeled on bodily desire. They have the brute facticity of desire; they have value only as *my* desires. In this sense, they have no reason about them at all.

This is a normative worldview that stands mired in the mind/body problem. There simply is no point of contact between mind and body, between reason and interest. These categories do not speak to each other. Liberalism begins as the empire of reason, but ends with the claims of the body itself. Reproduction, for example, has become a privacy issue. It is understood not as an issue of family, or as one of population policy, but as one of control over one's body. Homosexuality too becomes a discourse over the disposition of the body. Similarly, we struggle today with the issue of the right to suicide. The body itself

---

[37] See Y. Tamir, *Liberal Nationalism* (1993).
[38] See chap. 1.

has become the ground upon which we stand in asserting rights against the state, as if only there do we find a foundation for choice beyond reason's capacity for critique.[39]

There is, consequently, a flattening of the range of experience within the private—or, rather, a flattening of the understanding of experience. All that is not reason falls into a single category in which objects and actions get their value by virtue of the fact that they were chosen by a subject. They are not chosen because they are valuable, but valuable because they are chosen.[40] The paradigmatic expression of this notion of value is the contract and the idea of market value. Objects and activities get their value from a competition among freely choosing individuals, none of whom need to—or even can—offer a justification of their choices. They are simply the expression of an interest: to obtain the end is to satisfy the desire, which is explanation enough. Accordingly, there is a tendency to restructure every context on the model of contract—from family, to polity, to ethnicity.[41] Contract law offers us desire stripped of the coercion of context and harmful consequences to others.[42]

Just as the body absorbs the private, reason absorbs the "public." Liberal norms are not based upon what we might call habits of mind, intuition, or opinion. For liberalism, reason is a matter of objective presentation of argument. Reason always makes a claim independent of the fact that some individual expresses it. Opinions are "validated" by character and/or particular experience. Opinion, accordingly, is included in the domain of the private. It has the brute facticity of the body. My opinions are like my tastes. They can be observed and counted—for example, in opinion polls—but they cannot be reasoned with. To begin to reason, one needs to step outside of one's self, that

[39] There is a similar flattening in the opposite direction as all that is not chosen appears as a form of coercion. The failure of autonomy—and it must always fail at some point—produces proliferating claims of victimhood.

[40] See C. Taylor, *The Ethics of Authenticity* 36 (1991). ("The contemporary culture of authenticity slides towards soft relativism.")

[41] Consider the movement from status to contract in family law. See M. Regan, *Family Law and the Pursuit of Intimacy* 11 (1993), or the "Contract with America" of the 1994 political campaign.

[42] The contract law doctrines of coercion, unconscionability, and public policy are the paradigmatic expressions of this notion.

is, to give up the perspective of the body and its interests. Liberalism strives for "the view from nowhere."[43]

A liberal polity is never sure when it has finally satisfied the conditions of its own valuation of the private. It is, for this reason, a constant project of reform.[44] There is no area of social life that is not held up for scrutiny to assure that the conditions of free choice have been met. It is an endless project of identifying the coercive character of context and laying bare the harms that we suffer from that context. No social formation passes these tests. The result is that the empire of reason is driven past the social to the body itself. In the control of our own bodies, we purport to find a ground of free choice beyond the need for reason's repair. Thus, the politics of reason becomes the empire of interests; the voice of reason is silent before the mute particularity of desire.

The problem, of course, is that reason does not willingly stop at even this boundary. The body itself offers no firm foundation; it too is the subject of the critique of reason. The body is no less a social formation than the church. Belief in the body structures the imagination in a way that once again can be exposed as coercing and harming. To expose these limits has been a major part of contemporary critical theory.[45] Life and death, gender and sexuality have all been deprived of their claimed foundation in the private body.

Liberalism begins with the privileged position of reason, but under modern conditions can easily collapse into an ideology of the body.[46] It is not that the body simply displaces reason. Rather, the distinction of mind and body simply is elided, leaving us with a reason that extends no further than the body's interests and a body that purports to define the reach of a universal reason.[47]

---

[43] See T. Nagel, *The View From Nowhere* (1986).

[44] Habermas, speaking generally of the conditions of liberalism, would make it an endless project of discourse.

[45] See, e.g., T. Lacquer, *Making Sex: Body and Gender from the Greeks to Freud* (1992).

[46] See G. Agamben, *Homo Sacer: Power and Bare Life* (D. Heller-Roazen, trans., 1998).

[47] As I show below, reason is deployed to support positive interests in the market; it is deployed to support negative interests in the human rights agenda. Both moves demonstrate the nexus of reason and the body in the liberal state.

CATEGORY CONFUSION AMONG
THE PUBLIC AND THE PRIVATE

Public reason, I have argued, is never quite done with the private—at least not until it reaches the limits of the body itself. Even that limit proves to be only a temporary stopping point from the perspective of theory. The instability of the line separating the public and private is equally evident when approached from the other direction. Starting with the private, we quickly find ourselves in a public space.

Three spheres of the private have been particularly important in the American tradition and, more broadly, in the West: religion, market, and family. Liberalism's origins are in the protection of a private domain of religion. As markets displaced faith as the source of individual identity, liberalism shifted too. It now identified the market as the protected domain of the private. As markets have come to be seen as a domain requiring public regulation, a new ideal of the romanticized family has become the central image of the private.[48] For this reason, some of our most intractable contemporary debates are over the authority of government to shape the family: gay marriage and adoption, to take but two examples.

Each of these three—religion, market, and family—regularly moves from a position in which it is the opposite of the public order to one in which it is the very condition of the well-functioning state. Each is both the means to achieving a successful political order and the end of that order. Thus, each can switch places from the private to the public, becoming the fundamental truth of the public order.[49] The result is that familiar elision of categories that we see in American history. President Reagan expressed this idea rather precisely: "Private values must be at the heart of public policies."[50]

Throughout much of the nineteenth century, American public discourse regularly expressed the view that this is a Christian nation:

---

[48] See conclusion, below.

[49] Compare the double-role of the individual body both as the source of private rights against the state and as the source of the public health end of legitimate governmental action.

[50] Speech to Joint Session of Congress, quoted in *The New York Times*, Feb. 6, 1986.

"American life, as expressed by its laws, its business, its customs and its society" shows that "this is a Christian nation." [51] This assertion of the Supreme Court rested only in part on the historical fact that it was predominately Christians who had immigrated here. The nation was not Christian because it was occupied by Christians. Rather, there was thought to be a necessary relationship between the public order of the state and Christianity. Civilization advanced both Christianity and the order of reason. This was one project, carried forward by the same individuals in the same political form. To be against religion—meaning Christianity—was to be unreasonable. An advanced civilization had, with respect to the rest of the world, a single civilizing mission that included the extension of both science and revealed religion. Both converged in support of the American nation-state. The American constitutional order was the product of reason, but reason brought one closer to the truth of God's revealed religion.

Religion, accordingly, was both means and end for the state. Without religious training and belief, it was feared that citizens would not have the kind of public-regarding character that is a condition of a democratic state. The irreligious would be sunk in the private interests of the body. A successful democratic state had first to be a Christian community. Religion was a part of the public order, and both were opposed to the private-regarding values of the market in the emerging industrial age. Washington appeals to this idea in his Farewell Address, when he says that "reason and experience both forbid us to expect that national morality can prevail in exclusion of religious principle."[52]

Christianity was not just a means; it provided a teleology for the state. Lincoln's Second Inaugural is an elegant statement of this view. He invokes divine providence to give meaning to the central dynamic of American history in the nineteenth century. Lincoln thinks we cannot understand the violence of politics, the suffering of men for the state, without a belief that there is a just God in whose sovereign service we labor: "the judgments of the Lord, are true and right altogether." Thomas Cooley, the leading constitutional authority of the

---

[51] *Holy Trinity Church v. United States*, 143 U.S. 457, 471 (1892).

[52] Washington's Farewell Address (Sept. 16, 1796), in 1 *Documents of American History* 173 (H. S. Commager, ed., 1973).

second half of that century, gives doctrinal recognition to this idea: "the American constitutions contain no provisions which prohibit authorities from solemn recognition of a superintending Providence."[53] This is an old theme linking American political history to the millennial aspirations of Christian communities. This did not make the American political order a kind of secret theocracy. That would be a decidedly anachronistic reading. Rather, it suggests that religion and reason appeared as aspects of a single experience of meaning. Politics was not a secular activity, to be walled off from religious meaning. It could not be, if there was a convergence of religious truth and truth of reason. This belief in convergence explains why Darwin's theory appeared as such a challenge to the polity's self-understanding. For it suggests that there may be no such convergence at all, that the truth of reason challenges, rather than supports, faith.

None of this is surprising given the religious origins of many of the colonial communities. Yet it does suggest a problem with the formal division of spheres characteristic of liberalism, that is, a division between the public and the private. When we consider the state as an ongoing set of institutions that must present themselves as meaningful in the life of citizens, the borders of the private and the public appear so fluid as not to be borders at all. Religion is just one example of this fluidity in which we cannot establish a normative hierarchy between spheres—which is means and which is end?—or prevent their deep interpenetration. Modern liberal theory does indeed relegate religion to the private, but the explanation does not lie in the "inherently" private character of religion. Rather, it lies in our sense of the limits of reason. If religion has moved to the domain of the private because it is "without reason," it becomes an open question whether we continue to respect it as a substantive good or devalue it as a source of heteronomy. The political conservative fears that liberals are not neutral with respect to religion, but rather disrespectful of religious claims; this fear is not altogether groundless.[54] If theory would push religion into the private sphere, there nevertheless remains a substan-

---

[53] T. Cooley, *A Treatise on the Constitutional Limitations* 668–69 (7th ed., [1868] 1903).

[54] See S. Carter, *The Culture of Disbelief: How American Law and Politics Trivialize Religious Devotion* (1993).

tial body of citizens who continue to insist that our liberal political culture must recognize God's provenance.

This same indeterminate relationship of private to public creates confusion over the place of a free-market economic order in the public order of the nation. Exactly the same pattern of thought emerges. We are not sure whether our constitutional institutions include the market order.[55] Does political liberalism necessarily include a liberal market order? Does it do so as means or end? We often assume that the democratic order of the state depends on the market order not merely for productive efficiency but normatively. As in the Cold War, state ownership of the means of production represents far more than a competing theory of economic organization.

The normative importance of the market is signaled in its replication of the shifting place of religion from private to public, and from means to ends. Modern business, like religion in the nineteenth century, is supposed to create the kind of character necessary for public service: now a dedication to efficiency, bureaucratic rationality, and service. Would-be politicians emphasize their experience in the market, as opposed to their exposure to the corrupting effects of political life. This is the private as training ground for the public. More than that, this business training presents itself as purer than public life with its attendant corruptions. The business-trained candidate always promises to "clean up" the corruption of ordinary politics. That corruption is not so much criminal as the presence of the influence of "special interests." Business has stepped into the place of religion as providing a purer character type than the professional politician.

Just as religion moved from means to ends, so does the market. The telos of the market becomes identified with that of the state. Our public ends are, first, to increase the GDP and, second, and perhaps more controversially, to assure each individual the economic means of obtaining his or her own ends. Successful political campaigns repeat the mantra, "It's the economy, stupid." The success of the liberal state is

---

[55] Doctrinally, the constitutionalization of the market gains formal expression in the early twentieth-century Court and its development of the idea of a constitutional right of contract. In *Hammer v. Dagenhart*, for example, the Court includes protection of freedom of commerce as "essential to the preservation of our institutions," 247 U.S. 251, 275 (1918).

directly proportional to the productivity of its economy. The state's first responsibility is to maintain the conditions of a well-functioning market order. Thus, we measure the success of the political order by looking to the growth of the economy. We see this not just in the United States, but in the modern transformation of Europe as well. The displacement of national politics in European states has been overwhelmingly driven by the judgment that the creation of a European Union will be of substantial economic benefit. The idea that there can be a political end independent of this market judgment is increasingly unimaginable.[56] That the state could act against the economic interests of its citizens is becoming as unimaginable as acting against their religious interests would have been in the nineteenth century.

We condemn *Lochner*-era constitutionalism for identifying the political and economic orders in the protection of laissez-faire capitalism. In fact, the identification of the political and economic orders is far stronger today among all of our political institutions—with the sole exception of the Supreme Court, which still bears the burden of *Lochner's* defeat. The government assumes responsibility for the economy; it is judged by the others on the basis of economic performance. Similarly, a virtuous citizen is one who is economically productive. Unemployment suggests both moral and political stigma. Thus, modern welfare reform concentrates less on support and more on moving individuals into the workforce. Unemployment is so stigmatized that welfare programs continue with this ambition even when there are no jobs to be had.

The collapse of the distinction between the private market and the public order is expressed from the other direction in pluralist political theories, under which the behavior of both politicians and voters is modeled on market behavior. Instead of the public reason of the state pursuing market ends, market reasoning is understood to extend deeply into the political decision-making process.[57] Politics becomes a

[56] This is Siedentop's indictment of the rapid process of European integration and his plea for recovery of political values independent of the market. L. Siedentop, *Democracy in Europe* (2001).

[57] See, e.g., J. Buchanan and G. Tollock, *The Calculus of Consent: Logical Foundations of Constitutional Democracy* (1962); D. Mayhew, *Congress: The Electoral Connection* (1974); R. Dahl, *Pluralist Democracy in the United States* (1971); J. Buchanan,

literal extension of market interests, with different groups deploying their capacities to influence political decisions as a complement to their market power. Citizens are expected to vote their "interests," which are indistinguishable as a conceptual matter from those interests they seek to realize through market transactions. Politicians too are expected to realize their interests, which are personal—staying in office—in just the same way that the interests of those in the market are personal. The public, on this view, becomes an alternative organization of the private. In both of these forms of market ends coopting the public values of the state, we see the same normative process at work: the science of economics has come to dominate reason. Economics thus becomes both the model for public reason and for the explanation of free choice by the individual. The content is different but the analogy to theologically based public reason of the nineteenth century remains.

This collapse of the public and market orders represents one form of the cooptation of reason by interest—the positive side, modeled on the paradigm of bodily satisfaction. Conversely, much of the contemporary human rights movement represents a similar cooptation, but from the perspective of privation—pain—rather than satisfaction. At the foundation of the universal claim of human rights is an image of the suffering body—in particular, the suffering body of the concentration camp victim. Human rights, as both a political and a legal movement, is founded on the common understanding of the experience of pain.[58] The development of human rights law is, in substantial part, the application of reason to the negative economy of pain. That is why human rights law is simultaneously so thin and so all-encompassing. Its primary end is the avoidance of pain and of that which pain mimics, death itself. In an inverse reflection of a politics that has become merely an alternative form of the market, the discourse of human rights too is easily stripped of the autonomy of political meanings, focusing instead on the negative task of preventing pain. Claims to political and civil rights do not disappear, but they only have force

---

The Limits of Liberty (1975); G. Becker, "A Theory of Competition Among Pressure Groups for Political Influence," 98 Q.J. Econ. 371 (1973).

[58] See M. Ignatieff, Human Rights as Politics and Idolatry 88–90 (2001).

when linked to physical deprivation: to be tortured, jailed, or murdered for one's beliefs.

Because pain, like material need, is endless under conditions of finitude, there is no dimension of experience that cannot found a claim of human rights.[59] Accordingly, there has been an endless proliferation of these claims of right, well beyond their origin in murder and torture: rights of the child, of women, of ethnic groups; rights to environmental well-being, to social welfare, to health and education; rights to economic well-being, jobs, and communication.[60] Deprivation is always a source of pain; in a world of human rights, all pain is the enemy. Yet while rights claims proliferate endlessly, the contribution of reason is so thin as to be nothing more than a repetition of the body's interest in avoiding pain. The human rights movement claims to be a new form of global politics—the liberal politics of reason—but at its heart is has virtually nothing to say. As Michael Ignatieff writes, "There is . . . a deliberate silence at the heart of human rights culture."[61] There is no point to political deliberation; there is simply the reciprocal identification of pain and a claim of right.[62] For this reason, the effort actually to discuss human rights as a culturally specific project often appears to human rights advocates as a betrayal rather than as a serious invitation for political deliberation and debate.

We can discern the same pattern of elision with respect to the third prevalent idea of the private: the ideal of family life. We cannot really

[59] The idea of freedom from pain as the foundation for a claim of right does not necessarily produce a regime of negative, as opposed to positive, rights. Hunger is a condition to be negated, but a right to subsistence is a positive right.

[60] See, e.g., Universal Declaration of Human Rights (Dec. 10, 1948); International Covenant on Economic, Social, and Cultural Rights (Dec. 16, 1966); International Covenant on Civil and Political Rights (Dec. 16, 1966); International Convention on the Elimination of All Forms of Racial Discrimination (Dec. 21, 1965); Convention on the Elimination of All Forms of Discrimination Against Women (Dec. 18, 1979); Convention on the Political Rights of Women (Dec. 20, 1952); Declaration on the Elimination of All Forms of Intolerance and of Discrimination Based on Religion or Belief (Nov. 25, 1981); Declaration on Right to Development (Dec. 4, 1986); Convention on the Rights of the Child (Nov. 20, 1989); Declaration on the Rights of Persons Belonging to National or Ethnic, Religious, and Linguistic Minorities (Dec. 18, 1992).

[61] Ignatieff, *Human Rights* 78.

[62] See *ibid.* 95 ("The basic intuition that what is pain and humiliation for you is bound to be pain and humiliation for me").

answer the question of whether the family is a private or a public institution.[63] The family is the material source of citizens and, just as importantly, it too is a source of training in citizenship. The virtues of domesticity are the means toward a training in political virtue. Even as a nation of immigrants, we decidedly prefer that our future citizens be the products of existing families rather than new entrants from abroad. As with religion and markets, the political candidate will claim that he practices and indeed has been formed by the virtues of the private family. It is the rare candidate who does not put his or her family on public display. This is true not just of candidates but of a virtuous citizenry generally. We hear endlessly that problems of public values are to be met by a reaffirmation of "family values."

Again, we see a rapid movement of the familial from private means to public ends. Family is always more than just one of a number of possible means to public ends. Indeed, family can entirely displace the public ends of the state, such that public life appears as nothing more than a means to the preservation of our domestic lives. To say that, however, is to recognize that domesticity has become a public telos, just as religion and the economy have been. The narrative of the individual adult citizen is ideally to present the successful realization of the virtues of domesticity: to have a successful marriage, to raise children, to have the support of a loving family in old age. These are not means to a stable politics, but the very ends for which we form a political union.

Modern skepticism about government is matched by a virtually unchallenged faith in the family.[64] We admire those who give up a public life in order to return to their families. This often seems the only explanation ever offered by an official leaving public life or a candidate withdrawing from a contest. Of course, we appreciate the sacrifices that an individual may have to make of family life in order to pursue public positions, but except in extraordinary times we do not expect the public figure to appeal to us on the basis of his or her sacrifice

[63] This confusion arises as far back as bk. 5 of Plato's *Republic*.

[64] As with all such generalizations, there are exceptions. For example, there is a debate within the gay community over the place of marriage and family values. Despite these doubts among some members of that community, by far the more powerful political issue today is over extending access to family to "nontraditional arrangements."

of family. In ordinary times, we have more sympathy for the person returning to family than for the person sacrificing family for the state.[65] Ideally, we want both family and polity. This ideal is projected on that image of family domesticity as the public good, which is the iconography of the White House—an iconography violated by President Clinton at substantial cost. In moments of true crisis, we think of sacrifice for the state as equally a sacrifice for the family. Wars are fought not just for the Constitution, but for the protection of the family as a potent symbol of the meaning of that broader cultural entity that is "the American way of life."[66] This centrality of the family to the ideal of political order causes some of our deepest problems in understanding the role of gender in politics: specifically the conundrums over the participation of women in combat.

Liberal theory would locate the family in the private. But the modern liberal state is always transforming itself into the social-welfare state. The public end of the state's social-welfare function is a concern for children and the elderly. The liberal state is endlessly occupied with providing for the well-being of *its* children and the health of *its* seniors. This is the traditional image of the family assumed now by the state itself. This is not the family as bloodline present in the ethnic or aristocratic state, but it is no less a cooptation of public order by the values and discourse of domesticity.

If we ask how this has happened, we find the same double-set of reasons that characterized the private orders of religion and markets in their relationship to the public order of the state. First, without turning to private ends, the discourse of public reason is empty: what is justice, if not care for the most vulnerable among us?[67] Second, the model of public reasoning is deeply affected by the logic of family. Public reasoning becomes a debate about care: health care, child care, senior care. Care, like faith and markets before it, becomes the founda-

---

[65] We quite openly disapprove of those who would sacrifice the virtues of family to their own advancement in the market, although we recognize that this is often the norm. We do not characterize this as a valuable "sacrifice" at all, but rather are more likely to speak of "neglect" of the family.

[66] The film *Saving Private Ryan* explores this double-nature of family—both private and public—and the dynamics of sacrifice.

[67] See R. Unger, *Knowledge and Politics* 135 (1975) (liberal morality of reason is too abstract to do any actual work).

tion for a science of our public institutions. Even the political party associated with the economic conservatism of business interests campaigns today on a platform of "compassionate conservatism." What politician does not put care of the family at the center of his or her campaign? There is a reason that the most trite—and yet most expected—image of the candidate for public office is one in which he or she is pictured with a baby.

CONCLUSION

The relentless, critical quality of reason pushes toward a position in which the individual character of the subject can rest on nothing but the particularity of the body: its desires, interests, and satisfactions. This produces that familiar antinomy in which liberal theory seems ever more abstract, pursuing the conditions of pure practical reason, on the one hand, yet ever more focused on the body, abortion, suicide, homosexuality, health, et cetera, on the other. Intermediate positions—whether of families, religions, or communities—are always subject to the double-move of this antinomy. They are deconstructed by the critique of reason and then reconstructed as a matter of individual interest. But if this is one side of liberalism—the side most often criticized by liberalism's critics—the other side is the inability of a liberal polity actually to live within the terms of the distinction of the private from the public. Instead of finding a clear separation of the public from the private, we find a constant movement of the private into the public. The liberal state, like every other, leads its life in the middle range, that is, in the domain of meaning that is neither the product of reason nor the expression of the body.

This chapter began with the distinction between rules and meaning. Neither respect for the demands of law, reasonable as they may be, nor satisfaction of personal interests is an adequate ground for a meaningful life. Of course, we want to satisfy these interests and meet these demands, but in themselves they leave us asking whether there is not something more to a life well led. If we can understand this question, then we must ask whether a particular form of political or moral theory has a place for values that are derived neither from reason nor interest. Just here, liberalism is particularly problematic. For liberalism is stuck in a dichotomy between the discursive claims of reason and the mute claims of desire; it can perceive no middle ground. Without a middle ground, reason and desire—mind and body—continually collapse into each other.[68]

Berlin's "Two Conceptions" essay ends with the puzzle of the relationship of liberalism to the newly emerging, decolonized states. He notes that the Western debate over the appropriate scope of the science of politics makes little contact with the claims for freedom that have characterized the modern era of decolonization. He is struck by the absence in those debates of arguments based on reason and reason's truth. Instead, he observes claims for recognition of group identity by populations that had not been extended such recognition by the colonial powers. The puzzle here is how postcolonial self-government, which often tended to operate without the appearance of Western-style public reason, could be seen as advancing any conception of freedom at all. To Berlin it looks like Kantian heteronomy—not order, but disorder. A disordered life is one lost to either form of freedom. There is an absence of self-legislation as well as a failure to meet the conditions under which autonomous choices could be realized.

Berlin sees that the challenge in the postwar world is no longer the rise of antiliberal ideologies in the West, but the rise of a postcolonial politics driven by ideas of nationalism that are neither liberal nor totalitarian in their origins. They are not the products of a Western-style faith in reason at all, but of a romantic conception of the self that has found a new political foothold. Berlin, however, is much more comfortable arguing against the totalitarians than he is in arguing against the rising nationalists. A dispute over the appropriate domain of reason is one that he thinks he can win. The dispute between liberalism and nationalism is no longer a conflict over the character of reason's truth in the political domain.

This, however, is just the debate that we have to face when confronting the problems of cultural pluralism. Those problems are not going to be resolved by getting our political science right. The liberal's effort

---

[68] For a discussion of the growing intersection between neuropsychology and philosophy, see generally P. Churchland, *Neurophilosophy: Toward a Unified Theory of the Mind-Brain* (1986).

to deploy reason to resolve this debate is not an answer to it, but the very problem stated all over again. We need additional categories beyond reason and interest to understand what is at issue. We need to question liberalism's belief that the political order—our own political order, as well as that of others—can be the product of reason.

Reason exhausts itself early in the constitution of the self. Standing in the long Pauline tradition of the West, we can say that beyond reason is love, and without love even a just life is not a meaningful life. If meaning is the product of love, then adequate tools of explanation may not be present in the philosophical tradition that begins with Descartes's effort to chart the self from the perspective of reason alone.[69]

The liberal vision of love is that of an individual affair—a matter of private concern and choice. It sees love as a condition of a single subject—"to be in love." It pushes love toward a contractual model of relationships. It thereby confuses love and desire. Liberalism is a political philosophy of a loveless world. This is a world in which the faculty of will operates only as the agent of reason or the vehicle of desire; it is not the soul's opening to grace. Yet when we turn from theory to the experience of a public dimension, we find neither mind nor body, neither the universality of reason nor the particularity of desire. We find, instead, a meaningful world.

Love has an irrepressible public dimension; love always founds a public order. The communities within which we find ourselves often make claims upon us to which we respond as if what were at stake were a part of ourselves. In their dispute with the liberals, the communitarians got this right. They did not, however, go nearly far enough in developing a language adequate to the experience, or one that could begin to make normative distinctions among and within these communities. To do so, we have to develop a conception of the will separate from reason and interest; a new conception of the objective value of a world realized by will—an idea traditionally linked to grace—and of sacrifice as the action of linking oneself to this world. These are the terms of the inquiry of part II.

[69] See, e.g., I. Berlin, "On the Rise of Nationalism," in the *Crooked Timber of Humanity: Chapters in the History of Ideas* 238–61 (1992) (no philosophical school in the nineteenth century saw a future for nationalism); see also Unger, *Knowledge and Politics* 106–19.

Meaning exists in between mind and body, reason and desire. The structure of meaning is captured in the great Western metaphor of the "idea become flesh." The source of the idea become flesh is love: "God so loved the world" that the divine took on a human form. Love is the source of meaning, and all meaning is miraculous. This is a world beyond the conceptual capacities of liberalism. Yet it is our world. The feverish turning from private to public, and public to private—the mixing and elision of the categories—characteristic of the self-reflection within the liberal state expresses just this disjunction between the experience of meaning and the categories of liberal thought. Because meaning is neither public nor private, neither mind nor body, liberalism ends in a hopeless confusion of categories as it tries to account for the experience of the political.

PART II

■ ■ ■ ■

LOVE AND POLITICS

Liberalism is a doctrine of freedom but it often seems unwilling, if not unable, to take up the question, freedom for whom? This is why Berlin staunchly defends negative liberty over positive liberty, why Rawls projects his liberal inquiry behind the veil of ignorance and why Ackerman imagines a discourse in outer space. In the last chapter, I traced the way in which the rational, discursive subject of the liberal imagination easily transforms itself into the mute body. Actual subjects, however, exist at the intersection of mind and body. We see this clearly when we turn to the family, but it is no less true of the subject as citizen of the modern nation-state. The inquiry into love and family in chapter 5, accordingly, provides the foundation for the inquiry into the character of political experience in the final chapter.

My ambition in this part is to offer a kind of phenomenology of our most compelling secular forms of meaning: the experience of love and of politics. Before I take up these topics, however, I need to lay the groundwork by pursuing further the inquiry into political psychology. If liberalism's conception of the subject is too thin, what more is needed? In chapter 4, I argue that what is needed is the recovery of a much richer conception of the will, along with the normative order made possible by a psychology of the will. Once again, my point is not to displace liberalism, but to put it in a broader context. Our lives are rich in the multiple forms of self-conception. We need to bring this richness of the sources of the self into our understanding of the place of liberalism in our political life.

Liberalism's turn to contract displaced an earlier idea that the origins of the state are in the family and that the state itself is a kind of enlarged family. The unity of this preliberal state was realized in the mystical corpus that was the body of the sovereign. Liberalism rejects all such concepts as neither rational nor secular. The experience to which these concepts referred, however, does not simply disappear. It continues as the underside of our bond to others. We want not only to respect boundaries of individual autonomy, but to overcome them. Our name for this general experience of overcoming the self is "love." Love works through a kind of double-movement that is simultaneously a realization and a sacrifice of the self. We do not have to look to other cultures to find a questioning of the idea of the self as a rational, autonomous agent. We need only look to our experience of love. Against liberalism's conception of love as private, we must see the way in which love is public. For the end of love is creation of a meaningful world.

To escape the liberal understanding of self and polity, I will turn to some of our most familiar biblical and classical texts. These texts still speak to us. My hope is that the interpretation of these canonical Western texts will serve to illuminate elements of our experience that thrive just below the surface of our liberalism. Against this descriptive endeavor, however, liberalism can claim that its norms are secure and untouched. Demonstrating the persistence of illiberal inclinations hardly amounts to showing that liberal norms are in error. But the point is not to show that liberalism is wrong, but rather that it is incomplete even as an account of the operation of a liberal polity.

Liberalism purports to have monopolized the language of reason. Yet, from where else are we to draw our norms, if not from reason? That, however, is just the point: our experience of meaning is as much normative as positive. Philosophy is not the only point of normative reflection. In love, we experience a claim that is no less objective than that of reason. We may not be able to justify its norms through logical demonstrations, but they remain constitutive of our sense of what it means to find life worth living. To see this, we must once again expand the objects of inquiry, looking now at a variety of representations of the nature of eros, first in the individual and then in the polity. Love and politics are not opposed phenomena, but different expressions of the same structural possibility of experiencing a meaningful world.[1]

---

[1] There is an inevitable problem in speaking of eros in English: the word "love" has to cover a number of related but different meanings. I use "love" to refer to both the erotic domain of the family, as opposed to that of the polity, but also as the translation of eros, of which both family and polity are expressions. Thus love is both the general category of eros, and a particular form of its manifestation. For this reason, politics is both a form of love, eros, and a phenomenon set against love, familial. The context of expression should make clear which usage I have in mind.

CHAPTER 4

■ ■ ■ ■

THE FACULTIES OF THE SOUL: BEYOND REASON AND INTEREST

In the West, we live with a complex conceptual inheritance that draws equally on the thought of classical Greece, Christianity, and the Enlightenment. Oversimplifying greatly, we can say that the Greeks formulated the ambition to subject the soul and the state to the order of reason; the Christians turned from reason to a will informed by grace; and the Enlightenment turned both reason and will toward a new appreciation of the ordinary as the object of desire and the limit of experience.[2] All of these elements continue to inform our experience of the political.

The classical Greeks first conceived of a hierarchy of faculties within the soul and projected that logos of the psyche onto the order of the state. The first great work of political theory, Plato's *Republic*, explicitly deploys an analogy between polity and soul. In order to discern justice in the soul, Plato turns to an inquiry into the state, seeking there an "enlarged, visible" image of justice.

Reason, in the classical view, was an active faculty, the function of which was to rule internally, that is, over the other faculties and dispositions of the soul, and externally, that is, over the conflicting claims of individuals and classes within the polity. Just as a wise ruler would carefully deliberate among the polity's options in order to separate the course of reason from that of impulse or desire, a virtuous individual would rule himself through a similar internal deliberation.[3]

---

[2] See C. Taylor, *The Sources of the Self* 285–302 (1989).

[3] See e.g., Thucydides, Book 5. 84–116 (The Melian Dialogue, in which a dispute over possible Athenian destruction of Melos is presented as a dialogue between "Athenians" and "Melians" on the justice of each city's position).

Plato's philosopher-king is just one version of this common assumption that political rule and self rule are both a function of reason, and ideally, the identical function. The form of Plato's political inquiry—seeking that set of conditions under which the political order can be a function of reason—remains central to Western political theory and practice, even if deliberative assemblies and administrative agencies have replaced philosopher-kings. Similarly, the moral inquiry he pursued—whether the virtues of the good man are the same as those of the good citizen—remains central to Western normative inquiry.

To the classical philosopher, the problem for both the state and the individual was to subordinate the intemperate desires of the moment to the conclusions of principled deliberation. Reason was a political virtue as well as a psychological faculty. Education cultivated that faculty in order to produce a virtuous political practice. One educated reason through an appropriate discursive engagement. Both Aristotle and Plato confront the problem that the virtue of reasonableness is simultaneously the product and condition of the well-ordered polity: a good state produces good men, but only good men will produce a good state. This meant that the virtuous soul required a community of like-minded individuals. Where might such a community come from, if it is not already present? This is the paradox of the *Republic*; it remains the paradox for all political thought that seeks to appeal to both reason and democracy. How might a people become better than itself? How can a democratic polity recognize the conditions of rational excellence? The distribution of political authority in the liberal state between a constitutional court and a democratic legislature is a modern response to this classical problem.[4]

Early Christians recoiled from these claims for reason, believing that the most important truths were beyond the capacity of man's limited understanding. Man stood in need of revelation. The paradox of establishing the political conditions for the rule of reason is displaced by the paradox of the human condition: how can finite man achieve the infinite? This paradox could no longer be overcome by the accident

---

[4] For example, Alexander Bickel argued that the justices have the intellectual virtues of academics. A. Bickel, *The Least Dangerous Branch: The Supreme Court at the Bar of Politics* 25–26 (1962). The turn to the administrative agency is a parallel effort to deploy particular forms of rational expertise within the democratic polity.

that a king may come to have an interest in philosophy, which was Plato's answer, or by the cultivation of virtuous habits, which was Aristotle's, but only by divine intervention. This belief in revelation required a reconceptualization of the faculties of the soul, and thus a different ordering of psyche and polity.

No element of the classical conception of the soul had as its object anything like revelation.[5] This new source of substantive truth led to the introduction of the faculty of will. The Christian conception of the will is best understood as the faculty of the soul that corresponds to the substantive idea of grace. Will is the potential to realize God's grace; it is the faculty by which one puts the soul into a condition to receive that grace. The failure of the will is no longer weakness before temptation or the lack of habits that support political virtues like courage and moderation. The failure of the will now is that fall from grace that the Christian experiences as sin.

Grace is not a product of human reasoning; it is not even accessible to reason.[6] Beyond comprehension, grace marks the limits of reason and even of man himself. No amount of pursuit of the classical virtue of justice through the rule of reason will bring the soul into the presence of the sacred. The wise man may still be fallen. Indeed, Christianity's appeal was at first—and still is—to the "least among us": the suffering poor, the uneducated, women. Nor is grace a function of desire, as if grace could be ranked among the body's interests. Grace requires a turning of the soul, not the taking of an object.

Grace expresses the complete otherness of that which gives an ultimate meaning to life.[7] Grace is as inexplicable as creation ex nihilo. Indeed, Saint Augustine understood grace as the continuing presence of divine creativity.[8] Since God's actions cannot be explained, they are conceptualized as acts without antecedent cause. To receive God's

---

[5] See M. Forster, "The Christian Doctrine of Creation and the Rise of Modern Natural Science," 43 *Mind* 446 (1934).

[6] See M. Ignatieff, *The Needs of Strangers* 74 (1984). ("The language of Christian ecstasy which derives from Paul insists on the radical insufficiency of the natural human conception of our own alienation.")

[7] See K. Rahner, *Foundations of Christian Faith* 190 (W. Dych, trans., 1999) ("This immediate self-communication of God to spiritual creatures takes place in what we call 'grace.' ").

[8] See G. Wills, *Saint Augustine* 96–97 (1999).

grace is to be "chosen." This idea of the "chosen" expresses the incommensurability between the mundane and the sacred. This choice is wholly a function of the chooser.

Even if divine choice is not the product of one's being deserving, there must be limits to the idea of sacred otherness. Without such limits, the sacred would become as irrelevant to a life plan as the accidents of nature.[9] That otherness is cabined through the linkage of grace and will. Grace is the response of an omnipotent God to the act of willed confession by the individual. By confession, I refer not just to the ritual of the Catholic Church, but more broadly to a purification and opening to the sacred. Through will one puts oneself in a position to receive grace.

In classical thought, the virtue of speech was "logos," which meant both speech and reason. Confession does not participate in the logos. It is rather a kind of emptying out of the self and an accompanying recognition of pure need. Confession marks the turning of the will toward God, and thus the abandonment of the finite self. It is beyond reason and without desire. As Simone Weil writes, "[g]race fills empty spaces, but it can only enter where there is a void to receive it, and it is grace itself which makes this void."[10] Confession is the paradigmatic act of speech in a Christian metaphysics of the will. It is a speech that brings one to the edge of the sacred, while recognizing that speech cannot cross the boundary. Thus, the deliberative community of the Greek polis is displaced by the confessional community of the church. This is a community, however, that is unbound in space or time.

The will is that capacity man must have in a world in which meaning is wholly within the possession of God's act of grace. In an echo of the Platonic homology of city/man, the reconceived soul of man now operates in a new homology of God/man. Thus, just as will represents the openness of man to revelation, will is the source of revelation in

[9] Perry Miller saw the problem of working out predestination in a social context as the key to the entire intellectual history of Puritan New England. "If men may sit all their lives as obtuse as the walls and pillars," and yet be saved or not saved all the same, "with what face could ministers blame sinful people for afflictions or treat sin as avoidable?" P. Miller, *The New England Mind: From Colony to Province* 54 (1953). To combat this problem, the New England Puritans began to say that persons should be "prepared" for the experience of grace. Ibid. 53–82.

[10] S. Weil, *Gravity and Grace* 55 (1952).

God. God *wills* the world into existence; every manifestation of the divine—grace—is a renewed expression of God's will. No longer reason, but will binds the world into a single whole.

Thus, man's faculty of will represents the reconceptualization of man in the image of this new God, just as this new God represents a reconceptualization of man. Man's longing for God requires the will; God's response to that longing requires grace. A new metaphysics of the will replaces the metaphysics of reason. This is a world that is full of "signs." Reading these signs is not a function of discerning the works of reason—Plato's Forms or Aristotle's formal causes. It is a function of opening the soul through a will that rests on faith. The correspondence of man and God under the conception of will is not— at least not yet—the Hobbesian claim that, in the creation of the state, man's will mimics and displaces God's. Hobbes's will no longer exists in a sacred world of grace and faith. To understand Hobbes, we have to ask what happens to the Christian faculty of the will in a desacralized world.[11]

Every metaphysics supports a moral and political practice that "makes sense" within such a world. A community of individuals linked through a will directed at God's grace is no longer the deliberative association of ancient Athens. It is, instead, the church as the body of Christ. The realization of grace is not a matter of comprehending an object apart from the soul. It is experienced as a "new birth." It remakes the nature of the body itself, which becomes a part of the miraculous appearance of the infinite. Christ is the paradigmatic moment of this identity of the finite and the infinite. Every reappearance of this miracle of meaning is Christ-like.[12] This is the experience given expression in the church: a new form of community sustaining a new form of meaning.

For the Greeks, the problem of the will was conceived of as that of controlling a weak will—a will that would not comply with the demands of reason even when one knew what should be done. Accordingly, the virtues of the will were temperance and courage, the capacity

[11] See below at 170–71, 175–76.

[12] This is most evident in the sacraments; it is at the heart of the Gospel of Saint John.

to do what was right under extreme conditions of either pleasure or pain.[13] But what was right remained a matter of reason. Training of the will was a matter of forming correct habits within a context of reasonable community expectations. These habits could then be relied upon when circumstances become strained. This normative sensibility leads the Greeks to produce the first works of history in the West. These works present narratives of heroic actions, that is, of overcoming weakness of the will by deploying the virtues of reason under extreme conditions. This, for example, is the special virtue of Odysseus.

In his autobiography, Augustine describes his confrontation with, and ultimate rejection of, this classical conception of the will. The experience he describes begins from the problem of weakness of the will: *akrasia*. Despite his education, and despite his powers of deliberation, he is without the power to form his character under the guidance of reason. Indeed, reason just makes matters worse. It becomes a source of radical doubt. Augustine is the first to record the experience of existential angst.[14] Existence itself has become a problem, and the only answer to this problem is through a faith that reaches beyond reason.

This experience of failure of the autonomous individual—an experience of the terror of meaninglessness for finite man—is conceptualized in the mythic form of original sin. The source of sin is now reason. Knowledge becomes man's burden; reason, his weakness. Man's knowledge is never more than a kind of "carnal knowledge"; it is bound to the body. Reason has moved from the classical model of a faculty understood in opposition to the body to a position of individualization within the body. History is the passing on of this sin from one generation to the next. Time itself has been corrupted. The atemporal perfection of the Platonic Forms is now located in the divine, which is beyond man's reason.

The idea of original sin simultaneously gives voice to an experience of man's lack, and of the divine as the only possible resource by which to overcome that lack. Reason is wholly of this world, which means

---

[13] See Aristotle, *Nicomachean Ethics* 3., 6–12.

[14] Augustine, *The Confessions* 7, 21, 27. See Taylor, *Sources of the Self* 131. ("It is hardly an exaggeration to say that it was Augustine who introduced the inwardness of radical reflexivity and bequeathed it to the Western tradition of thought.")

it is tainted with death. The moral task, accordingly, is self-consciously to realize one's fallen state in order to place the soul in a position from which it is open to divine grace. If the opening of the will to God is the source of meaning, then political order too must be reconceived.

A polity organized on the principles of reason can never do more than replicate the limits of the individual soul and the incompleteness of finite efforts at justice. Organized political life comes to be seen, therefore, as the condition of fallen man. This corrupt political life is to be transcended in a new community of faith. Modern politics continues to bear remnants of this Christian idea of the corruption of the body. Politics, we often feel, is all too much of this world. When we take up politics, we inevitably dirty our hands.

The state too must have a will, if it is to become a possible representation of the divine. Politics is no longer a matter of justice under the guidance of reason, but of faith within a community of those sharing a common will. This idea of a community of the faithful begins in the church, but becomes central to the Western concept of nationhood. A political community is not merely an organized structure for the development and deployment of reason. Its foundation lies in will, not reason. Modern political thought expressed this idea in the notion of "sovereignty." The sovereign is the point of reification of the common will of the nation. The sovereign has will, not reason and not desire. Indeed, we come to the idea of the sovereign through that of the will: Because there must be a national will, there must be a subject in possession of that will. This is the sovereign.

For centuries, the sovereign will was quite literally embodied in a subject: the monarch was the mystical corpus of the state. That incorporation borrowed explicitly from Christology. The sovereign did not just claim a "divine right" to rule—a claim about the derivation of legitimacy. Rather, the sovereign was an appearance of the divine. He or she was Christ-like, in claiming, for example, a miraculous power to heal the sick.[15] This substantive claim of the monarch cannot survive the desacralization of the modern world. Yet the understanding of the form of the sovereign will remains.

---

[15] See M. Walzer, introduction to *Regicide and Revolution: Speeches at the Trial of Louis XVI* (1974).

The deeper point that survives the death of the king concerns the operation of the metaphysics of the will in the construction of the community's self-understanding. Just as the will of the individual appears in and through a metaphysics of faith, so too does the will of the nation. The nation is a community of faith. To this, the idea of sovereignty is critical, while the representation of the sovereign in the monarch is not. The monarch claimed to be the "mystical corpus of the state," but was vulnerable to competing symbolic representations of the national will. Modernity begins with a competition among claims to represent the nation's sovereign will. The monarchy loses this competition to representative institutions that appeal to the idea of popular sovereignty. The sovereign as mystical corpus, however, survives long after monarchs disappear. Revolution kills the king, but also announces the presence of a new sovereign: We the People.

Liberal political theorists fail to understand the foundation of sovereignty in the metaphysics of the will. They are likely to see popular sovereignty as a voting mechanism, rather than as an expression of a faith in a transtemporal, plural subject. They see a two-termed world of reason and interest. But that is exactly their problem: they produce theories of politics that fail to grasp the distinctive character of modern politics—a character founded on the will. Prior to the will, there was no sovereign. Without sovereignty, we do not have modern politics. Oddly, liberalism is a political theory for a world without politics.[16] For neither reason nor interest has any need of that distinctive domain, history, which is both the condition and the product of politics. Liberal theory, we might say, is not of this world.

The Enlightenment offers a kind of secular synthesis of the classical and Christian contributions—one in which the substantive meaning of each is fundamentally transformed. The desire for systematic knowledge under the norm of reason remains, as does the focus on will as the source of individual character. Now, however, will is stripped from grace, while reason is given a new object in the absence of a concept of the transcendent, whether Platonic Ideas or Christian

---

[16] See U. Preuss, *Constitutional Revolution: The Link Between Constitutionalism and Progress* (D. Schneider, trans., 1995) (on velvet revolutions of 1989 as efforts to depoliticize).

revelation. There is a new valuation of ordinary experience, which shapes the objects of both reason and will. Reason's task is to understand this mundane world, while the will's task is to create order among the ordinary objects of desire. The result is a new science of politics, entirely different from the classical inquiry into the ideal of justice.

The turn toward the ordinary represents a great democratization of thought. This democratization itself owes much to the Christian experience of the equality of all men before a transcendent God. In the modern age, however, neither philosophy nor claims of divine revelation appear to be self-legitimating. Only the immediacy of common experience—whether of pleasure or pain—speaks with a universal moral authority. Ours may be an age of reason, but we remain slightly embarrassed when asked what it is that is the object of our deliberations. We cannot seem to detach reason from the body itself.[17] In this respect, there is not a great deal of difference between the theory of the moral sentiments of someone like Hume and the theory of the erotic sentiments of his contemporary, the Marquis de Sade. Each offers a philosophy of the sentiments; each can find no source of value outside of "ordinary" experience. The miraculous no longer shines through the ordinary. The nature of man is to be a part of this ordinary world.

To value the everyday is also to transform the place of individual desires and interests in the moral and political imagination.[18] The paradigmatic act of will becomes the contract: will in the service of the body's interests. The will of the political entity too is reconceived on the model of contract: the social contract. Justice becomes a matter of distribution; it is no longer a question of ordering the soul. Of course, religious experience doesn't simply disappear in the face of this new value of the ordinary. It remains a vibrant claim on many, particularly in the United States. Characteristic forms of modern political reason must bridge these conflicting sources of meanings—religious faith and ordinary experience. This distinction leads to the two variants on liberalism that I described in chapter 2—the liberalism of faith and that of speech.

[17] See chap. 3 above.
[18] See Taylor, *The Sources of the Self* 211–14.

The new science of politics appears first as an effort to set forth the terms of the social contract. This is the tradition that extends from Hobbes to Rawls. The object of political organization remains deeply influenced by the classical tradition: reason is set against desire. Reason must bring order to the chaotic character of bodily interests. Writing the social contract is an exercise of pure reason. Yet reason is now in the service of interest; it brings no substantive ends of its own. This produces the primacy of the private, which I traced in chapter 3.

An incapacity to transcend the immediate perspective of self-interest disqualifies one from participating in the drafting of the social contract, even as an imagined act. One cannot write into this contract a special position for one's own personal interests. Rather, one must agree to act on reasons that can be accepted by all. Modern liberalism stands within this social-contract tradition. Different forms of liberal theory deploy different devices to filter interest from reason: Rawls's veil of ignorance, Ackerman's constrained discourse, or Habermas's ideal speech conditions.

Despite the classical origins of this claim concerning the ordering power of reason, there has been a subtle shift, captured in the idea of contract. Contract suggests that each individual, as a contracting party, has reasons of his own to agree to the political arrangement. Those reasons, in their particularity, don't affect the terms of the contract, but neither do the terms describe an order of reason independent of interests. Plato would strip the guardians of personal interests—the interests of the individual body—in order to have them embrace the political order of reason. But in the social-contract tradition, reason is seen as a mechanism of coordination—a means—while the motivating force for the particular individual remains interest. Individuals should agree to the social contract because it is in their own interests. This may require distinguishing long-term from immediate interests, but it does not require eliminating the ends of interest. The social contract promises a life that is more than short, nasty, and brutish—that should be enough. In contemporary terms, it promises to overcome the problems of social coordination by addressing the problem of defection.

This is hardly the whole story, however, since justice is not merely the answer to a coordination problem. As I argued in chapter 2, justice inevitably comes to be valued in itself; its pursuit is seen as a good separate from the satisfaction of particular interests. The ambiguous value of the social contract—as a means and end—is a function of the double-appeal to interest and reason in its production. The oldest philosophical psychology we possess values reason in and for itself. The appeal to reason in the construction of the contract, even if based originally on the motive of satisfying everyday interests, will inevitably cross the boundary from means to end. The construction of justice on the basis of reason will appear to be a valuable project in and of itself—indeed, the highest value. Thus, liberalism may begin by valuing interest, but always seems to end on the side of the party of reason. The result is the fundamental confusion that I described in chapter 3 in terms of the shifting normative places of the private and the public. We can never quite decide whether the value of the polity is set against the private or is in its preservation of the private.

Apart from this social-contract tradition, a second form of political science appears as an aspect of the general scientific program of understanding the objects of ordinary experience that characterizes the Enlightenment conception of reason. This is an analytic science of politics. It aspires to a positive understanding of political phenomena in the same way that any other domain of experience can be the object of a discipline of scientific inquiry. Its task is not the construction of the social contract, but understanding the character and sources of the political order as we actually find it. The task of political science, like other empirical sciences, is to offer a new set of categories that allow experts to describe and explain phenomena in ways not visible in ordinary experience. Politics, on this view, is epiphenomenal, and the task of social science is to reveal its deep structure. Political reason is stripped of its classical connection to public deliberation; it becomes instead the explanation of those sources of order that the nonexpert cannot even see. Regardless of what we may have thought about public deliberation and self-construction as the exercise of reason, both are now exposed as, at best, mere rationalizations. Political reason is in the exclusive possession of the scholar.

The appeal to a scientific discourse to explain politics puts this form of reason beyond the reach of the social-contract tradition. One does not deliberate about historical materialism anymore than one deliberates about geographical determinism. Nevertheless, there is an inevitable shift in the locus of political authority as a result of the development of this new science of politics. Precisely because the new science perceives ordinary political behavior as a product of some deeper set of truths that are not part of our everyday discourse, the virtues and vices of a political order now appear to be structural. Knowledge of this structure becomes a source of authority for a new form of political expert who is capable of designing "systems." Here, we find the origin of the modern phenomenon of the political scientist, who claims a kind of authority just by virtue of his knowledge. On this view, a constitutional order can be constructed more or less well. Its excellence depends not on public deliberation, but on the framers' understanding the deep structure of political order. The American founders' understanding of the constitutional order as a system of checks and balances that would encourage political moderation and reasonableness is one example.[19] Opposed to such "republican" forms of systemic knowledge are those that understand the political order to stand on material interests. Political science from this perspective has tended to collapse into the science of economics—whether that of Richard Posner or Karl Marx.[20] Nothing about the systemic claims of reason resolves the deeper issue of the source and character of political value.

The authority of reason in politics today derives from both of these traditions—that of the social contract and that of the expert system. Both are drawn upon by modern liberal theorists. This produces the ambiguous quality of works like Rawls's *Theory of Justice*, which is simultaneously contractual and systemic. Universalizing the contractual moment, he develops a system of pure reason. Thus, he models a pure political discourse, which allows him to make systemic claims for the design of the just polity, which is also a democratic polity. Such a system of just political order could be put into place, however,

---

[19] These virtues of the system can be distinguished from the legitimacy of the Constitution. The latter can remain a product of popular consent, even while the former are products of systematic knowledge. See P. Kahn, "Reason and Will in the Origins of American Constitutionalism," 98 *Yale L.J.* 449 (1989). The contemporary study of comparative constitutionalism continues in this tradition of expert design. See P. Kahn, "Comparative Constitutionalism in a New Key," 101 *Mich. L. Rev.* 2677 (2003).

[20] Economics may dominate the positive science of our own politics, but anthropology plays that role as the political system studied becomes more distant from our own.

without every citizen understanding the course of expert reasoning that produced it or sustains it.[21] Possession of right principles is a matter for elites: constitutional designers originally, and those with ongoing responsibility for maintaining the systemic virtues of the state thereafter.[22] The same ambiguity is found in the contemporary "Washington consensus" on Third World reform.[23] Emerging states must put in place an expert system of economic and political order, but they must also be democratic. Unlike the harmony of the original position, actual politics often faces an unresolvable crisis in the competition between these demands.[24]

All of the forms of experience that we describe through these three faculties of reason, will, and interest remain present. Faculties do not exist as components of the soul that are added onto or subtracted from some neutral frame. They are efforts to articulate a self-understanding; that is, to put into a coherent conceptual form experiences that are widely shared. We imagine the soul as a person within the person; we imagine faculties of the soul as if they were parties competing for governance of a state. In the end, however, these forms of political psychology are only reifications of common forms of experience.

Although these different conceptions of the self enter Western culture in different periods, the new never wholly displaces the old. Each struggles against the others. For example, economics is the leading social science today, reflecting the dominant place we tend to give the perspective of interest. Although much of our life is organized around market behavior, a prominent part of political and legal theory in the last generation has been an effort to recapture the civic republican tradition. That tradition reaches back to a classical conception of

---

[21] Compare Hart's location of the rule of recognition in the knowledge of an elite class of decision makers. H.L.A. Hart, *The Concept of Law* 112–13 (1961).

[22] There is, for this reason, always a substantial effort to educate the Supreme Court on the latest theory of political justice. Constitutional law professors play this role of mediating between Court and academic political theory. Consider, for example, F. Michelman, "In Pursuit of Constitutional Welfare Rights: One View of Rawls' Theory of Justice," 121 *U. Pa. L. Rev.* 962 (1973); C. Sunstein, "Beyond the Republican Revival," 97 *Yale L.J.* 1539, 1550 (1988) (on Pocock).

[23] See, e.g., J. Stiglitz, "The World Bank at the Millennium," 109 *Econ. J.* F577–97 (1999).

[24] See A. Chua, *World on Fire* (2002).

reason, in which political deliberation is valued not just for the correctness of its products—that is, its contribution to GDP—but also as an experience of common, civic engagement. We deliberate, not just to overcome our collective-action problems, but for the sake of realizing a common experience of virtuous action in the deployment of reason. The puzzle for many has been how to reconcile the reason of the ancients with the science of the moderns. Similarly, conceptions of will and grace that originated in Christian thought have hardly disappeared. They operate as a kind of background set of norms, always available as a source of critique of our "materialistic" age, on the one hand, and as a source of skepticism about the claims of reason, on the other. Neither quite reaches that experience of being enthralled by a meaning larger than the self. The result is that we live within competing ideas of the truth of the self: reason, will, and interest. Each can serve as the basis of a metaphysics, a moral psychology, and a political theory.

These sources point in very different directions when we theorize about values and sources of meaning. Reason points toward the universal; will points toward the history of a confessional community; interest points toward the satisfaction of the body's desires. Reason appears with a kind of timelessness; will appears in and through the narrative of a uniquely valued community; interest appears with the immediacy of the body's demands in the present moment. Individual subjects, as well as the collective polity, orient themselves in each of these dimensions of timeless truth (the perspective of justice), historical continuity (the perspective of nationalism and sacrifice), and immediate interests (the perspective of markets). Each generates a different attitude toward the future into which the polity is moving: the reformist ambition of reaching closer and closer to an ideal of justice; the maintenance of an historical legacy; or the present value of future satisfactions. Similarly, each generates a different perspective on the relationship between self and others. That relationship can move from justice to sacrifice to contract.

We can best conceive of the shifts in normative political psychology of the three periods as differences produced by allowing each of the three faculties to become the prism through which we view the other two. Thus, the Greeks sought to control self and state through deliberative reason; they thought of both desire and will as impulses to be controlled by reason.[25] Early Christians maintained the subordination of body to soul, but understood the soul from the perspective of the will.[26] On this view, reason becomes hermeneutics and desire the domain of self-denial. Finally, the moderns place the body and its interest at the base of their implicit metaphysics, viewing reason and will as agents of the body's interests. Moderns tend to see the order-giving function of reason as never rising above the interests of everyday experience, just as will finds its expression in contract.[27] This is true of both utilitarian and deontological approaches to liberal theory. Thus, the success of the modern political order tends to be measured by the success of the economic order, on the one hand, and by the physical health of its citizens, on the other. Contemporary politics can seem to be a matter of GDP and morbidity rates.

THREE FORMS OF POLITICAL PSYCHOLOGY

A full understanding of our experience of political meanings requires that we keep in mind all three faculties as sources. We need to examine the ways in which each faculty relates to the others. Liberal theory's greatest failure is its blindness to the continuing place of the will in the politics of modern nation-states. Liberalism is caught in a kind of dialectic of reason and interest, yet modern political experience has been centrally a phenomenon of the will.

Politics and the Metaphysics of Will

The more we take the perspective of the will, the more we emphasize a normative perspective that places a revelatory act at the foundation of the community's self-understanding. This is a politics that borrows from the religious linkage of will and revelation. Will and grace, I argued above, are linked as faculty and object. Just like reason and its object, the distinction of will and grace is never complete. We know the faculty in each case only in and through its object. In the apprehension

---

[25] See Plato, *Republic* 4., 439–41.
[26] See Augustine, *Confessions.* 7.21.27.
[27] See chap. 3 above.

of a mathematical principle, for example, we cannot distinguish the object of knowledge (an idea) from the faculty of knowing. Faculty and object provide two perspectives on a single experience of meaning. Similarly, grace is a function of will, and will a function of grace. The tendency of early Christian thought to collapse across this line, such that man becomes a part of the divine, was a danger resisted as a form of heresy.[28] The rise of modern political theology, however, embraces this heresy. The revelatory act, the moment of grace, is now that of self-revelation by the popular sovereign. In the politics of the nation-state, man, understood as the popular sovereign, has become divine. The source of the state's creation is the will of the popular sovereign. That will reveals only itself: faculty and object have become identical.

The modern, democratic polity is founded on a transcendent act of self-revelation: revolution. The political value of revolution cannot be explained either by appeal to abstract norm (justice) or by analysis of the empirical causes (material need) leading to revolution at a particular moment in time. Revolution is not the effect of any cause, although the circumstances that are the occasion for revolution can be described. They are not its cause, because replication of those circumstances will not necessarily lead to revolution. At best, those circumstances "invite" revolution. Revolution breaks into ordinary time as a new moment of creation. It is self-validating. It can never be reduced to its antecedent causes; neither can it be exhausted in the subsequent history it makes possible. It is politics in the form of a democratic metaphysics of the will.

Whether a modern nation-state can exist without a revolutionary consciousness is an open question. Even nations as ethnically and culturally stable as France or England maintain a narrative of popular revolution. More importantly, every modern nation-state believes that it is subject to a potential revolution—a new mobilization of the sovereign people outside of law. Constitutions may not have sunset clauses, but neither can they declare illegitimate an investment of the popular sovereign in a new constitution. This is part of the nation-state's sense

---

[28] The idea that matter is nothing but a deterioration of the spirit is cental to Gnostic thought, as well as the idea that man's end is a return and reunion with the Godhead.

of its own democratic legitimacy. Indeed, it is a necessary structure of the contemporary idea of a political will. The will of the popular sovereign is always deeper and richer than its particular terms of expression in a constitution.[29] That will is an inexhaustible source of meaning for the state.

Successful revolution is followed by constitutional construction. The constitution preserves that sacred appearance of the popular sovereign and organizes political life around it. The constitution provides access to the sovereign revelation, but is never fully adequate to it. It translates into the idiom of the ordinary the extraordinary experience of revolution. This juxtaposition of the extraordinary and the ordinary produces the problems of constitutional hermeneutics. On the one hand, constitutions appear as law, to which the ordinary canons of legal construction should apply. On the other hand, constitutions appear as an endless resource of self-understanding for the state. They preserve that original act of self-revelation by the popular sovereign.

Comparing the originalism of revolution to the original position of Rawlsian liberalism, we see two quite different normative structures. One we value because it is ours; the other because it is no one's in particular. One has value because it happened; the other has value only as a regulative ideal. This produces a paradox in the constitutional jurisprudence of democratic self-government: the more the nation believes itself to be a product of the will of the popular sovereign, the less democratic it becomes—if by democratic, we mean, subject to control through broadly participatory electoral mechanisms. Constitutional law maintains the revelatory act of the popular sovereign, which may not make direct contact with the contemporary wishes of a majority of the electorate. American constitutional theory has been focused on this problem since Alexander Bickel first labeled it the "countermajoritarian difficulty."[30] This is the modern form of Rousseau's distinction of the general will from the will of all.[31]

---

[29] This intuition of the limits of law leads Carl Schmitt to locate sovereignty at the point of the power to declare an "exception" to legal rule. See C. Schmitt, *Political Theology: Four Chapters on the Concept of Sovereignty* (G. Schwab, trans., 1986).

[30] Bickel, *The Least Dangerous Branch* 16–23.

[31] See J. Rousseau, *The Social Contract*, bk. II, chap. 3 (C. Sherover, trans., 1974).

Originalism as a mode of constitutional thought is inseparable from this experience of self-revelation by the popular sovereign.[32] American debates over the appropriate form of constitutional interpretation always occur within a broadly originalist framework. All participants in the debate take seriously the claim that constitutionalism is a matter of giving effect to a text with its own history. All ask what it means to be "true" to the text.[33] Originalism is sometimes presented as a doctrine designed to constrain judicial activism.[34] Not only does this seem false as a practical matter, but it fails to explain the passion with which originalism is pursued.[35] The originalist seeks to preserve and make operational a sacred, revelatory past. The nonoriginalist does not challenge this end so much as the manner in which that sacred past can continue to live in the present. This whole endeavor is a form of practical reasoning that appears simply irrational from the perspective of reason. Appeals to originalism seem to the liberal theoretician a methodological category mistake. But this is only because it is the mode of interpretation deployed by will, and against reason. We cannot measure faith by logic. The sacred is always beyond reason.

Will privileges the narrative of self-creation of a particular community. There is no universal will, no will in the abstract. On this view, the origins of the political community represent a perfect state of grace, in which there is a complete transparency of the individual will to the sovereign will. This revolutionary community has a kind of transtemporal existence: all individuals—present and future—are participants as members of the popular sovereign. For this reason, the actions of the founders can continue to bind future generations: all are part of a single We. The atemporality of Christ has moved from church to sov-

[32] This is not to suggest that originalism is the only legitimate mode of constitutional interpretation. On the dialectical relationship between originalist and nonoriginalist interpretations of a "sacred" text, see Kahn, *The Reign of Law* 220.

[33] See, e.g., Lessig's critique of a hermeneutics of strict originalism in the name of an originalist value. L. Lessig, "Fidelity in Translation," 71 *Tex. L. Rev.* 1165 (1993).

[34] See, e.g., R. Bork, "Neutral Principles and Some First Amendment Problems," 47 *Ind. L.J.* 1 (1971).

[35] Consider, for example, the contemporary revolution in federalism doctrine. See *United States v. Lopez*, 514 U.S. 598 (1995); *United States v. Morrison*, 529 U.S. 598 (2000).

ereign monarch to the popular sovereign. Such a nation cannot be conceived on the model of reason or interest. It is the product of a revolutionary act of will that has become a self-validating source of revelation. It is the nation-state become a church in which all citizens are part of the body—the mystical corpus—of the state.

Reason's role in a system of the will is neither that of identifying universal truths nor that of discovering the implicit logic of a market order; its method is neither deductive nor inductive. Rather, reason's task is hermeneutical: it must interpret manifestations of the sacred. Hermeneutics had its origins in the recognition that there is a unique demand on reason in the interpretation of a biblical text. A constitutionalism of popular sovereignty requires a similar approach to the sacred text of the civic religion. The task of political hermeneutics is to explain who we are as a community that has engaged in an act of self-creation. Its object is "We the People," never "we, the present voters." In its judicial form, hermeneutics interprets the constitutional text as the material representation of the sovereign people. Thus, the Supreme Court aims to speak in the voice of the sovereign people. If it fails, if it speaks only in the contemporary voice of politics, it is without legitimacy.[36] Constitutional hermeneutics treats the text not as a source of just political principles, but as the revelatory source of our deepest common meaning.[37] In its nonjudicial form, this same subordination of reason to the metaphysics of the will produces the political rhetoric of sacrifice: the call to the individual citizen to realize his or her deepest meaning in the giving over of the embodied self wholly to the maintenance of the sacred meaning of the state.[38]

Political rhetoric does not call the individual to sacrifice for the rule of a universal ideal of justice, or for satisfaction of the interests of any particular citizen or group of citizens. It is a call to *be* as a part of the

[36] See Kahn, *The Reign of Law* 208–9.

[37] For examples of two classic forms of constitutional misreading, consider Beard's interest analysis and Perry's turn to human rights. Neither makes contact with our constitutional practice as a hermeneutics of popular sovereignty. C. Beard, *An Economic Interpretation of the Constitution* (1965); M. Perry, *The Constitution, the Courts and Human Rights* (1982).

[38] On political rhetoric and sacrifice, see chap. 6 below.

transtemporal unity of the state that is the popular sovereign. Just as liberal political thought cannot understand reason as hermeneutics, it has no understanding of the rhetoric of political sacrifice—except as a dangerous appeal to irrational passion. Nevertheless, a state that operated without constitutional hermeneutics or political rhetoric would be a postmodern political form that made little contact with the politics of the nation-state as we have experienced it over the last two centuries. It would imagine the global reach of both a law based on reason and a market based on interests. Will would disappear from political ontology. For many, of course, this sounds like the appropriate aspiration in an era of globalization.

The sovereign will as the source of political creation, and hermeneutics as the method of reasoning, are remnants of the Christian confessional community that have become parts of our secular political tradition. So too is that understanding of the third faculty of the soul— interest—which sees the desires of the body as obstacles to be overcome. They remain "the temptations of the flesh" that turn the individual away from the source of meaning and to a kind of hopeless anomie. Indeed, individualization through personal interests could serve as a definition of political sin. In its most immediate form, it produces the problem of political corruption. But corruption is only the criminal form of a deeper problem of substituting individual interest for a conception of the self as a part of the popular sovereign. We know this more broadly as the problem of "special interests," or factions, that subvert the public good.

The politics of modern nation-states remains a world of symbols and miraculous appearances. The body of the citizen is to become a symbol—a point at which the popular sovereign shows itself by displacing interest. This is a politics of citizen sacrifice, which ranges from the battlefield to the voting booth to the courtroom. A virtuous political citizen willingly sacrifices his or her own interests. Sacrifice may appear first as the language of warfare, but it is more generally the language of "public-spiritedness." Just as with the church, sin in its political form is the ordinary condition in which we find ourselves. Church and nation-state are always calling on us to overcome the individualism of interest. Both appeal to a revelatory past and look forward to a redemptive future.

From the perspective of the will, the most basic structure of political reality is the transtemporal community. For the individual, contact with the sacred origins of the community requires an overcoming—a sacrifice—of private interests. The need to act as a public citizen is often expressed in contemporary constitutional thought.[39] The liberal tenor of that thought, however, tends to understand this demand on the individual as a precondition for public deliberation based on reason. But reason is no less a problem from the perspective of will than is interest. The political community founded on the will of the popular sovereign requires a deliberate suspension of belief in the powers of a universal reason, no less than it requires sacrifice of individual interests. Political deliberation is not an abstract consideration of justice. It is, instead, the hermeneutic enterprise of constitutional interpretation. The sacred political community exists in the traditional paradox of Christianity: by sacrificing the subject, the self will be reborn; by abandoning reason and interest, one will find the truth.

Of course, the revolutionary consciousness of the popular sovereign makes a claim to justice. We inevitably bring our abstract understandings of justice to the task of performing a revolution, as well as to that of subsequently interpreting the meaning of the revolution. The popular sovereign must say something; it must produce a text. Where else can it look for the content of its discourse than to its moral and political ideals? Thus, the Declaration of Independence speaks of "self-evident truths," which only in retrospect become the revelatory speech of the popular sovereign.[40] That the American founders located their self-evident truths in substantial part in the classic liberal tradition is obviously important for the content of the politics of will in our tradition. Yet it is a mistake to see only the form of justice and not the politics of the will within which this tradition operates. The political community is not reducible to a collective effort to realize

---

[39] See, e.g., C. Sunstein, "Naked Preferences and the Constitution," 84 *Colum. L. Rev.* 1689 (1984); B. Ackerman, *We the People: Foundations* 230–94 (1992) (arguing a dualist conception of the "private citizen" that includes a public function of higher law making).

[40] See Kahn, *Legitimacy and History* 54–55; H. Jaffa, *Crisis in the House Divided* 227 (1982).

these liberal norms. Politics is not just something that gets in the way of liberalism.

Similarly, even revolutionary communities must be concerned about individual interests. The demands of the body must be met. Politics—even a politics of will—is not a kind of practical eschatology. A political community demands sacrifice, but it is not a suicide pact. While a politics of will must still respond to the claims of interest and reason, these intersections are not only incomplete, they also represent a kind of boundary crossing as we find ourselves responding to very different claims. Thus, the American politics of the will occurs within a general understanding of markets as the means of meeting interests. This does not mean that economics displaces the politics of the will, but rather that the construction of a narrative of the national will makes room for an account of markets. I described the particular form of this American narrative—with its ambiguous understanding of the private as familial, sacred, and economic—in chapter 2.

The political perspective of will is that of a community whose identity is constituted by the narrative of its own self-creation. History, prior to that founding act, lacks meaning. Prerevolutionary history gains whatever meaning it has retrospectively, that is, its meaning is only as a kind of preparation for the revolution. The American colonial experience, for example, is not understood as an aspect of British life, but as a kind of training for independence.[41] The same is true in the modern, postcolonial world as each new state makes a claim to its colonial past.[42] That past is reinscribed in the narrative of revolution; it is dispossessed of its place in a competing narrative of empire.

The birth of the postcolonial state was made possible by the metaphysics of will. Revolution breaks the link with a colonial, and even a precolonial, past; it begins history over. This is the means by which the arbitrariness of the boundaries of the postcolonial state—a legacy of European, not indigenous, history—is simply eliminated from the narrative of political meaning. Within those boundaries, the popular sovereign reveals itself as a self-validating source of political meaning.

[41] See, e.g., J. Butler, *Becoming American: The Revolution Before 1776* (2000).

[42] See B. Anderson, *Imagined Communities: Reflections on the Origin and Spread of Nationalism* 170–85 (1991) (on maps, museums, and the postcolonial).

This political metaphysics of the will is just what Isaiah Berlin could not see when he bemoaned the loss of reason.[43] The postcolonial state is, then, a legacy of a Western idea of politics that traces directly to a Christian conception of the will. It should not be surprising that the actual politics of these states has, for the most part, failed to match the conceptual foundations of the polity.

So far, I have elaborated the modern political psychology of the perspective of will. The will, however, does not have a privileged position in contemporary political theory—as opposed to in constitutional theory.[44] Indeed, this is the perspective that liberalism resists, and for that reason is worth elaborating in some detail. Although liberalism may deny its continued existence, this is the only perspective that makes sense of much of modern political practice, especially that of the United States. American constitutionalism looks strangely irrational and anachronistic to the elites of much of the rest of the modern West precisely because we remain enthralled by the perspective of the will. Our actual politics remains distinctly less liberal than our political theory, because we remain a sacred, political community.

Of course, American elites no less than their equivalents in other developed countries are deeply attracted to an emerging regime of globalization of markets and of law. They, too, are cultivating a sense of transnational—not transtemporal—identity; they, too, speak of the breakdown of traditional political boundaries. Yet, most Americans—and certainly the political leadership—remain conflicted over the virtues of globalization, for two reasons: first, a deep tradition of constitutional law as a hermeneutics of the will; and second, the enduring persistence of a belief in American exceptionalism. These two points are reverse images of each other: American exceptionalism is grounded in a political psychology that privileges the perspective of the will.[45] Even abroad, however, we should not too quickly judge the tenor of a nation's political form by looking only to expressions of

[43] See chap. 3 above.

[44] Work on constitutional theory in this vein includes not only that of Ackerman and my own, but also that of Jed Rubenfeld. See J. Rubenfeld, *A Theory of Constitutional Self-Government: Freedom and Time* (2001). It is not too much to speak of a "New Haven School" of constitutional thought in referring to all three.

[45] I elaborate the structure of American exceptionalism in chap. 6, below.

political and legal theory. The European Union, the model of community after the age of sovereignty, has hardly begun to displace the sense of identity through nationhood in citizens' political imaginations. Europeans may not yet be done with the politics of will, and Americans remain firmly in its grasp.

The Politics of Interests

If we shift perspective from will to interest, our conception of the other faculties changes as well. We now take up the point of view of a market orientation in which interest is modeled on bodily desire. This does not mean that every interest expresses a physical taste or aversion, but only that each shares the characteristics of such desires. First, there is a primacy of the individual—interests count because they are *someone's* interests. Collective interests have value only as the aggregate product of individual interests. Second, interest is the imagined internal state that corresponds to the outward action of taking: a reaching out to an object to make it part of the self. An interest expresses itself by making a claim on something or someone outside of the self. An unexpressed interest has no politically cognizable value: thus the link between a political psychology of interest and a legal order of property. Third, there is no neutral perspective by which to judge or compare interests. Apart from the willingness of individuals to invest in and pursue their interests, there is no ground for comparison.

The generalized perspective of interest is that of the market. Markets coordinate the urge or need to take, turning it from a brutish competition of each against all to a stable order of exchange. A market does so by objectifying interests in the form of property, which then allows a process of valuation and exchange. In such a world of individuals with objectified interests, market norms become guides to political behavior. On this view, there is no fundamental difference between the ends of the market and of the polity. How can there be if interest is the source of meaning, and meaning is only the satisfaction of some individual's or individuals' interests? Such a view renders problematic any independent claim for preservation of past meanings. Meanings must be of interest to someone; the dead do not count in these calculations of value.

Markets are complex forms of satisfying the compulsion to take.[46] One takes in order to satisfy an interest. Those devoted to market models insist that they are metaphysical individualists; that is, all explanations must begin from the fact that there *is* only the individual. The image driving this form of analysis is the body itself, with its radical individuation and separation from others. These theorists do not worry much about a differentiation of faculties within the individual, because every faculty ultimately expresses itself in a market choice. Production within a market model has the same brute facticity as the body. The logic of the market is the aggregation of individual decisions about interests and aversions. There is no "reason" to be offered as to why one product rather than another succeeds; it simply does or does not. The idea of market perfection is found in the notion of the Pareto-optimal condition, in which no further exchanges would make any individual better-off without making someone else worse-off. There is not otherwise a "right" outcome; there are no grounds for intervening simply to secure the satisfactions of some over others. Justifications for intervention will, therefore, identify areas of market failure. Public goods, for example, may require a supplement to the self-regulation of the market.

Of course, markets do not serve only the needs of the body. There are markets for art, books, and music. The body hardly needs luxuries, but markets may be at their best in meeting the differentiated and discerning tastes of those with money to spend. Markets not only respond to needs, they create the interests that they are able to satisfy. They create a kind of spiral of desire and its satisfaction.[47]

From the perspective of interest, the role of political reason is to identify barriers to free entry and to correct for market failures. Government's role is to establish and secure the conditions under which markets can flourish. Economics is its own science, with its own measure of true and false propositions. We know that attempts to use reason to construct a nonmarket economy have for the most part proven to be "false sciences." This does not mean that the only viable

---

[46] See J. Locke, *An Essay Concerning the True Origin, Extent and End of Civil Government*, chap. 5 (1690).

[47] See R. Frank, *Choosing the Right Pond* (1985).

position is that of free markets unconstrained by government regulation—just the opposite. The scope of government intervention required to support market operations—for example, in the forms of
bodies of law, mechanisms for dispute-resolution, and responses to
market failures—are all complex questions requiring the active deployment of reason.

The point is not that economics has a kind of truth that makes it
the highest of the human sciences. Rather, economics will dominate
the conception of reason if we take up political psychology from the
perspective of individual interests. We can imagine political circumstances in which other sciences would be the source of governmental
decision making. If we were, for example, to approach political psychology from the perspective of a religious quest for salvation, theology would displace economics as the form of reason to which politics
must be responsive. Moreover, specialized governmental functions
may turn to other forms of social science even while privileging economics generally. No one thinks economics can displace medicine in
the government's maintenance of public health services. The same sort
of functional specialization occurs with respect to issues ranging from
penology to urban planning. These forms of expert knowledge nevertheless experience the dominance of economics in two ways: first,
there is a constant effort to deploy the methods of economics within
these disciplines, just as in the Law and Economics movement; second,
economics purports to provide an overall structure within which each
form of specialized knowledge must justify itself. The market model
of the social world that economics supports reflects the powerful attraction of an interest-based understanding of the self in many contemporary contexts in the West.

Like reason, will too changes its form when viewed from the perspective of the modern idea of interest. Will remains the representation
of a subjective capacity to locate the source of meaning outside the
self. Will, however, is now understood on the model of contract. Contract simultaneously invests objects with value and creates an intersubjective world of exchange. It expresses a commitment to regulate one's
own interest-seeking behavior in conjunction with others. Without
others with which to engage, will is indistinguishable from desire.
Thus, the simplest contract is for a purchase or sale: it sets a value on

an object and defines a relationship between two subjects committed to reciprocal recognition of that value. Will as contract changes what would otherwise be the unpredictable character of interests into a stable order of intersubjective satisfaction. This stabilization makes possible economics as a new science of the will.

The contemporary emphasis on contract expresses the stabilizing quality of will in a mobile world of interests. A market order is distinguishable from a system of theft just to the extent that it moderates immediate desires by a will formed in and through contract and property. Locke locates the origin of property, which is a necessary condition of a market order, in the investment of the individual's will in the object through labor.[48] He saw property as an objectification of the self made possible through such an investment of the will. Accordingly, property was a visible and enduring representation of interest. As value becomes less attached to real property, contract displaces property as the paradigmatic objectification of a will in the service of interest. Intangible property is just the power to enter into or prohibit contractual relations; real property itself becomes a special subject of contract.[49]

If the task of politics from this perspective is to maintain market values and institutions, the problem of politics is its tendency to interfere with markets. Politics becomes a distrusted form of action because too often it is a form of rent-seeking. Today, when we consider globalization, we see a lag between the logic of markets, which tend toward a global reach, and politics, which for the most part remains community-specific. This bounded state is continually tempted to intervene in the global market in inefficient ways. The logic of markets is one in which the politics of nations is to yield to the management by experts. It is a world in which the WTO and the IMF replace the national parliament. Of this, we might say that "it is one possible future," but it is not yet our present. Nor is it necessarily our destiny. Even some European states have resisted the Euro, despite its representation of the logic of the market.

[48] J. Locke, *Two Treatises on Government* 287–88 (P. Laslett, ed., 1988).
[49] See B. Ackerman, *Private Property and the Constitution* 27 (1977). ("For the fact [or is it the law?] of the matter is that property is not a thing, but a set of legal relations between persons governing the use of things.")

Liberalism at Home: The Politics of Reason

The first two perspectives—interest and will—generate disagreement across all of the inherited categories of our political psychology. Is the source of value individual interest or self-transcendence? Do individual interests gain value through their satisfaction or their sacrifice? Is will the source of contract and property or the faculty of participation in a transtemporal popular sovereign? Is the work of reason economics or hermeneutics? These are familiar yet irresolvable debates in the nation's law schools. The debates reflect larger conflicts within the nation's political self-understanding, which seems to move endlessly back and forth between a pride in American exceptionalism and a demand for lower taxes. The former makes prominent the collective memory of a unique history; the latter aims to put more discretionary power in the individual consumer who is seen as the ultimate source of his or her own meaning. To these debates, we must still add the third perspective—that of reason. Only here do we confront liberalism in its own right.

The ambition of reason is to put political life on the same sort of compelling foundation as is present in the sciences. The task is to construct order from first principles that would be self-evidently valid to all rational persons who confront the task of establishing a polity under the predictable conditions of material need and moderate scarcity of resources. This is the source of the modernist urge to build the political community from an imagined state of nature in which all that we can rely upon is our ability to reason and all that we can be sure of is that we confront a world of need and threat. Just as there is only one science of mathematics, there should be only one science of politics—despite our present disputes over the contents of that science. A perfect politics of reason would, therefore, imagine a single political order of global dimensions. As long as men can reason and have needs, the outcome should be the same. This does not necessarily mean a single empire. We cannot know in advance how far the application of reason will take us in the construction of political order. It may leave room for substantial variation within general parameters; it may set out alternative structures that are sensitive to contexts. If a plurality of reasonable states is possible, then the problem of creating an order of reason replicates itself in considering the proper relations among states. Thus, Rawls follows his works on justice within the state with a work on justice among states.[50]

The application of reason to the problem of political construction is to produce justice. We can see this in two ways. First, the critique that reason offers of existing arrangements is always one of exposing their injustices. A political arrangement that is "unreasonable" is one that makes an unjust claim: it favors one individual or group over another without offering an adequate reason for that difference or it suppresses a reform that would be to everyone's benefit. Every reform movement that speaks the language of reason makes a claim to justice. Second, the Kantian idea of giving the law to oneself through the appeal to reason, explored in the previous chapter, is a paradigm of justice. A law that makes an equal claim on every rational subject—and therefore can be imagined as given by each person to himself—is a just law.

Of course, there will be contention over the content of justice. Competing conceptions of the will and interest may enter this debate as elements of an idea of justice. It matters to our idea of justice whether we think of a relationship to the body on the model of interest or that of sacrifice. Justice on the battlefield is not the same as justice in markets. Reason cannot tell us whether individuals or transtemporal communities are the basic subjects to whom justice applies. Indeed, the inquiry into justice may lead us beyond politics as an organization of the state. Marx's science of politics, for example, famously described the "withering away of the state." Competing versions of nineteenth-century political science were similarly disinterested in the state as an actual historical community.[51]

All who enter this debate are committed not merely to their own conception of justice, but to the idea that we can reach agreement if

---

[50] See J. Rawls, *The Law of Peoples* (1999). Ackerman and Habermas are similarly inclined to advance from the liberal state to a liberal international order. See, e.g., B. Ackerman, "The Rise of World Constitutionalism," 83 *Va. L. Rev.* 771 (1997); J. Habermas, "The European Nation-State: On the Past and Future of Sovereignty and Citizenship," 10 *Pub. Culture* 397 (Winter 1998).

[51] See I. Berlin, "The Bent Twig: On the Rise of Nationalism," in *The Crooked Timber of Humanity* 243–51 (1990).

we set the appropriate conditions for our mutual deliberations such that the outcomes are the product of reason. This is the origin of liberalism's search for the set of ideal conditions of deliberation—whether construction of a veil of ignorance, establishment of constraints on the domain of possible reasons, or agreement on procedures to hold open for reconsideration every substantive proposition. Neither reason nor justice can be the unique possession of an elite.

To take up the perspective of reason does not entail indifference to the conditions of production and to the satisfactions achieved through markets. Reason does not deny the existence of interest. Reason seeks only a metaphorical death in its denial of any place for personal interests behind the veil of ignorance. This is the same death of which Plato spoke in the *Phaedo* when he said philosophy is a kind of practice of death.[52] Nevertheless, the fact that some object or action is of interest to an individual or individuals is not in itself a sufficient condition of value from the perspective of reason. A standard of justice is separate from that of market efficiency. Rawls's "maximin" principle, for example, is derived from an analytic of reason; it is not a value internal to the idea of a market.[53] Value now comes from the autonomous operation of reason, not from reason's capacity to contribute to the satisfaction of individual interests.

The same is true with respect to the expressions of a sovereign will that define and create a single historical community. Reason need not deny that individuals may understand themselves as members of a transtemporal community for the sake of which they are willing to endure sacrifice. As with interests, however, the community's will must pass a test of reason if it is to be valued. What is valuable is a community's success at constructing itself according to reasonable principles of justice. Maintenance of an unjust arrangement has no value in and of itself, even if it expresses the self-understanding of the citizen as a part of a transtemporal popular sovereign. The dead hand of the past has no privileged position from the perspective of justice. Absent justice, reason sees only the political pathologies of nationalism in this direction. Not only the internal order, but equally the temporal and geo-

---

[52] Plato, *Phaedo* 64a–b.
[53] J. Rawls, *A Theory of Justice* 132–35 (1971).

graphical boundaries of the political community must pass the test of reason. These boundaries, for example, should constitute a just allocation of resources among peoples. Reason does not privilege one community over another.[54] The accidents of place and time must be replaced by the ordering principles of reason, that is, by justice. That these borders have defined the domain within which the sovereign will has been formed and maintained is not a value to be balanced against justice. It is only a fact, not a value. It is relevant only to the degree that it advances—or obstructs—the realization of justice.

What happens, then, to will and interest when we adopt the perspective of reason? There are two possibilities. One is that they simply disappear from view; the other is that they are banished to the domain of the private. An example of the first is the odd position of the will in Rawls's *Theory of Justice*. Rawls places his work in the long tradition of social-contract theory. Yet, for him the will has no independent content by which it makes itself known behind the veil of ignorance. This originating will is structurally required to assert whatever conclusions reason reaches. Before history or any other sort of individualizing principle emerges, there can be no ground by which the will can separate itself from reason. The will of the individual within the confessional community—political or religious—is specifically excluded from the original position. So too is the will as the means of individual investment in contract. There is no moment of choice separate from that of deliberation. Pure practical reason does all the work.

The actual will makes no appearance until after the ideal public reason has established the fundamental principles—justice—for the basic order of the state. Indeed, Rawls provides a careful, multistep scheme for the introduction of will and interest into the theoretical project of establishing just norms and constitutions: "[A]ny knowledge that is likely to give rise to bias and distortion and to set men against one another is ruled out. The notion of the rational and impartial application of principles defines the kind of knowledge that is admissible."[55] Will and interest are allowed to reappear at the same

[54] See, e.g., A. Gutman, "Democratic Citizenship," in *For Love of Country* 66–71 (J. Cohen, ed., 1996) ("[A] philosophy of democratic education rejects the idea that national boundaries are morally salient.").

[55] Rawls, *Law of Peoples* 200.

moment because both present the same problem to reason: the threat of the irrational. The transition from ideal to actual is always a process that threatens the corruption of pure reason. No actual political process will meet all the conditions that reason imposes; the legislative and regulatory output of even a "fairly well-made" state will be corrupted by individual and group interests. From the perspective of reason, the problem of the human condition is that we are embodied—we are not pure reason. The body will always present itself as irrational. One aspect of the liberal project, accordingly, is to institutionalize the presence of a critical reason within the structures of governance. This is the source of courts, and of constitutional courts in particular, which are ritualistically disembodied—they have neither will nor interest.[56]

Interest and will are suppressed in the original position—that is, in the mythic origins of the state. They are suppressed again in the ideal end of the state. The modern state is, accordingly, in a constant process of reform as one area after another is subject to the scrutiny of reason. Reform is the process by which the products of will and interest are purified by reason. Because interests are essentially irrational and without end, we are never done with the project of reform. Interests must be held in check by a will that accepts the critique of reason. Ackerman provides a model for this ideal of reform as the engine of reason's suppression of interests: every assertion of an interest or a claim to a scarce resource can be challenged and that challenge must be met by a reasoned discourse of justification.[57] This is true for both the state and the individual. Just as legislative policy is always open to challenge, and then to reform if it cannot meet the challenge, so too is every individual's choice. Education becomes a lifelong process of critically evaluating habits and interests. In both cases, the ambition is that the will should be invested only in those interests of which reason approves.

From the standpoint of reason, there is not a substantial difference between reform and revolution. These exist on a single continuum, measuring the scope of the application of reason. A gradualist agenda of reform can produce, over time, a political order that is as just as the

---

[56] Hamilton spoke of courts having "no influence over either the sword or the purse." *The Federalist No. 78*, at 465 (Hamilton) (C. Rossiter, ed., 1961).

[57] See B. Ackerman, *Social Justice in the Liberal State* 4 (1980).

outcome of dramatic revolutionary change. The common law evolution of a political order—for example, in England—may compete on the scale of reason and justice with the revolutionary constitutional construction of the United States.[58] Only from the perspective of the will does revolution show itself to be different in kind from reform.[59] Theorists who ignore the place of the will in American constitutionalism are likely to assimilate the constitutional tradition of Supreme Court adjudication to the common law working out of the order of reason.[60]

The first strategy of reason, then, is to suppress recognition of interest and will, and only extend recognition to that which passes the test of reason. The second strategy is to allocate both interest and will to the domain of the private. Again, we see reason dealing with what it perceives as the recalcitrant irrationality of the body, which is now cabined, rather than suppressed. To the degree that will and interest prove impenetrable to reason, a domain of the private is recognized as the proper place of man's inevitable irrationality. Because it is defined by this impenetrability to reason, the private has an incredibly broad sweep. It contains both the trivial desires of the body and the confessional community of the church. It includes both the familial domicile and the marketplace. All that unites these vastly different enterprises is their rejection of reason as the measure of value. Indeed, the line separating the private from the public is only as secure as the belief that reason can go no further. Rationalization pushed too far produces the extremism of the variety of forms of authoritarianism that have plagued Western politics since the French Revolution. But the practice of limiting the reach of reason derives not from reason itself, but from a cultural context within which reason operates.[61]

[58] William Gladstone expressed this idea: "As the British Constitution is the most subtle organism which has proceeded from the womb and long gestation of progressive history, so the American Constitution is . . . the most powerful work ever struck off at a given time by the brain and purpose of man." W. Gladstone, "Kin Beyond Sea," *N. Am. Rev.* (Sept. 1878).

[59] Failure to recognize this difference in conceptual models produces the normative confusion of Ackerman's dualism. He needs a theory of the will, but does not want to abandon his liberal commitment to reason. See my critique in P. Kahn, "Community in Contemporary Constitutional Theory," 99 *Yale L.J.* 1 (1989).

[60] See, e.g., D. Strauss, "Common Law Constitutional Interpretation," 63 *U. Chi. L. Rev.* 877 (1996).

[61] See chap. 3, above.

Belief in the fundamental irrationality of the private explains, in part, the American reluctance to speak of "civil society." The concept of civil society suggests an alternative organization of the social. We can identify the principles of reason that should operate in civil society. Indeed, we can even give them weight in the construction of a just political order. Thus, Europeans can speak of the conditions of civil society that are a necessary predicate for a liberal, democratic, political order. For Americans, however, the public domain tends to absorb the entirety of reason. If there is a place for reason, there is a place for public establishment and enforcement of norms. If civil society is private, then reason must be mute.

CONCLUSION: THE DIVERSITY OF POLITICAL MEANINGS

As my mention of American resistance to the idea of civil society should suggest, my account of the three perspectives on political meaning was systematic without purporting to be complete. Most of all, it was informed by my understanding of the competition of perspectives within American political culture and politico-legal theory. Other permutations and applications of these categories are realized elsewhere. Nevertheless, here these three different normative perspectives provide the shape for many of our deepest political dilemmas at the level not just of national policy, but equally at that of the individual and the global. Consider the multiple norms to which the individual citizen feels drawn. He or she simultaneously affirms the virtues of participation in public deliberation over the character of justice, of satisfaction of interests through participation in a well-functioning market, and of responding to a call for sacrifice for the maintenance of the state. At the international level, we affirm the justice of universal human rights, the appeal of transnational markets, and the importance of state sovereignty. The problems here are not just those of incommensurable values. Each value stands upon an entire metaphysics that grounds a political psychology. We live simultaneously in distinct universes, that is, among diverse symbolic forms. There is no neutral perspective, no reality, separate from the forms themselves.

Although we can understand the institutions and values produced by each, these relationships among reason, will, and interest cannot be stabilized in any one order. Consider, for example, the different attitude toward the future each adopts. From the perspective of will, the future always poses a threat of corruption, of a falling away from the meaning that created and sustains the community. From the perspective of reason, this fear of change is nothing less than submission to the dead hand of the past. Reason looks to a future of endless reform, moving ever closer to an ideal order of justice. Interest rejects both the reverence for the past and the hope for the future, looking to present satisfactions; it measures the future in terms of present value.

We live with radically different and conflicting values, both in our personal lives and in our political communities. Each of these faculties can provide a dominant perspective by which we order the other two. Thus, we can think of the role of reason as that of articulating a public order of individual rights—human rights—that should be universal in scope. But we can also think of the state's deployment of reason as essentially filling in the space of market failure: the modern state must engage in constant monitoring of, and interventions in, the economy. Or, we can think of reason as the hermeneutic enterprise of maintaining the meaning of founding texts. Similarly, if we begin from the fact of individual interests, we can affirm the value of their satisfaction as the end of the state or, conversely, we can see those same interests as the temptations of bodily desire. Temptation can be a threat either to the virtuous politics of reason or to the effort to maintain the politics of popular sovereignty. Alternatively, if we consider reason and will to be only superstructures built on to the satisfaction of the individual's needs and desires, we will move toward a market-based conception of political perfectionism.

We can prioritize the will such that maintenance of the historical identity of *this* community as a single entity expressing the continuity of the popular sovereign becomes the ground of legitimacy and the telos of the state. Now the threat of interest is not the threat of the irrational, but the threat of forgetting the past out of a concern for the satisfactions of the present. The same threat of forgetting, however, can arise out of too great a concern with abstract justice—a criticism often made of nonoriginalist, judicial opinions.

What is important to see is that none of this is true in and of itself. Nor is it true that the multiple perspectives and structures that we deploy constitute a complete account of possibilities, even for ourselves, let alone others. We could, for example, see interest as the product of character, and character as the product of a life built within a community. We could locate even the body's desires in the historical narrative of a particular community.[62] This is no more right or wrong than seeing desire as the domain of sin to be fought against by reason and will. All of our structures of thought have their own histories, their own genealogies. We are in no position to make universal claims when our own conceptual resources are so diverse and incommensurable.

Together these three perspectives produce just that clash of political values that characterize the contemporary, cosmopolitan moment: we simultaneously affirm an international legal order of human rights; a global order of sovereign states; and a single market that knows no geographic bounds. These are the perspectives of reason, will, and desire. Each can make a global claim, geographically and conceptually. We are replicating at the international level just those conflicts of faculties, values, and perspectives that we have been managing in our conceptions of domestic order since the modern nation-state emerged as a product of a revolutionary act expressing the will of the popular sovereign in an age of reason, and at a point in time when the promise of markets to satisfy the social question first became imaginable.

We do not have the resources for managing this clash at the international level. Indeed, at this level of analysis, liberal theory is itself part of the political problem. Its vision of rights and markets puts it into direct conflict with the claims of state sovereignty—the traditional basis of international law and international relations. Liberals tend to think that the post–Cold War international order has transcended the state, which appears increasingly anachronistic in a global order of rights and markets. Reason, on this view, has triumphed over will. That vision is very far from the reality in places like the former Yugoslavia, the Caucasus, the Middle East, and the postcolonial order of Africa and Southeast Asia. It is, I believe, equally far from the continuing reality of American politics and self-understanding. Afghanistan and Iraq may represent the intersection of both of these sources of contemporary antiliberalism: Islamic fundamentalism and American

---

[62] See Aristotle, *Nicomachean Ethics* 2. 1. 1103b4–5 (character is a function of community's law).

exceptionalism. We forget the intensity of nationalism and claims of state sovereignty only at our peril.

The strengths and weaknesses of liberalism are best understood by placing liberalism within this conceptual and normative matrix. Liberalism represents a rough melding of normative perspectives of reason and interest. The combination of the two produces the general modesty of its claims for reason, unlike the extremism of competing forms of the politics of reason. That modesty is expressed in liberalism's recognition of the distinction between the public and the private. Only the public is subject to the norms of reason. Reason determines the basic structures of the political order; interests are only suspended, not expelled. The value of the private expresses the continuing presence of the perspective of interest. Characteristic problems of liberalism are produced by the need to manage the intersection of public reason and private interests.[63]

This marriage of reason and interest produces the odd spectacle of competing liberalisms that move across a spectrum that extends from libertarianism to the social-welfare state, from Bentham's utilitarianism to Rawls's theory of justice. Liberalism, I have argued, stabilizes a number of conceptual resources available within the Western tradition. Different liberalisms can be understood as "local equilibria" of these conflicting resources. This approach explains the historical ambiguity in the meaning of liberalism, which points simultaneously to a conception of politics founded on notions of individual rights and to a market order. The former emphasizes the role of reason in liberal theory, while the latter emphasizes the role of interest. The instabilities of liberalism, however, are produced not only by this tension, but also by that which liberalism cannot see at all.

Liberalism leaves out of the account those norms that have their origin in the faculty of the will as it enters the Western tradition through the experience of Christianity. Will and grace are the terms of our inheritance from a postclassical world of monotheistic values and concepts. In the age of democratic states, there is a collapse of these terms: the people, as popular sovereign, endow their own revolutionary act of will with its sacred meaning. Every manifestation of the will of the popular sovereign has the aura of grace. We are a chosen

---

[63] See chap. 3 above.

people because we will ourselves into being and thus choose ourselves as a people. This is neither a matter of reason nor of interest, but of will and of the norms generated by a particular conception of the will. These concepts remain a part of the construction of meaning for the individual and the polity within the democratic, constitutional state. In chapter 6, I will argue that they are not just a part, but indeed central to the felt-meaning of the politics of the American nation-state.

Seen from the perspective of American political history and experience, liberalism is a political theory without an understanding of politics. For our politics is neither reason nor interest, but a reading of the body as an "idea become flesh." The paradigmatic political act is sacrifice, not contract and not deliberation. Liberalism, however, has no conceptual space for sacrifice. In the next chapter, I begin the description of that space, which is only revealed when we turn from reason and interest to love.

Finally, a word of caution. I have offered a kind of schema of conceptual relations. This chapter has, like the first, been an exploration of conceptual architecture. Yet we should not confuse a schema with actual experience. In that experience, relationships among these concepts and categories are much more fluid than in the architectural account. Appeals to the different sources of norms are made on an ad hoc basis; there are always attempts to meld the traditions, to find points of synthesis and mutual appeal. Conceptual resources are not like material resources. Our ambition cannot be to find that single, coherent position that makes the best use of the totality of resources at hand. Rather, the concepts are in genuine tension, pointing toward different worlds of experience and meaning. Different forms of argument appear to be more or less convincing in different contexts.

If I am right about the deep attraction of incommensurable forms, consistency is too much to ask. The most we can do is to observe patterns of practice and thought, examining the way different possibilities are emphasized or come to a dominant position. Architectural inquiry must, for this reason, always be supplemented by genealogical inquiry.

CHAPTER 5

■　■　■　■

THE EROTIC BODY

The most immediate description of the subject that we expect of others and offer of ourselves refers to age, gender, and family. Before any other set of meanings appears, one finds oneself already within a world of family, attached through the body itself. Family is the site of birth and death, of childhood and reproduction. Moreover, through family the connection to the polity is ordinarily established. In the family, we learn language and group identity.

When family works well, it is a center of love and support. When it works poorly, it is the center of pain and tragedy. Either way, we cannot answer the question of identity without locating the self within a familial order that brought it into being and will see it out of existence. This is not just a matter of placing the body on a family tree as an exercise in human cartography. Participation in the family, even a tragic family life, is neither a matter of choice nor a contingent fact about which we can express indifference. Even the tragic family makes a claim, not a request. We confront such tragedies as our own. We make our lives in the context of these claims, even if we might wish it otherwise. We can turn away, but for the most part we cannot leave behind the family that claims us.[1]

Family is first of all an organization of sexuality—of bodies understood in their reproductive capacities. More than that, it is an organization of the comings and goings of life itself. Of course, not every family relationship produces children, and not every relationship should be held to some standard of child-production. But families, even if only the married couple, are not just close friends. In the family, we feel we are near to the deepest mysteries of life and death. For this

[1] Perhaps the greatest fictional representation of the tragic claim of family is Tolstoy's *Anna Karenina* (1877).

reason, and not just for the bureaucratic and legal benefits, many gay couples insist on the right to marriage. While the heterosexual family frames the discussion that follows, nothing I say is meant to preclude the possibility of "nonconventional families" or gay marriage; indeed, just the opposite.

Family maintains a set of meanings that control and direct the explosive potential of love and death, both for individuals and for the community. Because of this, no polity can be indifferent to familial order. Neither, however, can it simply impose its own conception of order on familial love. If the polity contests that love, it may lose. As with so many other things in our democratic age, we have generalized a concern that previously found its symbolic, and legal, expression in the monarch as sovereign: the state could never be indifferent to the family formation of its royal line. That same concern is now extended to the familial generation of the popular sovereign.

FAMILY AND POLITY BEFORE LIBERALISM

In the story of Adam and Eve, the problem of time does not emerge until after they eat of the Tree of Knowledge. Before that point, they live in a timeless present in which they are fulfilled through each other: "they become one flesh." This atemporal fulfillment is marked by their lack of shame. Sexuality has not yet entered the domain of morality. Neither has it entered the domain of generation. There is no mention of children in this union.[2] The story is an image of complete fullness in and through the other—an ideal, at the center of the romantic, but also, as I will argue below, of the pornographic.

In the Garden, man is said to have been created in the "image" of God. Image here has the connotation of subordination—of a lesser reality—as the image in a mirror is less than the reality.[3] Although man is an image of God, he does not have the knowledge of good and evil. Just this knowledge, however, was the source of creation. Thus, at the end of each day of creation, God looks at his work and sees that

---

[2] As a myth of origins, the image is very similar to that of Aristophanes' circle people recounted in Plato's *Symposium*.

[3] Plato's divided line, *Republic* 6, 509d–11c, provides a useful ontology of the image.

it is "good." Without this knowledge, man's power is exhausted in the act of naming: God brings each of the creatures before man to see "what he would call them."[4] Naming is to creation as man is to God, that is, the name is an "image" of the named object. To move from namer to maker, man must eat of the Tree of Knowledge. To do so is to aspire to be not a lesser image, but "like God"—just the temptation that the serpent offers Eve.

Unlike God, for man to have knowledge of good and evil is to be subject to the pain of labor. This is labor in its double-sense of bringing forth offspring and of craft. To know the good is to have to struggle to achieve the good. God speaks the universe into existence, but for man making and speaking are not the same.[5] The fact of labor characterizes a life bound to time: "you are dust, and to dust you shall return."[6] Man's power to create fights against this measure of its own exhaustion, for man is a wasting asset. There is always something of ourselves in the products of our power and we are not endless.

Man gains the power to produce by knowing the good. Power is not represented here as resting upon a natural base of reproduction. Rather, the intergenerational project of reproduction is itself a manifestation of power. It too is a domain of labor, and labor is always a matter of bringing the good, an idea, into material existence. If the work of man is the exercise of power, then we see in this story the claim that the family is work, not nature. Family, no less than the state, is the product of an effort to create the good. If family is the domain of love, then love too is linked to power, production, and the good.

These ideas are sharpened considerably when we turn to the story of Abraham. In this story, the knowledge of good and evil is displaced by the covenant with God. No longer is the source of power the knowledge that man shares with God; rather, it is the relationship to God. The covenant makes possible human history in its double-sense of political and familial continuity through time.

---

[4] *Gen.* 2:19.

[5] God's omniscience and his omnipotence paradoxically intersect at this point, generating traditional theological debates. Knowing the good, could God have not created the world? Does perfection require creation and thus limit omnipotence?

[6] *Gen.* 3:19.

The fundamental point of the story of Abraham is that his relationship with Sarah cannot produce children before he enters the covenant. Again, we see that there is nothing natural about the family. The family, no less than the polity, must be founded upon an in-forming idea of the sacred. God promises Abraham a future in return for entering the covenant. That future is not immortality. Rather, Abraham is promised that he shall found a great nation: nation and patriarch are simultaneously political and familial ideas.

The production of a family is conditioned upon Abraham's acceptance of the covenant. The family must mean something before it can be a display of power. Like all man's creations, reproductive labor must be directed at the production of the good; it must embody an idea of the good. The source of that norm cannot be located in the merely natural. This founding idea is now simply that of the covenant itself, which is the source of all meaning. The divine must manifest itself in time to found the nation, for all meaning is an appearance of the divine.

The Abraham story carries this idea of embodiment significantly further. It tells us that meanings must be borne directly on the body. The covenant requires circumcision: "So shall my covenant be in your flesh an everlasting covenant."[7] The flesh must bear the idea; it must appear as a text already named. Instead of man naming the products of creation, man himself becomes a name. This particular mark on the flesh is singled out because of its sexual, intergenerational connotations. The very organs of reproduction are marked. Sex is the source of family and politics. They are the same not because the polity must be based in familial relations, but because all products of labor must bear a divine meaning. What might appear most personal is given significance as a mark of the intertemporal project represented by the covenant. Naked, man still finds himself a representation of the covenant.

Abraham, as the story of the sacrifice of Isaac makes clear, stands completely in the presence of the idea. Thus, Abraham's repetition of the most simple line of confession to God: "Here am I." This is the measure of his faith, the founding moment of a political community, and the origin of the intergenerational family. Not the social contract,

---

[7] *Gen.* 17:13.

but the covenant; neither reason nor desire, but faith: without faith, man's labor will produce nothing that is not undermined by its inevitable return to dust.

This same theme is suggested in two other aspects of the story. First, in the destruction of Sodom, we find a linking of corrupt sexuality with a corrupt politics. The destruction of Sodom represents a failure of human time, that is, a failure in the construction of political history. That failure is brought on by the corruption of sexuality, vividly portrayed in the attempted rape by the men of Sodom of the messengers of God. That rape is a kind of counterpoint to circumcision as the presence of the sacred within the sexual act itself. The covenant with God, which makes possible a meaningful history, is embodied in the sexuality of the family. This is what Abraham achieves as a result of the covenant; it is what Sodom lacks.

Yet, Sodom tells a story about the dangers of sexuality as well. It tells us that the possibility of alternative readings of the body and of its sexuality are always latent. They remain there to challenge the covenantal reading of family. What, after all, is Sodom but a vision of the pornographic as a representation of a kind of political freedom? The homosexual appears here as paradigmatic of an affirmative reading of the body as the source of its own meanings, and thus a denial of the covenant. This assertion of completeness within the body—the denial of the body as an image of the divine covenant—calls forth God's wrath. Sodom is, therefore, an image of danger, not a denial of the possibility of alternative readings of the body's sexuality. Contemporary homophobia remains embedded in this same worldview linking family, politics, and covenant.

This central idea—that the body must gain a symbolic meaning, and that that meaning is always contestable—is portrayed on the personal level in the practice of circumcision and on the political level in the destruction of Sodom. The story of the sacrifice of Isaac makes the same point yet again. The act of sacrifice is the conversion of the ordinary into the sacred. It is quite literally an act of embodiment of an idea: a rereading of the body. Rituals of sacrifice are the routinization of the miraculous.[8]

---

[8] I owe this point to Roger Scruton.

The sacrifice of Isaac makes clear the conditions under which the intergenerational project of family and nation becomes possible. Isaac is not the product of a natural union of Abraham and Sarah. He is instead the expression of the divine in human time. Faith in the divine is the source of nation, which is a political organization of human sexuality. Isaac exists at the intersection of all of these. His birth represents the end of natural time, in which man simply returns to dust, leaving no trace; it is the beginning of history. He literally embodies the continuation of the covenant between God and Abraham. That is the meaning he carries forth into the future, but it is only that meaning that makes Isaac—and so the nation of Israel—possible. His life is a miracle, and thus already a test of Abraham's faith. What is true of Isaac is true of every child: to be a child of a particular family or nation is to carry forward a meaning. The possibility of history must precede the child, if his production is to be seen as good—that is, the embodiment of an idea. An unwanted child—claimed by neither family nor community—challenges the very idea of humanity.

The production of the child, accordingly, is not a natural act, but an expression of power. The child is the product of labor and love under divine provenance; more exactly, the child is the product of love's labor, which is always divine. In the loved child, we experience the power to overcome our own finitude. This requires that succession be seen as the expression of an idea. We must, in the language of Genesis, be able to see that "it is good." We are, of course, free to deny this. Man is free to insist that God is dead and that, along with God, good and evil died. In that case, the body would no longer be the point of representation of the miraculous. In the terms of Genesis, that denial would be the end of history.

Genesis portrays human power as a twofold product of grace and faith. It is grace because there is no explanation of how Abraham is chosen. That choice is as miraculous as the saving of Isaac. The presence of meaning in a world of suffering is always without explanation. That we exist as subjects claimed by a world filled with meaning is without explanation. Abraham's faith is not an explanation of the miraculous. He may be tested, but the test does not explain how or why the divine enters history through Abraham. Yet his faith is equally a condition of the appearance of meaning. Faith is the opening of the subject to this experience of grace.[9] Without faith, grace could not be received. This is the meaning of the "test" that is the sacrifice of Isaac.

Abraham must accept God's word on faith; that is all he has. We cannot appeal from the meanings we experience to some "objective" test, some neutral position by which to evaluate the universe we occupy. Abraham must have faith beyond reason. He must have faith that he can sacrifice his only legitimate son and still found a nation.[10] That we die is a fact; that death can be an act of sacrifice and birth the expression of an idea are matters of faith.

In Genesis, then, we find a claim that the source of power is in the act of reading the body as a sign of the divine. There is no domain of the private family held out as separate from politics because the covenant is the source of all meaning. This does not make family—or polity—any less the domain of love. Rather, both are love's proper domain. There is never any question but that Abraham loves Isaac. Love is not something separate from power; it is the subject's experience of the creative act. Abraham's love finds its completion in the act of founding a great nation. Interestingly, these same ideas are found at the core of Plato's thought about the nature of eros.[11]

The Platonic account of origins is similar to the biblical account in the priority it gives to the political community over family. Plato places the origin of the political in the arts, that is, in the common space generated by and required for the variety of *techné*. Human community begins with the need to exchange the products of the arts; the family fits within the public space that the arts make possible. The difference between the biblical and Platonic accounts is located in the contrasting images of the entry of the divine into time—that is, of the creation of the possibility of history. This is a contrast between the idea of an art—a techné—and of the covenant. A techné is the knowledge of a set of ideas, as well as the skill to embody them within

[9] See chap. 4, above.

[10] This is Kierkegaard's "leap of faith." See S. Kierkegaard, *Fear and Trembling and the Sickness Unto Death* (W. Lowrie, trans., [1849] 1954).

[11] Plato's thought finds a distant mirror in Freud's account of the family in *Civilization and its Discontents*, in which family is both the "germ-cell of civilization" and a force powerfully "in opposition to civilization." S. Freud, *Civilization and its Discontents* (1930), reprinted in 21 *The Standard Edition of the Complete Psychological Works of Sigmond Freud* 57 (J. Strachey, ed. and trans., 1961).

a changing world. Man as possessor of techné is a laborer. Both techné and covenant point to a source of meaning that can organize experience. Both suggest the man mediates between a timeless ideal—or divine—world and the endlessly changing world of time and space.[12] For Plato, the divine is inextricably linked to reason, the ultimate object of which is the domain of Ideas. In the Judeo-Christian tradition, faith not reason is the point of access to the divine.

Plato emphasizes the social dimension of the techné when he argues that the origin of the city is located in the coming-together of a number of artisans. From the perspective of the city of artisans, the question of sexuality emerges just where one would expect: the city must tend to its own reproduction. Accordingly, Plato introduces the family only after the contours of a class-based political order, devoted to the project of maintaining the self-sufficiency of the polis, have become clear. Sexuality must be managed to achieve the historical continuity of the city. The natural act of generation must come to bear the idea of the city: it must be shaped by the techné of the political artisan.[13] The city's guardians will decide who marries and what becomes of children.

The techné of politics works in the medium of beliefs. The rulers must instill those beliefs that will support the political order. Individuals must understand their own sexuality as the embodiment of the idea of the good maintained by the political community. Plato makes this clear by organizing human sexuality on a false idea: what he calls a "noble lie"—the myth of earth-born men.[14] It is noble because it is

---

[12] Just as the biblical account is both a representation and an instance of the covenant, Plato offers not just an account of political acts, but an instance. For Plato's project in the *Republic* is itself a form of techné: Socrates and his interlocutors are making a city. They are engaged in a project of mediation between the idea of a city and the construction of a city, that is, human space organized under an idea of justice. If the techné is a paradigm of power, then there is no human activity that cannot be understood within the paradigm. Every action can be seen as an effort to bring unity to changing experience.

[13] Rawls takes a parallel approach to the family when he writes that "in a democratic regime the government's legitimate interest is that public law and policy should support and regulate . . . the institutions needed to reproduce political society over time. These include the family (in a form that is just)." J. Rawls, "The Idea of Public Reason Revisited," in *The Law of Peoples* 147 (1999).

[14] Plato, *Republic*, 3. 415a–d.

necessary to the establishment and maintenance of a human community; it is a lie because there is no "natural" origin of this community.

According to the myth, the original members of the city were born of the earth and were each of a distinct quality: gold, silver, or iron and brass. These metals in the soul determine the citizen's place within the political class structure. The moral of the Platonic myth is that "the first and chief injunction that the god lays upon the rulers" is to assign each new child to that political position that corresponds to the metal of his soul—regardless of the political position of the parents. The metals in the soul are a marking of the body as a part of the nation in just the same way as circumcision is in the biblical account. The myth simultaneously establishes identity (all are brothers, born of the same mother) and difference (the different metals in the soul). This is the mythical foundation for a political order founded on merit.

The myth ironically substitutes nature for politics. Instead of representing itself as an advance beyond a state of nature, politics seeks its security in a myth of its own naturalness. Thus, family may appear to be natural, but that naturalness is itself a product of political power. Nature is a construction of politics, not a prepolitical fact. There is no escape from the political to the natural family. Family is, from the beginning, the means by which the power of the political embodies itself in time. This is no less true of the biblical account: Abraham and Sarah are, by nature, childless.

Plato's myth of the earth-born men tells us that the political order is never indifferent to the familial order. The city's dependence on generation for its own endurance means that human sexuality must be given a political shape. Sexuality makes possible the political order by creating a space for history, but politics makes sexuality possible by creating a meaning to fill that space. This reciprocal relationship of dependence between politics and family is reflected in the confused temporality of the myth. From the perspective of the dialogue, the myth is a product of the political art. From the perspective of the city, politics follows the myth.

Plato's noble lie is by no means the end of his reflections on the relationship between politics and the family in the *Republic*. The myth introduces the idea that sexuality is a malleable object for political construction. Accordingly, as the meaning of the political order shifts, so must the shape of sexuality. This takes Plato into the great paradoxes at the center of the *Republic*. These are paradoxes in the literal sense of proposals that go against common opinion. Most paradoxical is his proposed deconstruction of the ordinary understanding of the family and its reconstruction to match the shape of the re-formed political order. Ultimately, this leads to the complete displacement of the private family and gender roles. All children and women are common; all perform in a way that most contributes to the city's well-being. The state has become one family in which all relations are public relations. As numerous theorists of political ideals, from Leninists to Maoists to kibbutzniks have learned since then, the family may be less malleable in fact than in theory. Family may shape politics as much as politics shapes family. This is not because the family is natural in a way that politics is not. Rather, it is because the love within a family can as easily compete with, as support, the love of the polity. If the polity would take away all the children—as Plato proposes—it must first have parents willing to give them up.

That Plato is aware of these limits is clear from the further progression of the *Republic*. This ideally constructed political order begins to break down precisely with the resistance that originates in the family: family members will pursue meanings apart from those upon which the ideal city depends. Plato portrays this symbolically with an image of reproduction occurring outside of the cycles of cosmic harmony.[15] The point of this image is only that political power cannot wholly penetrate familial love. Political order is not the only form of meaning within a community. Every site of meaning can become a site of contestation. Family is no different.

This idea is given substance in the cycles of political decline that Plato describes in the latter part of the *Republic*. In each case, political decline is linked to a failure of inculcation of political beliefs within the family. Family becomes an alternative locus of power that can then stand in opposition to the polis. Alternative sources of value emerge when the child asks why parental authority does not coincide with political authority. Individual identity is now caught in a contest be-

---

[15] Ibid. 8. 546a–47c.

tween family and city. Love within the family challenges belief in the noble lie. Abraham could have refused to sacrifice Isaac.

Political power inheres in the set of beliefs about self and other that inform the child as he comes of age. When relationships among family members are no longer isomorphic with political relationships, power within the family can become a basis for comparison with political power. This is a familiar phenomenon today in the politics of multiculturalism. The child who links identity with ethnicity will ask why political power does not reflect that set of meanings. A subordinated minority culture may compete with the state in the inculcation of beliefs. It will pursue a form of oppositional politics that begins in a challenge to the content of education but aims for a reconstruction of political power to match a different familial understanding.

Running through classical and biblical thought, therefore, is a close connection between the organization of familial life and the maintenance of political life. A failure in the sexual order will lead to political disaster. There is no break between the political and the familial. Both are manifestations of eros, of reading a meaning in the body itself. Expressed so directly, this theme suggests another classical text: Sophocles' *Antigone*. The whole of the Oedipus story is a striking illustration of the connection between familial order and political order. The horror of Oedipus's fate is his violation of the terms of the familial order. His mother becomes his wife, his children are his siblings and his father, the king, is his victim. This sexual confusion brings about the disastrous political consequences with which *Oedipus the King* begins. The city is suffering a terrible death:

> There are no growing children in this famous land;
> there are no women bearing the pangs of childbirth.
>
> . . . .
>
> In the unnumbered deaths of its people the city dies;[16]

This is the classical equivalent of the story of Sodom and Gomorrah in which sexual disorder brought about political ruin. For Sophocles, this sexual disorder has been localized in the family of the ruling household. The political consequences, however, are the same.

---

[16] Sophocles, *Oedipus the King* 171–79.

Antigone takes up directly the terms of this inquiry into the relationship between the body, the family, and the state. The play begins with the body of Polynices, Antigone's brother, lying before the walls of the city. The ruler, Creon, would disown and dishonor that body by reducing it to just that: a body making no claim upon the human community, but fit only to be food for animals. Because he attacked the city, Polynices is to be denied his personhood in death. Without a place in the political life of the city, he is cast into the natural world in which he is nothing but rotting flesh.

It is authority's privilege to define the relationship between state and an individual: "A king is fortunate in many ways, and most, that he can act and speak at will."[17] This is the message that Ismene gives her sister, Antigone, at the beginning of the play: "We'll perish terribly if we force law and try to cross the royal vote and power."[18] It reflects as well Creon's understanding of his own power: "The man the state has put in place must have obedient hearing to his least command when it is right, and even when it's not."[19] On such obedience depends the order of the city and the family: "[Disobedience] ruins cities, this tears down our homes, this breaks the battle-front in panic-rout."[20]

Yet human order does not exist within the single dimension of political authority. Politics does include a technical element of forming the order of the state, but ultimately it rests upon the citizens' self-understanding. Antigone tells Creon that she "cannot share in hatred, but in love."[21] From the perspective of authority, love is mad. The Chorus states that "who has [love] within him is mad." But from the perspective of those in love, love appears to have a "power as strong as the founded world."[22] This double-perspective—of love and of authority—is the source of the "quarrel of kindred."

Sophocles is misunderstood if this quarrel is seen simply as a conflict between family and polis. Love and authority each generate their own idea of justice and, thus, each can give an account of order. Each sub-

---

[17] Sophocles, *Antigone*, 506–7.
[18] Ibid. 62.
[19] Ibid. 676.
[20] Ibid. 672.
[21] Ibid. 525.
[22] Ibid. 790.

ject is struggling to give expression to a vision of justice, which simultaneously has a familial and political form. This is captured most directly in Haemon's exchange with his father, Creon, about the source of order within the authoritarian state:

> CREON: Is the town to tell me how I ought to rule?
> HAEMON: Now there you speak just like a boy yourself.
> CREON: Am I to rule by other mind than mine?
> HAEMON: No city is property of a single man.
> CREON: But custom gives possession to the ruler.
> HAEMON: You'd rule a desert beautifully alone.[23]

Authority reaches its limit in love. The love among the citizens limits the capacity of those with authority to reorder relationships already secure. What those limits are is indeterminate in the abstract. They become concrete at the moment of sacrifice, as Creon learns when Haemon, his son, sacrifices himself for his love of Antigone, who will also martyr herself for familial love. Ismene, on the other hand, subordinates love to authority. Plotting the possibilities of this conflict was part of Plato's task in the *Republic*. Moreover, the ruler's own love limits his power. Creon is destroyed not because he is disobeyed, but because obedience destroys the objects of his love.

Creon is not pure authority; rather, he too is stretched across this conflict of love and authority. At first, he has an Ismene-like respect for authority. Thus, on hearing of Antigone's refusal to comply with his authority, he states that "[s]he is my sister's child, but were she child / of closer kin than any at my hearth, / she and her sister should not so escape / their death and doom."[24] This must be so because only if he applies the same rules of order within his own household can he appear just within the state:

> If I allow disorder in my house
> I'd surely have to licence it abroad.
> A man who deals in fairness with his own
> He can make manifest justice in the state.[25]

[23] Ibid. 734–39.
[24] Ibid. 485–89.
[25] Ibid. 659–63.

In the end, however, he is overcome by an Antigone-like love for family. Creon understands the consequences of his vision of political justice within the family, when he hears the prophecies that he will give "corpse for these corpses." He says that "[t]o yield is dreadful. But to stand against him. Dreadful to strike my spirit to destruction."[26] And, of course, the dreadfulness comes. The exercise of authority brings about the undoing of his own world of love: "Son, you have died too soon." And, then his second death, learning of his wife's suicide: "Servants, take me away, out of the sight of men. I who am nothing more than nothing now."[27] Creon has become a mere body, outside of the state. A nothing who lives more appropriately within the animal world than in the city. By the end of the play, he has personally performed the libations of the dead for Polynices and has himself become "a breathing corpse."[28]

Sophocles ends *Antigone* with a plea for wisdom: "Our happiness depends on wisdom all the way." The wisdom that *Antigone* teaches is the lesson that Creon learns: authority must respect love. The family is not some private domain of necessity that the citizen transcends in his or her public life. Rather, the play reveals the dependence of politics on family. A politics without love would be the rule of a lone man on a desert island. Creon never lacks authority, but he nevertheless suffers disaster. The wisdom of political rule is to respect in the self, family, and citizens the order of love.

Of course, we know from *Oedipus the King* that the order of love, which authority must respect, is not simply the play of desire. Oedipus falls, not because he lacks love in the ordinary sense, but because he has confused the appropriate objects of love. Love does not take its meaning only from subjective experience, but from the character of its object. Similarly, Creon confuses the appropriate objects of political authority: sending the living (Antigone) to a tomb and holding the dead (Polynices) within the domain of the living. The point is not that objective authority must respect subjective interests, but that there is an appropriate order that must be respected in both family and state.

---

[26] Ibid. 1095–96.
[27] Ibid. 1320–21.
[28] Ibid. 1067.

Creon and Oedipus for different reasons fail to realize that order, and they suffer the consequence of rejection from the ordinary human community of family and polity.

There is no political world that transcends the family. Children pull polity and family together and make them one. Thus, the Oedipus trilogy opens with the dying of the city because of the barrenness of the women and it closes with the political death of Creon because of the death of his child. Similarly, there is no public world of authority that men can occupy apart from women. Creon accuses his son, when he seems to side with Antigone, of being a "woman's slave" and he says of himself that "I won't be called weaker than womankind."[29] But this is where Creon begins, not where he ends. He is destroyed, made "nothing more than nothing" precisely by the self-sufficiency of women. Antigone and Eurydice act without political power; they take their own lives and thus destroy him, even without touching his authority.

The royal house of Thebes is a symbol of the interpenetration of familial and political life that is true of each household. The state depends upon the well-ordered sexuality of the household; it inheres in the intergenerational movement of the family. But the family equally depends upon the state. Violating the order of the family disorders the state, but the disorder of the state similarly undermines familial order.

LOVE AND POWER: A MODERN MISREADING

All of these stories are about reading the body: Polynices outside of the walls, the body marked by circumcision, or defined by the quality of the metal of its soul. All emphasize that the act of reading never occurs in a state of nature or from an absolute beginning. We don't first recognize the body as our own and then decide whether to place it into relationships with others. Rather, we find ourselves already claimed by family, and we find the family already within a political order. Family and polity draw upon each other to express the meaning of the self. Yet, it is in the nature of power that each can also provide a resource for opposing the other. All of these accounts show that

[29] Ibid. 680.

opposition as a contest over the meaning of the public order, not as an assertion of the private against the public.

This reading of the classical texts stands in sharp opposition to that put forth by Hannah Arendt in *The Human Condition*. Arendt's is one of the more prominent modern accounts of the relationship between sexuality and the state in classical thought. Because her ambition is to undermine a conception of liberal politics that understands political action as nothing more than the expression of private interests—an interest-group conception of political pluralism—she turns to classical thought to draw a sharp distinction between the private and the public.

For Arendt, the distinction between the private and public is at the core of classical theory. The private is the domain of the household, while the public is the domain of political action. While the former makes the latter possible—that is, the possibility of political action depends upon the satisfaction of need in the household—they represent different orders of meaning. The citizen must be released from the household before he can pursue the words and deeds appropriate for the public space of politics. Conversely, anyone bound to labor within the household—women and slaves—cannot possibly participate in the life of the city.

Arendt believes that "[a]ccording to Greek thought, the human capacity for political organization is not only different from but stands in direct opposition to that natural association whose center is the home and the family."[30] Within the household, individuals hardly rise above their biological foundation: "The distinctive trait of the household sphere was that in it men lived together because they were driven by their wants and needs. The driving force was life itself."[31] The organization of the household is a function of nature, a nature man shares with all other animals. Only in the political domain could man rise above mere life into a uniquely human domain of freedom: "What all Greek philosophers . . . took for granted is that freedom is exclusively located in the political realm, that necessity is primarily a prepolitical phenomenon, characteristic of the private household organization."[32]

[30] H. Arendt, *The Human Condition* 24 (1958).
[31] Ibid. 30.
[32] Ibid. 31.

This domain of freedom was constituted by free citizens—"to move in a sphere where neither rule nor being ruled existed"—whose words and deeds make up a common world. The public domain is a world of appearances, not in the Platonic sense of a world dependent upon, and so less valuable than, the world of Ideas, but in the active sense in which the reciprocity of acting and being seen to act holds together a common world.

The common space constituted by actions and words "transcends our lifespan into past and future alike. . . . It is what we have in common not only with those who live with us, but also with those who were here before and with those who will come after us."[33] The creation and maintenance of this common space is a function of power: "Power is what keeps the public realm, the potential space of appearance between acting and speaking men, in existence."[34] In understanding power as the capacity to embody an idea, Arendt follows the Platonic understanding of eros. But she parts company with Plato, and I with her, in the opposition she draws between the power of the public and the powerlessness of the private.[35]

For Arendt, sexuality and the domain of the family tie man to mere life, to the conditions of animal existence. Public action must be defined against this lesser form of behavior:

> The only activity which corresponds strictly to the experience of world-lessness, or rather to the loss of world that occurs in pain, is laboring, where the human body, its activity notwithstanding, is also thrown back upon itself, concentrates upon nothing but its own being alive, and remains imprisoned in its metabolism with nature without ever transcending or freeing itself from the recurring cycle of its own functioning. We mentioned before the twofold pain connected with the life process for which language has but one word and which according to the Bible was imposed upon the life of man together, the painful effort involved in the reproduction of one's own life and the life of the species.[36]

[33] Ibid. 55.
[34] Ibid. 200.
[35] For support, she turns from Plato to Aristotle, who does share her view of the break between the private and the public. See Aristotle, *Politics*, I. 2.
[36] Arendt, *Human Condition* 115.

Arendt connects pain to labor, and both to slavery, because they are below the horizon of the public world of acting and speaking. They focus the subject on the limits of his or her own body: "Nothing . . . ejects one more radically from the world than exclusive concentration upon the body's life, a concentration forced upon man in slavery or in the extremity of unbearable pain."[37]

This whole discussion, however, is profoundly wrong. Man is not first an animal, laboring for self and species in a meaningless world of pain. This is hardly the meaning of the biblical story in which labor is the result of knowledge of good and evil, not a condition that precedes that knowledge. Similarly in Plato's account, the labor of reproduction follows the founding of the city and is a part of the public enterprise of sustaining the good. Men and women, in all that they do, differ from the animal world. The divine character of human life, what Plato calls "eros" and what the Bible locates in eating of the forbidden fruit, penetrates all of the way down into those very activities that maintain the body and the species. Nature, *Antigone* and *The Republic* tell us, is a postpolitical phenomenon. Surely this is the lesson of twentieth-century genocide, from which we learn that it takes a tremendous political effort to slaughter people as if they were nothing but animals. This is hardly a return to a prepolitical nature. To see the other as less than human is the end point of a totalizing politics.

Arendt seems strangely indifferent, if not hostile, to the family. She reduces this domain of love to the pain of species-generation. But no one conceives of one's own children as a contribution to the maintenance of the species. My children are mine because they embody an idea of the self: not a narrow idea of the self as a natural body, but an idea as rich as the subject I take myself to be. They, just as much as the political world of actions and words, connect me to a world that was and a world that will be. Indeed, they connect me to that same political world.

Similarly, the pain of childbirth is hardly the breaking out of a natural violence in the human world. Arendt can see courage on the battlefield as the subjective side of a process by which an idea is made real in the world, but she cannot see childbirth as just the same process.

[37] Ibid. 112.

"Labor" is a term common to the activities both of creating and of maintaining a meaningful world. The common use of the term points only incidentally to the pain of the body that characterizes each. Pain is not the opposite of meaning, but the condition of its production for the finite creatures that we are. The unity of labor is the common effort at creating a world of meaning. Arendt sees this with respect to the work of the crafts, but not the work of the family. Yet our entire world is one we have built and must maintain. This is true of craft and politics; it is no less true of family.

Arendt's blindness to the meaning of family is marked by her failure to treat love in a book on "the human condition." Of love, Arendt writes only that "love, in distinction from friendship, is killed, or rather extinguished, the moment it is displayed in public."[38] But familial love is constantly displayed in public. This is not a hidden or private love. No one hides from the larger public the love of one's family members. It is not a violation of an appropriately public life to appear with spouse, children, and parents. Indeed, we distrust the public actor who does not show this familial love. Kept hidden, love is more likely to fail than to thrive. Indeed, Arendt confuses the pornographic/romantic with love. She would put friendship in the place of love because her idea of friendship is built on the public political virtues of speaking and acting.[39]

We proclaim familial love loudly as an essential part of our selves. It is not hidden from our public actions and words. The end of our political action is the well-being of our children, just as the well-being of our children is the only source of the polity's future. As I argued in chapter 3, family and polity will always circle around each other as reciprocal ends and means. Of course, conflicts can arise between familial and political duties. Yet the possibility of conflict hardly suggests a need for wholesale "transcendence" of the familial.[40] Conflicts arise as well within the family and within the polity, quite independently of conflicts between them. What is most striking is not the occasional conflict, but the deep compatibility between the domains of

[38] Ibid. 51.
[39] See H. Arendt, *Men in Dark Times* 24–26 (1968).
[40] See A. Bellow, *In Praise of Nepotism: A Natural History* (2003).

politics and family. This is not to deny that forms of family have been strained as conditions of production shift and as our expectations about the form and character of political participation shift. Family, like very other institution in the modern state, is an object of continual reform, that is, it too is subject to the critique of reason. Yet, the deeper point remains: the family produces citizens in both the material and the cultural dimensions. The modern nation-state has demanded of families that they give up their children for the sake of the state.[41] For the most part, families have done so.

PORNOGRAPHY AND ROMANCE

Approached from the perspective of meaning, the conflict over the body is not that seen by Arendt and modern liberalism—the public versus the private. Rather, it is a conflict between love, on the one hand, and the pornographic, on the other. Pornography is simultaneously the object of condemnation by the state and a flourishing practice within the state. Pornography may be legally tolerated, but it is generally condemned. Even liberals who defend the pornographic as a matter of law do not defend it as a matter of morality, politics, or ethics. Their defense focuses on the dangers of government suppression of any speech, rather than on the message of the pornographic.

When we find a flourishing practice, however, it is a mistake to characterize it first of all as the result of a failure of a policy of suppression—as if the pornographic is always slipping just beyond our capacities for political control, moral education, and social reform. We need to recognize that the main consumers of the pornographic are not the fringe elements of the social order. The social phenomena that reveal the shape of the pornographic imagination are not the practices of the sociopath, but the widely available pornographic materials of ordinary life—those available at the video store, the drugstore, or, increasingly, on television. The consumers of this material are the same people who otherwise maintain the ordinary forms of familial sexuality.[42] Of course, every social formation, including the pornographic, is avail-

---

[41] See chap. 6, below, on sacrifice and conscription.
[42] See F. Rich, "Naked Capitalists," *New York Times Magazine*, May 20, 2001.

able for use by the sociopathic, from child molesters to misogynists to murderers. But for the ordinary citizen, what is at stake in the pornographic is not the satisfaction of a criminal lust, but a claim of freedom. This understanding of freedom, not the speculative, criminal consequences of the pornographic, is the underlying source of the opposition between polity and the pornographic. Pornography challenges the state's claim to the body, which works first of all and most of the time through the family. In this challenge, the pornographic works in the same dimension as the romantic.

Pornography is always a form of display. It is not a style of life, but a kind of ritualized, performative sexuality. This is not just because it is a form of entertainment. Rather, the traditional pornographic plot is about the formation of consciousness. The plot revolves around an awakening sexual consciousness of the main character. That character's transformation echoes the transformation of the audience that is to move through the same awakening in the act of watching the sexual performance. Since all sexual activity already includes an element of voyeurism, the distinction between actor and audience is elided at multiple levels. In acting out an awakening self-consciousness, the performer simultaneously represents the audience-observer.

To grasp the formation of the pornographic imagination that is at stake in the performance, we must begin with what that performance leaves out. Pornography is a representation of self-possession through a kind of absence. The first great absence is children. I don't mean children as they appear in child pornography. I mean children as the ordinary consequence of human sexuality. The pornographic begins with a severing of sex from generation, of sexuality from reproduction. Second, the state is absent. The pornographic tale is a kind of morality play in which the state does not appear. If politics does appear, it is only to make the claim that the politician too is deeply attracted by the pornographic, even if he or she attacks it publicly. Third, economic labor is absent. Without labor, there are no class distinctions. The pornographic subject is no more defined by labor or profession than by political affiliation. Pornography presents us the body detached from family, state, and market. If we ask, who owns the pornographic body? the answer is, the individual. The characteristic plot is one in which the subject makes a claim to possession of his or her body against the claims of the ordinary institutions of institutional-ized power: family, government, and markets. This act of taking pos-session is represented as a discovery of the self such that the truth of the subject is located in that experience of the body.

Pornography is a form of sexuality shorn of the ordinary, generative characteristics of the body. The pornographic act produces no off-spring: no children, no discourse, no enduring relationship to an other, no useful products. It is marked by the absence of labor in both of the biblical senses. It is episodic; it exists neither as a form of historical memory nor as a claim upon the future. Its only temporal condition is the present. Because the pornographic is sexuality without children, it is sex freed of the state's demand upon the body. Sex without chil-dren is sex taken out of both the political construction of time and the familial economics of providing for a secure future. The pornographic event happens instantaneously. There is no symbolic continuation of the pornographic moment in a representation of an other—the child. The event is not a symbolic reference point for a more complex, con-tinuing involvement of two individuals in a common life. This is a representation of a radical claim to freedom.

If history is understood as the organization of power in the familiar institutional forms of family, polity, and economy, then pornography is a response to the burdens of history. The pornographic represents a denial of the historical character of power. Ultimately, it denies the appearance of our own finitude. The pornographic does not recognize aging: No one is ever too old for the pornographic. To the degree that it recognizes death, it is as a limit phenomenon. In a kind of parody of power over death, it incorporates a death-like experience into the pornographic moment. Figuratively, this has long been captured in the identification of orgasm and death. This metaphor stands opposed to both that of sexual intercourse as a kind of knowledge and that of sexual activity as labor. Labor and knowledge, I argued above, are the constitutive elements of power and power is always generative of a community. Nor is erotic death the death of sacrifice. Indeed, it is just the opposite—a kind of antisacrifice in its denial of the symbolic character of the body. The body and its meaning coincide in the porno-graphic. There is no reading of the body as a symbol of an idea.

The pornographic is both the simplest and the most compelling form of fleeing from the burdens of history. Those burdens are experienced psychologically in the fear of death; socially in the commitment to family; economically in the labor of production; and politically in the state's call for sacrifice. Pornography excludes these burdens by denying any recognition of death, including the institutions of family, market, and state by which we ordinarily deploy power to counter death. Contrary to the claims of some of its opponents, pornography is not so much a form of power over others as a reaction to the ultimate lack of power that individuals experience.[43] For most people, men as well as women, power is experienced not as something they have, but as something they lack. They find themselves within immense, and seemingly unchangeable, structures of power—power that ranges across the political, the economic, the familial, and the religious. Empowerment is inseparable from the burden of labor.

The pornographic offers a deeply antistatist meaning, directly challenging the state's claim on the individual's body. The pornographic

---

[43] Compare C. MacKinnon, *Only Words* (1996). Catherine MacKinnon insists that we see pornography as men doing things to women. For her, in pornography words become action. To represent women is to make women in this image. Power represented is power deployed. The ideological message she reads in this performance is a masturbatory fantasy that merges directly into the political power of men over women.

MacKinnon is not wrong in pointing out that the sexual is a domain of power and should be analyzed from the perspective of power. But she has picked the wrong enemy in associating the pornographic with support of political power. Instead of collapsing sexuality and politics, we need to explore the ways in which sexuality is deployed against the political. The primary domain of power, and its asymmetries, is not the pornographic imagination but the family. In the family, we should expect to find all of the inequalities of power that the state maintains and supports. This was a simple truism until quite recently. The family was the microcosm of the state. It produced boy-children who saw their highest destiny as sacrifice for the state and girl-children who understood their bodies as the vehicle for reproduction of the state.

I have argued in this chapter that we may not be as far from that familial-political order as we think. The political and the familial are deeply intertwined. It truly does take a terroristic act of the imagination to see these connections and to proclaim a kind of freedom from both. MacKinnon is wrong in failing to see the pornographic as a potential contributor to this terrorism of the imagination. Even a brief look at the role of the pornographic in the French Revolution, for example, shows the deep connection between freedom of the imagination in matters sexual and freedom from the power of the state. See R. Darnton, *The Forbidden Best-Sellers of Pre-Revolutionary France* 85–

representation of the body sees it as the individual's unique possession. The alternative social order of the pornographic is an antipolitics founded, like ordinary politics, on the body. Unlike the political body, however, the pornographic body does not reach out symbolically toward the past or the future. It is not a link in a chain connecting past and future. The antipolitics of the pornographic disavows any need for, or interest in, history. It sees the future only as an endless opportunity for more of the same: a succession of pornographic moments. The sociality of the pornographic is a world in which individuals relate to each other as possessors of bodies that are in themselves mutual sources of fulfillment.

This is a taking back of the body from its normal condition in which it is a complex signifier of meanings outside of itself. We read ourselves as citizens, parents, children, or occupants of a division of labor in a complex economy. We explain who we are by pointing to these structures of meaning that appear in and through the body. From citizen-soldier to familial matron, the body gains its meaning from its function in an extended political and temporal order. The pornographic sets itself against all of the ordinary dimensions of power within which the body figures. It proclaims the body the center of its own meanings, quite independent of the political order of power. The pornographic takes up the imagery of new birth and new body. But the newness discovered is wholly within the boundaries of the physical body. Arendt could see in such a turn only a collapse into the domain of necessity, but this is a claim of freedom of the most extreme sort. Thus, it is not surprising that pornography is associated with political revolution.[44] Political liberalism is no less threatened by the pornographic than is any other political arrangement, for politics in whatever form is the target of the pornographic imagination.

The stripping away of the symbolic in the pornographic is seen in the irrelevance of language to the pornographic representation. One can imagine a pornographic film, for example, in which the protago-

---

114 (1996). It is no accident that MacKinnon finds herself in the strange company of the conservative Right in her attack on the pornographic imagination.

[44] See, e.g., L. Hunt, "Pornography and the French Revolution," in *The Invention of Pornography: Obscenity and the Origins of Modernity 1500–1800* (L. Hunt, ed., 1996).

nists do not speak each other's language, in which there is no communication, but only the act. It has no need of language because it is a claim that the body can constitute its own meanings. It has no need to represent something outside of itself. Of course, it must be imagined as such a denial and affirmation.[45] There is no thing-in-itself that is the pure nature of sex. The pornographic is a postlinguistic phenomenon, not a return to prelinguistic nature. The failure of the pornographic imagination may leave only a perception of a representation of violence. This is what the critics of the pornographic see.[46]

Because meaning collapses into act, we are fundamentally voyeurs with respect to the pornographic. We do not engage it dialogically, but watch in our own form of speechlessness. Were we actually to speak of the pornographic as a form of freedom, it would itself be transformed into yet another political movement subject to the same historical conditions as every other form of politics. We cannot use language to get beyond language. Some critics worry that the pornographic leads to action, including rape. Whether or not this is true as a sociological phenomenon, it fails to grasp the ontological structure of the pornographic, and its deep attraction to the ordinary citizen who is not the sociopath. The meaning of the pornographic lies in its denial of action: representation collapses into the represented, seeing into experience.

Pornography is a fantasy of freedom and as such should be contrasted not only with historicized readings of the body but also with that other powerful fantasy of freedom from the body that operates in the West: the ascetic tradition within Christianity. Our imaginations—fictional and acted out—record numerous instances in which these fantasies coincide.[47] We recognize, for example, the operation of the pornographic imagination in the self-flagellation of the Christian ascetic; in art we see this coincide in the work of Hieronymous Bosch,

---

[45] One suspects that, in part, the outbreak of sexual violence in situations of political disorder—e.g., Bosnia—reflects a revolutionary nihilism on the part of the perpetrator. Not sharing this view, the victim perceives only violence and abuse, i.e., the destruction of a world of politics and family.

[46] See, e.g., R. Morgan, *Going Too Far* 169 (1978) ("Pornography is the theory; rape is the practice."); A. Dworkin, *Pornography: Men Possessing Women* (1989).

[47] Most famously perhaps is the priest-pornographer in the work of de Sade.

among others. Just as Foucault showed us the connection between repression and sexual identity in the Victorian era, the point holds as well for the larger relationship between the Christian morality of sexual denial and pornography.[48] The Christian ascetics' withdrawal of the self from the full range of our ordinary commitments—familial, communal, and political—always threatens to leave him or her in thrall to the pornographic. The pornographic threat shows us that there is no great distance at all between a transcendent god and the death of god. Or, should we say that Dionysus is never all that far from the Christian God? The claim that the body is nothing at all easily becomes a claim that the body is all that there is. Against both stands the construction of love/power as that experience of meaning in and through the body.

The pornographic is the ecstatic moment shorn of religion. It stands in the antipolitical tradition of the hierophantic. The sacred too can displace ordinary forms of language. In both, we are rendered speechless, without even that most rudimentary form of speech—our own name. In another age and another culture, this would be the moment of spiritual rapture and complete identification with the oneness of the universe: Freud's cosmic feeling of unity.[49] We should not be surprised that as the possibilities of religious transcendence diminish, the pornographic moment becomes the locus of an antistatist vision of freedom. The personification of this conceptual development was the life and image cultivated by Michel Foucault. Central to that image was a critique of liberal institutions as themselves structures of power that effectively deny individual freedom, that is, that deny the very value of autonomy upon which liberalism is founded. But if we push beyond the negative, superliberal critique of liberalism and look for his positive account of freedom, we find a turn to the body seen through the prism of the pornographic imagination.[50]

We view the pornographic as a kind of entertainment, but it is a deadly serious entertainment. It is about the denial of death, the state,

---

[48] See M. Foucault, *The History of Sexuality: An Introduction*, 49 (R. Huxley, trans., 1978).

[49] See Freud, *Civilization and its Discontents* 11–13.

[50] See J. Miller, *The Passion of Michel Foucault* (1994).

the family, history, markets, and even language. At the center of the pornographic moment, there is a vision of a total lack of responsibility extending beyond that moment itself. Responsibility is an acknowledgment of the claims of the other. It appears to the pornographic imagination as a diminution of the self. Ethically, we understand this as a form of immorality, politically as a revolutionary threat. In popular political culture, this convergence was expressed in the melding of "free love" into the antistatist vision of the counterculture of the 1960s.

The pornographic is epiphanic in a deeper sense as well. We do not live in the pornographic any more than we live in the constant presence of the sacred. We are inevitably drawn back into the profane world of language, family, markets, and politics. The world in which we are located has a history as well as a commitment to a future with a certain meaning. We bear on and in our bodies the complex representational meanings of this world. Saint Paul spoke of the true circumcision as a mark on the heart.[51] We all bear that mark; it is that by which we read ourselves. Nevertheless, we cannot deny that, whenever love fails, the claims of responsibility are experienced as submission to power. Without love, a life fully constituted by responsibilities can take on a sort of desperation as one loses a center to and of the self.

The necessary conditions of the portrayal of an antistatist freedom help explain another common feature of the pornographic: at the center of the pornographic tale is often a woman as the main character. The pornographic may be fundamentally a male phenomenon, but the tale that men are telling in the pornographic is one of women's equality as well—not an equality within the ordinary institutions of power, but an equality in the capacity to transcend those forms of power. Men cannot experience a freedom in the denial of state and family, if it appears as literal irresponsibility. There will always be a battle of self-perception between freedom and irresponsibility. If the family is present as counterclaim, then there is an inevitable perception of moral failing. In this fantasy of freedom, women must appear as equals, engaged in the same self-discovery as men.[52] Of course, it may be a male

[51] Rom. 2: 29.

[52] As I write this, I find AOL leading with a heading "top 10 sexual fantasies" of men and women. Unremarkably, most of the fantasies appear on both lists. (July 26, 2000).

fantasy that women will find the same meaning in the antipolitics of the pornographic representation, but women and men are no less bound together in fantasy than in reality.

The pornographic message is freedom. Today, freedom without guilt can only appear within a context in which all are free. I have no reason to think that this message of freedom from the burdens of history is of any less interest to women than to men. It may, however, be the case that its representation takes different forms. One need only look at the romantic fantasies portrayed in the popular women's magazines and romance novels. We need to ask of those representations: Where are children, politics, and markets? Where are death and the phenomenon of aging? Romance shares in the structure of the pornographic just to the extent that it claims that a life can be complete— that is, full of meaning—in and through the singular experience of the physical presence of the other.

In the end, the pornographic tale usually succumbs to the temptation to tell a moral tale. The social order's real defense against pornography is found not in the political condemnation of pornography, but in the cooptation of the pornographic representation. The pornographic representation is embedded in a larger morality play in which family is affirmed, and, through family, the ordinary forms of the political and social order. The pornographic—like the romantic—becomes a moment of "self-discovery," which then makes possible the reaffirmation of the traditional values of family and polity.[53] Thus, the pornographic representation takes up the temptation to speak. When it speaks, it has nothing to say beyond the representation of just those institutional structures of power against which it has set itself. In the end, it affirms normality.

Consistent with our own voyeurism, the pornographic moment is embedded in a morality play of quite ordinary dimensions. The pornographic experience is represented as a detour, a deviation, that does not fit into our ordinary time, but ultimately serves to reconcile us to the life we live. We turn off the television, and return to our families, our jobs, and our communities. This is not a demand of the pornographic itself, but a demand of the ordinary moral and political life

---

[53] Most conventionally this is the Playboy ethic.

that is put upon the pornographic. It is the cooptation of the pornographic, just as the state coopted the church. Like religious ecstasy, the pornographic becomes a liminal experience.[54] Attempts to institutionalize the pornographic or the sacred always fall back into our ordinary structures of experience: institutional hierarchies, claims of responsibility, temporal accountability. This is as true of the church as of the commune. Sex becomes family, which becomes a structure of intergenerational responsibility inextricably connected to the establishment and maintenance of political forms. The pornographic becomes a memory of—perhaps a longing for—freedom associated with an always receding youth. This is no less true of the romantic.

The embedding of the pornographic moment of freedom in a larger, but traditional, morality tale shows us the power of state and family as organizations of our experience of self and other. We dream of a freedom in which we are complete in ourselves, but we recognize that it is a dream. The pornographic is a particularly powerful form of that dream. It represents our capacity for self-transcendence poured into a contest of meaning over the body itself. Power encompasses us without fully defining us; it allows us to dream of a true self beyond that which we find ourselves already to be.

Like liberalism, the pornographic imagines a prepolitical moment that would found a new social order. It presents its own myth of overcoming the chaotic conditions of meaninglessness brought about by the fall. Aristophanes' account of the circle men in Plato's *Symposium* is one of the most powerful representations of the pornographic myth.[55] He presents the story of the circle people, their challenge to the gods, and Zeus's punishment of their hubristic action.

In Aristophanes' myth, our physical nature today is a consequence of this fall from an earlier state of fullness. Originally, people were "nothing like we are now." Instead, they were circular. Each was composed of two equal halves, and each pairing was either of individuals of the same or of different sexes. Homosexuality is just as grounded in our original natures as heterosexuality. Out of "arrogance," these

[54] See V. Turner, *Drama, Fields and Metaphors: Symbolic Action in Human Society* 231–33 (1974).

[55] Plato, *Symposium*, 189c–193d.

circle people tried to "set upon the gods." In response, Zeus split them in half. Each of us today is only a half of a whole. Love, he says, is the desire to return to that original state of completeness through a recoupling with our genuine other half. Love accomplished is the completion of the circle, the return to our true nature, which is to be one with an other.

Part of the attraction of Aristophanes' account is the vivid symbolism he uses to describe the experience of the fall—the sense of man's current state as a consequence of moral failure, and the deep longing to recover a lost wholeness. He ascribes the original moral failure to the circle people's "lofty notions." Their hubris was located in their philosophical inclinations: they thought too much. They believed themselves to be complete in themselves and without any need of the gods. He offers a comic rendition of the two main accusations against philosophy—accusations that have remained remarkably stable for two thousand years. First, philosophy places reason above faith; second, it ignores the way in which man is tied to the body. Man does indeed want to overcome the suffering of the body, the sense of incompleteness that goes with bodily existence, but according to Aristophanes the only way to overcome that suffering is through love, not reason. At stake is the possibility of realizing the truth about the self: that truth is inseparable from an identity bound to a particular body.

The heart of Aristophanes' account is his description of love as the resource by which we overcome our experience of the body as need. In his myth, the object of love extends no further than the experience of the beloved. In and through each other, lovers find the completion that was their former selves. The melding of their bodies into one, to which sexual union is incidental, is the response to the ontological condition of human need. Love is not about children or the satisfaction of physical desire; rather, it is about an experience of meaning in and through a union with a particular other who is our mythical other half.

Aristophanes' recovered lovers are speechless. Those who find their proper halves "are wondrously thrilled with affection and intimacy and love . . . though they could not even say what they would have of one another." Language itself is a twofold threat to love. First, as the potential for philosophy, it represents a hubristic claim to a divine—not human—completeness. Second, as the means of political governance, it makes possible life in the city regardless of love. Language either claims too much or makes do with too little. In neither case is it commensurate with the experience of fullness of meaning among true lovers.

Just as Aristophanes' understanding of love is of an experience outside of language, it is also of an experience outside of time. Time, in his myth, represents need, not resource.[56] If history is the source and outcome of politics, love, one might say, stops time. The atemporality of Aristophanes' love is represented symbolically in Hephaestus's offer to weld the lovers together so that "you can live your two lives in one, and, when the time comes, you can die a common death." Of this offer, Aristophanes says "no lover on earth would dream of refusing [it], for not one of them could imagine a happier fate."[57] Time stops for the lover in the presence of the other. In the completion that the other offers, there is no longer any need and so no longer any experience of human time.

The symbolism of Hephaestus's offer has its counterpart in the irrelevance of children in Artistophanes' account. Lovers find their completion in each other, not in what they produce. They are whole and complete in their mutuality. Children are represented as a merely incidental by-product of this search for completeness. They are not essential to the operation of love: "[I]n all these clippings and claspings [if] a man should chance upon a woman, conception would take place and the race would be continued." Similarly, work within the ordinary operations of the city is outside of the domain of love: "[I]f man should conjugate with man, he might at least obtain such satisfaction as would allow him to turn his attention and his energies to the everyday affairs of life."[58] City and family are both matters of indifference to lover and beloved.

At issue is the reading of the body, which Aristophanes tells us presents itself as a gaping wound. We find ourselves as if we are injured. Our deepest desire is to make ourselves whole. Wounded, Aristophanes' circle people still have in each other all of the resources needed to makes themselves whole. This is a story of the lovers' completeness in and through each other.

[56] In Socrates' speech in the *Symposium*, Love (eros) is represented as the child of Resource and Need (203b–c).

[57] Ibid. 192e.

[58] Ibid. 191c.

The myth portrays love as continuing the deeply hubristic attitude of the circle people, but now under the conditions of the fall. Individuals continue to believe that together they have the resources to be complete, to lack nothing. To experience the beloved is to experience this sense of completion; it is to lack nothing and thus to be ready to die. Aristophanes already grasps one of the deepest themes of Western culture: the link between love and death. This is death as redemption: in the presence of the beloved man is without need. Need pushes us endlessly into the future.[59] Aristophanes shows us this connection as comic; romance shows us the same connection as tragedy.

Love relieves man of the burden of labor in the dual senses identified in Genesis. For Aristophanes, love represents an end to labor, a return to that moment before man had to work to fill the needs that drive us endlessly into the future. To achieve love is to be as the gods. "[W]hen we are longing for and following after that primeval wholeness, we say we are in love. For there was a time . . . when we were one, but now, for our sins, God has scattered us abroad."[60] Of course, that which the gods can be endlessly, man in his current state can achieve only episodically. In love, we may feel we have escaped the burdens of labor in time, yet time continues to claim us. We may be done with time, but it is not done with us. We are not welded into one; we fall apart, as the center cannot hold.

There is something deeply attractive about the myth of the circle people. Aristophanes, as a writer of comedies, offers an account of love that has more to do with the pornographic than with the familial. It suggests the link between the pornographic and the romantic by showing us how both stand apart from politics and family. Aristophanes' lovers are simultaneously a romantic and a pornographic representation. Romance too is speechless, childless, and antipolitical in its claim of completeness. It too finds all of the resources it needs within the body of the beloved.

The most romantic play of our tradition is *Romeo and Juliet*. It shares many of the qualities of Aristophanes' myth. The attraction of the lovers for each other is without explanation or reason. It comes

[59] The other great myth of endless need in the West is, of course, that of original sin. There too redemption is linked to love.

[60] Plato, *Symposium* 193a.

over them as if it were a realization of meaning inherited from a primordial past; a response to an ontological need, but without justification in their ordinary experience. There is just the linkage of family and polity: the latter domesticates sexuality through the form of the family and thus assures its own continuation. Romance cannot justify itself against the demands of family and state; it exists in another dimension. Yet, not to acknowledge the demand of the beloved would be to live a life, no matter how successful in ordinary terms, of endless need and of profound meaninglessness. What do the lovers want? To be bound to each other forever. And to be bound to each other forever is just what they achieve. There is no turn toward generation of either a new familial order or a new political order. The real appearance of this romantic fantasy is death. Not the death as life that Hephaestus offers Aristophanes' lovers, but the real death delivered by those instruments of power that control our ordinary experience: family and polity. Our lives are securely within family and polity, which offers only tragedy to the lovers.

Pornography and romance pose equal challenges to familial love within the polity. In Genesis, we can find a similar point if we pair the image of Sodom with the life of Abram and Sarai before the covenant. Sodom is an image of the pornographic; Abram and Sarai are an image of the romantic. They too are without offspring; they too are failing to produce a future. These are linked images of the political and the familial outside the covenant. Indeed, we can see the same set of strategies of cooptation today in dealing with the pornographic/romantic: both must be led to an affirmation of the ordinary, familial order of the state. The romantic is represented as incomplete until and unless it enters into the familial; the pornographic is represented as a wild danger to be met by official suppression. The pornographic tends toward the comic and the romantic toward the tragic interpretation of a similar phenomenon of meaning. But these attitudes can be reversed. The God who destroys Sodom has no sense of humor. The romantic image of Abram and Sarai, on the other hand, is represented as comic rather than tragic: both laugh at the prospect of children.[61]

---

[61] *Gen.* 18:12. ("So Sarah laughed to herself as she thought 'After I am worn out and my master is old, will I now have this pleasure?' "). See also ibid. 17:17 (Abraham "laughed and said to himself 'will a son be born to a man a hundred years old? Will Sarah bear a child at the age of ninety?' ").

The blurring of the line between romance and the pornographic that characterizes Aristophanes' myth remains true of both genres today. No great insight is required to see the movement toward the pornographic in the representations of romance, or the move toward romance in the genre of the pornographic. This is the great secret inside the romantic: romantic lovers are coconspirators in the pornographic moment. The internalization of the pornographic moment is central to the contemporary imagination of the romantic. This is not sexuality domesticated into family and children, but the claim of completion outside of time and language. This is just the claim of the pornographic. For however briefly lovers meet, the romantic/pornographic engagement is a state to itself.[62] It needs no direction from others; it sets itself in opposition to all others. This claim of completeness is just what the Christian tradition labels as sin and the Greeks saw as hubris.

The pornographic and the romantic differ in that the romantic claims—as in Aristophanes' myth—that there is a unique beloved, while the pornographic seems unconcerned with the particular subjectivity of the other. Yet if the romantic other appears without explanation, without cause in our ordinary experience, then there is no great distance between the pornographic and the romantic. Each makes a claim to meaning through the "stranger" who appears as if from nowhere. Whether that stranger is one or many is a matter of aesthetic choice within the genre.

Both the pornographic and the romantic make claims to "love," but both stand opposed to that generative love that characterizes us as members of families and communities. Both can lead to such loving relationships, but neither does so necessarily.[63] Moreover, love can be equally hard on the romantic and the pornographic. It is not true that a marriage, for example, that lacks romance lacks love, any more than the pornographic presentation of the body is a necessary aspect of a loving familial relationship.

---

[62] For characteristic fictional representations of this theme, see K. Vonnegut, *Mother Night* (1966) (speaking of lovers as a "nation of two"); P. Roth, *The Human Stain* (2000); R. Hellenga, *The Fall of a Sparrow* (1998).

[63] The romantic is more traditionally enclosed within an account of cooptation: romance "leads" to family. But nothing is more romantic than the failure of love to become generative of family and the ordinary forms of relationships. Romance is true

Two points of contrast with Aristophanes' mythic representation of the pornographic/romantic are immediately evident when the *Symposium* goes on to present the Socratic account of love. First, the focus of the erotic in the Socratic account shifts from the immediate relationship between the lovers to their mutual relationship to procreation. Erotic longing, according to Socrates, is not for the other, but for creation in time. Procreation "is the one deathless and eternal element in our mortality."[64] Aristophanes denied this.

Second, for Aristophanes love is outside of politics; it is outside of the entire domain of human construction and thus outside of the ordinary relationships of power. Apart from myth, there is no explaining the attractions of love. Accordingly, love cannot be given an ordered form by the institutions of power. Again, the Socratic account is to the contrary. Love is now at the center of political order. Not only is political order a consequence and manifestation of love, but man's erotic nature is shaped by education. It is no longer beyond speech, but the subject of the most serious discourse. Politics is a practice of love. The politics of love, however, is neither romantic nor pornographic; it is generative.

In both of these respects, our contemporary understanding of love is closer to that of Socrates than that of Aristophanes. We think of love as generative; we know that there is a deep connection between the multiple forms of generative love—from family to community to nation. As I described in the first part of this chapter, this was a simple truism until quite recently. The family was understood as a microcosm of the state. It produced boy-children as citizen-soldiers—children who could see their highest destiny in sacrifice for the state. It produced girl-children who understood their bodies as the vehicle for reproduction of the state.[65] Familial and political identity remain essential aspects of

---

to itself in tragedy. Compare the tragedy of Shakespeare's *Romeo and Juliet* with the comedy of his *A Midsummer's Night Dream*.

[64] Plato, *Symposium* 206e.

[65] The same sentiment is expressed today in the context of the Palestinian-Israeli dispute. The third female Palestinian suicide bomber, Ms. Abu Eisheh, left the following message: "Let Sharon the coward know that every Palestinian woman will give birth to an army of suicide attackers, even if he tries to kill them while still in their mother's wombs, shooting them at the checkpoints of death" (*New York Times*, Mar. 1, 2002).

our understanding of the self. We speak of the "founding fathers" and of "love of nation." Similarly, the education of love remains high on our agenda. We are never done with our attack on the pornographic, for example. At stake symbolically is the continuation of the community—even the liberal community.

Yet, Aristophanes' reading of the body is not defeated; it does not disappear. Against the family and the state stands the pornographic/romantic. We experience the body's sexuality as a field of conflicting interpretations. We are of two minds on the question of who we are. We are parents and citizens, but we are also romantic voyeurs. This conflict is at times tragic, but just as often it is comic. Part of the attraction of liberalism no doubt arises from the fact that it leaves room for the pornographic/romantic. It does so by consigning love to the private, while insisting that the public order is to be the product of reason. Love, however, is not a private phenomenon. It is the foundation of a public world of meaning.

LOVE AND POWER RECONSIDERED

The classical accounts of family and polity resist two moves essential to liberalism. First, they do not begin with the individual as the elementary unit of explanation. Second, they resist the division between the public and the private. For the liberal, the problem is to generate the public out of a private world of individuals. The private, on the other hand, needs no explanation. The consequence of these dual assumptions of liberalism—that of metaphysical individualism and the primacy of the private—is a failure to understand the character of love. Thus, altruism is always a puzzle for liberalism. It is explained away as either a personal desire of some individuals or a rational act despite contrary appearances. It cannot be what it seems: a sacrifice for love.

The perennial problems of liberalism arise at just those points where its dual assumptions literally make no sense. Liberalism has never produced an adequate explanation of the family, for example, because we cannot understand children within either of these framing assumptions. It cannot settle whether the state should protect the child from the coercive influences of his or her own family, or whether the private family should be protected from the state. As a political position, the liberal state will often protect the family over the child. But it can do so only with a guilty conscience: from the perspective of liberal values, this looks as if the child is treated as property of the parents.[66]

What holds of liberalism and the family holds of liberalism and the multiple phenomena of eros. Of the generative qualities of love, liberalism has no better account than that of Aristophanes' comic image, in which children are simply the accidental production of the couplings of individuals. Aristophanes, however, offered the image as a way of conveying the antipolitical character of the pornographic/romantic. Liberalism can no more understand the pornographic rebellion against politics than it can understand the erotic foundation of the state. Indeed, one cannot understand the pornographic without first understanding the character of eros, against which it reacts. Every individual effort turned toward a public project—whether politics or philosophy—is a puzzle for liberalism.[67] The puzzle is demystified in contemporary thought by the turn to game theory, out of which has emerged a renewed interest in Hobbes.[68] When such public-spirited ideas resist rationalization, the mystery is allocated to the impenetrable character of different individuals' conception of the good. That love is not desire, that eros spans family and polity, that it can ground an ethos of sacrifice, that the pornographic and the romantic share an ontology—all of this can make no appearance within the conceptual framework of liberalism.

In the classical accounts, love is always experienced as empowering, even when its consequence is suffering.[69] This experience is as immediate as the perception of ourselves as individuals limited in space and time to the dimensions of our own physical existence. We find

[66] See, e.g., *Wisconsin v. Yoder*, 406 U.S. 205, 244–45 (Douglas, J., dissenting in part).

[67] This puzzle pushes Ackerman to a postliberal dualism. See B. Ackerman, *We the People: Foundations* 295–322 (1991).

[68] See, e.g., D. Gauthier, *The Logic of Leviathan* (1969); J. Hampton, *Hobbes and the Social Contract Tradition* (1986); G. Kavka, *Hobbesian Moral and Political Theory* (1986).

[69] This is closer in some sense to contemporary sociobiology, which is likely to see the individual as only a moment in a constant intergenerational process. Unity over time is what needs explanation, not an individual act. Sociobiologists, however, are not interested in the phenomenology of this experience of process.

ourselves, from the very beginning of consciousness, producing meanings that we share with others. Those with whom we share this experience of producing and maintaining a meaningful world are those we love. Thus, family and polity are the objects of our love because they are simultaneously the sources and the products of our power.

In love, we may be enthralled by an other, but the experience is never passive. Enthralled, we experience the creation of a new world. There are meanings present, both for the self and the other, that were not there before. This is the "labor" of love: the production of meaning in all its diverse forms. Love seeks to create an image of itself; it seeks to instantiate in the material world its own meaning. Loving, we see a world made new.

This experience of creating a universe of common meaning is characteristic of all of the domains of love. The wisdom of Diotima in Plato's *Symposium* is the knowledge that love is the source of procreation. Procreation is not just the production of children, but the production of meaning in any form. Every person maintains a universe of meaning. This is the central truth of the Talmudic saying that "if anyone destroys a single soul from the children of Man, Scripture charges him as though he had destroyed a whole universe."[70] Love is the internal experience of this character of ourselves as meaning-giving subjects. It is not just to experience the meanings, which we cannot help but do, but to experience the self as the power that is the source of those meanings. In love, we experience the most intense sense of ourselves as powerful—if necessary, a source of meaning against an entire world. For that reason, we feel most alive in and through love.

Love links us with others because it shows us a world that is "ours." That world claims us not because it somehow appears as independently worthy of our love. It claims us because we create and sustain it. Thus, there is no explanation of the object of our love that is independent of the act of love itself. To attempt such an explanation is to substitute contract for love. As the source of a meaningful universe, every subject overflows the boundaries of the self. We are already connected to the world that we see as the object and product of our love. It is our fecund self.

[70] Sanhedrin 4:5.

In the Judeo-Christian tradition, we carry forward the basic insight that our fundamental relationship to the world is one of love. Christians say that "God is Love," that God created the universe out of love. The source of God's Creation is love, and our relationship to the possibility of meaning within this created world is in and through love. The Christian community is a reciprocal relationship among subjects who love and are loved. The subject maintains the meaning of God's Creation by taking up a Christ-like love toward others. The appearance of meaning in the world—love's product—is always a manifestation of the divine. Liberalism turns away from this entire tradition of thought, in part because of its association with religion, and in part because this tradition resists the analytic form of reason. For liberalism, religion is individualized and privatized, and thus it cannot be used in the explanation or justification of a public space. If it does invade the public, it threatens irrationality. But religion is no less an effort to understand the character of our experience, and even a secular philosophy must not ignore that experience. We cannot simply deny what we cannot place within our categories of analysis.

Stripped of the sacred imagery, we can say that love is the experience of our ontological condition as the source of a meaningful universe. In this sense, love is stronger than violence.[71] Indeed, for man love is prior to violence. To experience the brute fact of violence, we have to struggle to overcome our ordinary readings of experience. We moralize endlessly, even about the facts of nature.[72]

The image of love conquering death is not just the story of the martyr, but a common possession of us all. Death, after all, is simply the ultimate threat of violence to the body. It does not bear its own meaning. That remains up to us, and the power to create meaning even in the face of death is love. We understand this not just when we read fiction, but in our daily experience when the family gathers around the dying person. There is, at that moment, an affirmation of a deathless love. That is what we want to hear in the presence of death; these are the only words we know how to speak in the face of death. Love

[71] See chap. 2 above, on sacrifice conquering violence.
[72] See P. Kahn, *Law and Love* 70–73 (2000).

endures because its source is not the desiring body, but the power to produce a common world of meaning.

If modern man is forgetting this language of the deathbed, he will be overcome by the fact of his own death. We have few other resources to make of death a public event. If it is merely private, it will be merely the end of an existence that never extended beyond the satisfaction of the body's interests, on the one hand, and the abstractions of reason, on the other. Such a life, we say, is "without meaning." It leaves no enduring memory of itself. Its particularity has exhausted itself in its own satisfactions. This is a world that takes concrete form as entertainment, and that world is at the extreme opposite from the world of love.[73] When contemporary man contemplates the moment of his own death, he secretly hopes that he will be sufficiently distracted—that is, entertained. Despite the pleasures of such a world, he fears that he lives a life without meaning. In love, we never fear that we lack meaning. Our world overflows us, pulling us into the future.

We say that we are "in love" when we experience that creativity—or even the potential for that creativity—in a particularly extreme fashion. But we want not just to experience the momentary peaks of love, but also to have lived a life well-loved. A full life is one that has been full of love. With that, we point to the most basic structures of our ordinary experience: family and polity. These ordinary sources of our experience must be felt as expressions of our love, embodiments of the power to create meaning. Love is not bound by the terms of the ordinary, but it surely starts there. The boundaries of love are only the boundaries of the possible range of meanings that the individual can experience as making a claim upon the self.

Because we are not gods, creativity is never "out of nothing" for us. Love is always both creation and discovery.[74] This sense of mediation between the ideal and the real, being and becoming, or the divine and the mundane, is characteristic of all experiences of love. This is the

---

[73] Nothing is more common in our popular entertainment than the countless deaths of individuals who are not subjects. George Lucas did not even give the Storm Troopers real faces in the Star Wars movies.

[74] In the *Symposium*, Socrates describes love as a daimon, mediating between the divine and the human. This imagery captures the idea of love as simultaneously an overcoming of the self and a discovery of a larger self.

domain of the will. The action of love is closer to aesthetic production than to the rule-governed understandings of the scientist or the liberal political philosopher. For the objects of our love are not instances of production under an ideal rule that can be grasped separately from the act of production—despite Plato's urging of a pure field of Ideas. Rather, love is bound to particulars. It is an interpretive act of reading meaning in the particular.

Just as there is no book in the abstract, there is no abstract object of our love.[75] Even the ambition to achieve a universal love of all mankind is not a love of the abstract idea of man. We must love the universal in the particular. The same is true of children: we think of them as embodying certain ideals, whether of beauty, courage, or familial respect. Loving them, we bring them up to try to realize these ideals. But we love them, not the ideal we hope they realize. We love them for themselves, but we do not love them as if it makes no difference who that self is. We love them because we participate in a meaningful universe that we share with them. This is not just the form of love in the family, it is that of the state as well—even the modern nation-state, as I will show in the next chapter.

Love is the experience of power through the creation/discovery of meaning. This combination of creation and discovery links us to others through love. The creations of love are expressions of a common universe of meanings. As subjects who love, we share that world with others. Love is the creation of a universe of meaning, but there is no singular experience of such a universe. A private universe would be like a private language—not a language at all.[76] Even the lonely artist, who creates all by himself, creates in response to ideals of beauty and truth that he expects will be shared by those who view his creations. The aesthetic object affirms the community in which its experience is possible.

In love, I can always answer the question, who am I? Indeed, in love I know with certainty who I am. The paradigmatic act of reading the loved body is sacrifice. In its essential form, sacrifice is a kind of

---

[75] We speak of "love" of justice, or other ideals. But this is a metaphoric use of the term. This love does not fall within the domain of eros. But compare H. Frankfurt, *The Reasons of Love* 41–42 (2004).

[76] See L. Wittgenstein, *Philosophical Investigations* 243–81 (on private languages).

transubstantiation: Christ was the Word become flesh through love. That is love's essential form. If it cost us nothing, we could not love. Thus, the Greek gods, who are embodied but immortal, desire but do not love. If we are unwilling to sacrifice, we cannot love. Sacrifice is the affirmation that the body is nothing but the vehicle for an idea. It is to read the materiality of the body as a sign; it is to see the other wholly and completely through the self. This is why the idea of sacrifice links the modern family—and state—to the very oldest forms of religious practice. At stake is the ideal content of an embodied life.

Sacrifice is at the heart of both politics and family. Both parent and citizen understand themselves as subject to a demand for sacrifice. They recognize the demand as legitimate because they live in the world of meanings that the sacrificial act affirms. Sacrifice is, accordingly, the way of being in a meaningful world. Sacrifice, we say, is an act of love.[77] In love, we are willing to sacrifice, and through that sacrifice we simultaneously create and discover the subject that we are.

Sacrifice is not extraordinary, but paradigmatic. What we explicitly call an act of sacrifice is only a point at which the symbolic structure of meaning that is always present becomes particularly evident. To imagine a family in which sacrifice was not ordinary is to imagine a dysfunctional family; the same is true of the state. Liberalism, however, is speechless in the face of sacrifice. Yet every parent understands sacrifice, just as every citizen-soldier understands the reading of the self as expression of an idea of the state. A political theory that finds sacrifice incomprehensible has failed to come to grips with the most elementary forms of our experience of meaning. We will never understand sacrifice, however, if we fail to embrace love.

In love, we find salvation from our own finitude. The only salvation that is possible is to read the self as the embodiment of an idea. The scope of the idea defines the reach of love. We can love narrowly or broadly. If our love is directed at that common world that all humanity shares, we realize a Christian love as *agapé*. This is broad, but thin—not thin in the sense of lacking depth, but lacking particularity. That

---

[77] To be sacrificed may be an act of violence, when the ideas affirmed in the act are not those that make a claim upon us. The thousands sacrificed by Montezuma were mostly drugged captives or slaves, and it was generally considered a most bitter thing to be sacrificed. See I. Clendinnen, *Aztecs: An Interpretation* 87–110 (1991).

which we share with everyone as a common world of meaning builds on the existential condition within which we find ourselves: we experience pleasure, suffer pain, seek particular loves, and fear death. As our love becomes more particular, through community and family, it becomes thicker. The world we share is one of many ideas and common values.

This idea of thick and thin worlds of love restates the Thomistic conception of the "orders of love."[78] This is also the idea behind Diotima's education of Socrates about the ladder of love in the *Symposium*. Both see that the demands of love can be set against one another. To believe that there is only a single ranking of love that brings order to the whole, one has to accept Platonic metaphysics or Thomistic theology. Without that, we are left on our own to balance the thick and the thin experiences of love, to recognize both intimacy and solidarity.

To say that conflicts are possible and that we are left on our own is not to say that it is a matter of indifference where we place ourselves on the ladder of love. In every encounter, we seek to create a common world of meanings. We seek to live in an entirely human world. One in which we see ourselves in all that we experience, not because we make a narrow claim to it, but because we share a potential universe of meanings with all whom we meet. Our ambition, as subjects who create a universe through love, is to be at home in the entire universe. Thus, we cannot withdraw our love without diminishing ourselves. Where we cannot love, we can only experience violence, and violence is always less than human.

Were we perfectly to read ourselves as an instance of humanity, we would have achieved an idea of moral sainthood. We cannot simply give up this idea or pretend it makes no claim upon us. Nor, however, can we give up the claim of particularity that we realize in family and nation. We want moral saints, but we do not want only moral saints.[79] We confront the order of love not as an order that takes care of itself through divine presence or metaphysical structure, but as a moral task. We want to love the particular in a way that opens us up to the

[78] See S. Pope, *The Evolution of Altruism and the Ordering of Love* 50–76 (1995); see also M. Walzer, *Thick and Thin: Moral Argument at Home and Abroad* (1994).
[79] See, Wolf, "Moral Saints."

universal. Our moral task is not to abandon the family for the life of Mother Teresa, but to love within the family in a way that connects us to those in Calcutta. When we fail—as we always do—we experience this absence of love as the cutting off of a part of the world.

CONCLUSION: LOVE AND LIBERALISM

Family and polity constitute the elementary forms of the symbolic universe that is the expression of man's power. Love is the internal experience of this fundamental relationship of the subject to this symbolic world. Because the labor of love expresses need as much as resource, love is always matched by an erotic vision of an ecstatic state in which we are free of family and polity, and thus free of the burdens of time itself. No individual can wholly repress the dream of the pornographic/romantic. Who does not long for a release from the burdens of labor, which are the burdens of time itself? We agree with Aristophanes that life is too hard, and too short. We want to feel complete in the instant. We do forget ourselves—our commitments to self and others. Yet we never forget for long. We are thrown back into the burdens of production of family and community. We wake up as if from the dream, and take up again the labor of loving. A theory of politics must equally take up this burden.

The pornographic/romantic myth of return is just that: a myth. Love is our first relationship to the world. The pornographic/romantic is always a rebellion, a taking back of the body from the symbolic labor of love. The pornographic/romantic sets at naught all efforts at ordered social construction, wherever they might appear. Eros, on this view, takes us over and in so doing takes us out of our ordinary lives. It is a kind of madness—a theme that Plato develops in his other great dialogue on love, the *Phaedrus*. To this mad soul, state and family appear as a kind of death. For this reason, the pornographic will always be seen by the state as an act of political rebellion. It is no less, because it is a reclaiming of the self from all of these attachments. State and family will accordingly make a common alliance against the pornographic. This is the politics of "family values."

Politics begins with the domestication of the erotic, the turning of love toward the labor of social and familial reproduction. The liberal state, no less than any other, must rely on the loving attachment of citizens to each other and to the intergenerational project that is the polity. It too needs citizens willing to sacrifice themselves to this particular state. It too needs families that inculcate the virtues of citizenship within this particular political order. No less than other political forms, it requires citizens who see themselves in the public history of the state, and see their future as bound to the maintenance of this state. Liberalism cannot explain the normative conditions of the political, which do not lie in reason but in love.

CHAPTER 6

■ ■ ■ ■

THE AUTONOMY OF THE POLITICAL IN THE MODERN NATION-STATE

There is a sense in which the inquiry into love can expand to include every dimension of meaning. This is the foundation of Plato's *Symposium*, in which the discourse on love spills across pedagogy, ethics, and metaphysics. If love is the experience of the generation of meaning, then there is no domain of life that cannot be perceived as an aspect of love. The attachment to the political order is a form of love. It involves loyalty, courage, self-identification, and participation in the intergenerational project of family and community. These were all touched on, to varying degrees, in the last chapter. But political meanings will not appear in their unique form unless we turn explicitly from love to power. Love, I argued, was the internal experience of power. Politics, correspondingly, is the outward face of power. The communitarians, in their argument with liberals, are reluctant to discuss power; the multiculturalists tend to see power primarily as a source of oppression. Neither sees the linked character of law, power, and love.

Examining love in the last chapter, I started with the obvious and unavoidable: the body's union with the other and the production of children. When we turn to politics and the body of the citizen, we must also start with the unavoidable. For political life, this is the knowledge of the possibility of killing and of being killed. The political order, we say, "defends a way of life." This defense appears to the state as a matter of ultimate seriousness. For the sake of this, every state claims the right to decide matters of life and death. Every citizen knows that the state has the power to require sacrifice for the maintenance of that set of meanings that is the state. Similarly, every state claims the right to kill those who it has identified as enemies. Most states have given up the death penalty for violations of their criminal law, but virtually none have given up their armies.[1]

The presence of the army is only an institutional expression of a pervasive—even if not explicit—understanding of the meaning of citizenship: to be a citizen is to stand in a relationship of authority in which life itself may be at issue. Citizenship includes the possibility of sacrifice for the state. To understand sacrifice, we have to examine a relationship of felt-identity between citizen and polity. This does not mean that we must celebrate this quality or believe that it somehow defines an essence of human nature. While romantic thought "assumes that the political domain should express the highest personal ideals of its members, and so refuses to envision the possibility that the political realm and other areas of social life may heed different priorities," I make no such normative claim.[2] The autonomy of the political, as I describe it, assumes that we live within diverse, incommensurable forms of meaning. Just as I am not describing the essential truth of the individual, I am not describing the essential truth of political arrangements wherever and whenever they appear. I do describe *a* claim of identity between the individual and the polity. I do believe that this was the dominant form of modern Western political experience. In the contemporary period, however, this form of political life is under great strain, particularly outside of the United States. Were this form of politics to disappear from our lives, that would not necessarily be grounds for regret.

I assume that most citizens most of the time hope that their capacity for sacrifice is never tested. Today many individuals seek postpolitical forms of association that would no longer have, or need, such a power over life. The fact remains, however, that the political character of the modern state has included this power and citizens have acknowledged this power over themselves.

The problem for political inquiry is not to imagine the conditions of justice in which sacrifice would not be required. Rather, the problem

---

[1] Costa Rica abolished its army in 1948; Panama did so in 1990. Japan has had no army since World War II; it does, however, have a growing self-defense force.

[2] C. Larmore, *Patterns of Moral Complexity* 92–93 (1987).

is to grasp the character of the political as a form of experience within which the modern Western citizen—particularly the American citizen—has imagined the possibility of sacrifice not as an alien eruption of violence into his or her life, but as the realization of an ultimate meaning. To accomplish this, I explore the way in which political meanings present themselves to the citizen—the inquiry into rhetoric—and the way in which the modern nation-state has rested upon a set of beliefs about popular sovereignty. These beliefs include the ideas that the popular sovereign creates and maintains itself, and that it knows no measure apart from its own existence. The former produces our deep commitment to the rule of law: the order the popular sovereign imposes upon itself. The latter produces our deep commitment to war as a matter of self-defense. The ultimate character of political meanings, like those of religious belief, is located in their closed or self-referential character. The popular sovereign knows only itself. That knowledge constitutes its past and forms it future.

KILLING AND BEING KILLED

No theory of the political is adequate if it fails to confront and explain the phenomena of sacrifice and killing. Although sacrifice for the state is linked to killing for the state—wars are a killing and a being killed—sacrifice is the more basic phenomenon.[3] A citizen may be excused from killing—the conscientious objector—but none are excused from the possibility of dying for the state. We recognize no countervailing moral claim for the latter, but only the political vices of cowardice or betrayal. Could we even speak of a political community if no one was willing to sacrifice for it? Of course, citizens can and do object to particular instances of the deployment of this power. They may find themselves opposing every instance of military action that occurs under a particular regime or even in the span of their lives. Yet, even so, they recognize that circumstances could be such that they could be called upon to sacrifice themselves and they would have no grounds to object. This is not just one possibility among others, but that possi-

---

[3] In chap. 2, I argued that martyrdom can be more powerful than murder. The martyr controls the meaning of his death in a way the killer can not equal.

bility that defines the extraordinary character of political power. Only the political has the power over life and death.

Reading liberal political theory, one might think that the state succeeds a violent state of nature by granting government a monopoly on the legitimate use of coercive force. The intention of that grant is to eliminate the actual use of violence by the threat of an overwhelming violence. Violence is displaced from the center of politics to the margins—literally in the form of protection of borders, and metaphorically in the suppression of crime. In either case, the reappearance of violence signals a failure of politics. The result of this set of assumptions is that liberal theory never confronts the experience of sacrifice.

For example, the problem for Hobbes is to understand how authority can emerge out of a violent world. Natural violence becomes political power through an act of consent that acknowledges the authority of an agent—the sovereign. At that point, a community is formed. Community is not possible without order, and order is possible only when individuals recognize relationships of authority. Authority is a privilege to use violence. Violence "legitimated" is political power. The endurance of the political community depends upon continued belief in that founding act. When that belief fails, sovereign authority becomes just another form of violence, and there is a return to the state of nature. The violent chaos of contemporary failed states—for example, Sierra Leone, Sudan, Afghanistan—illustrate Hobbes's argument.

By hypothesizing a state of nature, Hobbes secularizes death. Death is no longer understood as a release of the soul from the body, but as merely negation. As a negation, it can only be feared. Death, for Hobbes, marks the chaotic temporality of a natural world of mere violence. The political community begins when death is "put off." We establish a political order to escape the violence of nature, which in its simplest form is death. Correspondingly, freedom for Hobbes is measured by the absence of violence. An individual is freer to the extent that the boundaries of the state of nature have been pushed back, leaving a domain in which he can act without the fear of violence. Thus, Hobbes can couple a maximum of political power to a maximum of freedom.[4]

---

[4] See Q. Skinner, *Liberty Before Liberalism* (1998).

Of course, we don't actually experience the state of nature; we mythologize the time before ourselves as a prepolitical moment. We understand it as the time out of which the state arose. We imagine a world without meaning as one that is deficient in our meanings. We can't start with a perception of violence and trace the way in which violence becomes power. The process is the opposite. We understand violence as that which intrudes upon us without reason, meaning by that not without cause, but without justification. This idea was traditionally captured in the image of the city as a walled space protecting the populace from violent intrusion. The political community understands itself as the foundation and necessary condition of all meanings.[5] It understands itself to be under a constant threat from a violent nature. Often that natural violence takes the form of a competing community. These are the "barbarians" who threatened Greece and sacked Rome. Defeat means the killing of the men, the raping of the women, and the enslavement of the children. This is the end of the known world. In a nuclear age, political defeat can quite literally be the end of the world.

Strikingly, the face of evil is often perceived as the face of nature itself. When man becomes merely a natural object, there are no constraints on what can be done to him. We have seen this phenomenon repeatedly. The enemy is constructed as natural in order to justify atrocity. This is the history of the twentieth-century "camp," from Germany to Bosnia.[6] Hobbes's mistake is to assume that the natural precedes the political. Rather, the natural is more often a product of the political imagination. It is the violence that threatens the political world. The enemy has this ambiguous quality by which we simultaneously recognize and fail to recognize its humanity. Believing in different gods, the enemy very much belongs to the human world. But precisely because those beliefs threaten our world, we imagine the enemy as less than human.[7]

---

[5] See Aristotle, *Politics* 1. 2 (polity is prior to the individual who can only realize his own virtues as a citizen).

[6] See M. Ignatieff, "The Narcissism of Minor Difference," in *The Warrior's Honor: Ethnic War and the Modern Conscience* 34–71 (1997).

[7] For a good example, see T. Todorov, *The Conquest of America: The Question of the Other* (R. Howard, trans., 1984) (on Spanish attitude toward the Aztecs).

If the state of nature is a product of politics then so too is the violence with which it is associated. The state of nature is a way of representing the continuing demand upon citizens to defend a way of life. The transition from nature to politics is not past, but points to the continuing process by which death becomes sacrifice. This is not the transition from violence to peace, but from violence to power. The power of a political community is located neither in its contractual foundation nor in its capacity to threaten. The former confuses politics with morality, the latter with violence. Political power is present when individuals recognize in themselves a capacity for sacrifice for the state. In the act of sacrifice, polity and citizen, objective power and subjective faith, are one and the same.

Sacrifice is not an exclusively political ideal; it is not in itself a marker of the presence of the political. In the last chapter, I spoke of sacrifice within the family, and linked sacrifice to love. Just as I had to speak of diverse forms of love—from the particularism of romance to the universalism of a love of humanity—we should speak of sacrifice extending from the thick to the thin. Thus, sacrifice can happen even among perfect strangers. The heroic sacrifice to save the world from some impending disaster is a constant of science fiction. The moral message of this fictional tale of sacrifice is not different from that of the self-sacrifice of one person in the lifeboat that is sinking under the weight of all, or the sacrifice of the one person who must repair some dangerous technological device gone wrong, or even the sacrifice of the fireman who enters the burning building to save the unknown child.[8]

Political sacrifice rests on a kind of love, but it usually does not have quite the spontaneity of other expressions of love. It is often organized before the fact and, as such, subject to the demands of justice: it must not appear arbitrary from within the community. There is no single answer to this demand for justice. American law has experimented with a conscription lottery as well as other systems of ranking. Moreover, the most any such system can allocate is a risk, not sacrifice itself.

---

[8] What is the ethical responsibility of the fireman or the policeman to sacrifice himself for the unknown other? We expect them to act to the limits of their technology; we expect them to take risks. But sacrifice is beyond risk. On what grounds could we demand sacrifice?

Liberal theory confuses this demand for just allocation of the risk with the act of sacrifice itself. They are not the same.[9] Killing and being killed for the state will always support a sense of moral arbitrariness. There is no good answer to the question, why me? except for the arbitrary fact that you are in this place at this time. Political sacrifice, then, is not a product of justice, but neither is it wholly beyond the demands of justice. In this respect, it is like love within the family. The family too is not wholly beyond the reach of justice—members should treat each other justly to the degree they can—but there is nothing particularly just about the demands that love may happen to place upon an individual member.

Sacrifice is always an act of love, but it becomes a distinctly political act when it is linked to the reciprocal possibility of infliction of injury. Political sacrifice occurs in a context of political killing, or at least potential political killing. Carl Schmitt argues that the specifically political distinction is that between friend and enemy.[10] Friend and enemy are his terms for those from whom sacrifice can be demanded and those against whom the use of deadly force might be required. Without this distinction, we have not yet confronted the set of meanings that are constitutive of the political as a distinct form of experience.

Schmitt's appeal to the distinction of friends from enemies makes two independent points, both of which are outside of the liberal approach to politics. First, political meanings are plural; a political community is always one of many. Second, political meanings operate on a field in which violence or the threat of violence is always present. A fundamental fact of politics is plurality among communities. Every polity has an understanding of how it relates to other political communities—it has a foreign policy—and it has an understanding of its own internal order. It stands for something and in doing so it stands against others. Conversely, standing against others, it comes to stand for something. A community that stood for no particular political meaning would have nothing to defend. It would be politically indifferent to conflicting claims of authority because it would not matter whether it was a part of one state or another. Such a community might still

---

[9] See M. Walzer, *Obligations* 82–83 (1970).
[10] C. Schmitt, *The Concept of the Political* 26–27 (G. Schwab, trans., 1996).

bring nonpolitical values to the conflict: under which authority might it be better off materially, religiously, or ethnically? But there would be no separate issue of political identity. For example, failing to see that non-Europeans could maintain their own political communities, the colonial powers thought it a matter of indifference to the "native" population, which European political order they became a part of. No one asked the indigenous populations whether they preferred a French or British colonial master.

To stand for something is at least implicitly to identify an enemy. The issue is, who is perceived as threatening the way of life for which the polity stands? That may be an external or an internal threat. Political communities may encourage and protect diverse views, but they also recognize the possibility of betrayal and treason.[11] We cannot identify the enemy by any reasoning apart from the political calculus itself; how do we see self and other? It may never be the case that war is justified in economic terms; it is rarely justified in moral terms. Of course, we will use moral and economic terms to vilify the enemy once an enemy has been identified. But the chain of causation is the opposite from the rhetorical sequence. Those with whom we have religious, ethnic, and economic disagreements do not necessarily become our enemies. Competitors are not enemies; differences in worldviews can be celebrated. But if competitors are not necessarily enemies, it does not follow that enemies can come to be seen as only competitors. Sometimes they can, but there is no compelling logic to such a transition.[12]

Liberalism, however, reaches for unity across borders. It sees unity within or despite difference. It celebrates the fact that it is a global perspective and thus a negation of the specific experience of the political.[13] The goal of a liberal global order would be a single world market

---

[11] See G. Fletcher, *Loyalty: An Essay on the Morality of Relationships* 53–58 (1993).

[12] Compare Chantal Mouffe, who sees in the "domesticating of hostility" the possibility of a democratic politics in which the us/them distinction does not becomes literally that of friend/enemy. C. Mouffe, *The Democratic Paradox* 100–105 (2000). While I agree with much of Mouffe's critique of liberalism—she too believes that liberals tend to collapse the political into the ethical or the moral—I do not share her optimism that the antagonistic nature of the political can be transformed into a democratic agonism.

[13] See Schmitt, *The Concept of the Political* 70. ("Liberal thought evades or ignores state and politics and moves instead in a typical always recurring polarity of two heterogeneous spheres, namely ethics and economics.")

236 · CHAPTER 6

operating under common legal norms. In this world, contract would replace sacrifice. Competition within a single legal order replaces the perception of threat and counterthreat to differing ways of life. Correspondingly, the common legal norms would define a global order of human rights that are designed to mediate group identity through individual consent—again, the appeal to consent as the source of legitimacy. Group identity might continue to exist in the form of ethnic, religious, or ethical practices. But a liberal order—global or national—does not allow the politics of friends and enemies to define relations among these groups. In a single nation-state, all of these subgroups share a political identity as citizens; a global liberal order would be a postpolitical order.

These terms, friend and enemy, point to an autonomous domain of meaning, that is, a symbolic form of the political that cannot be reduced to any other set of norms. Thus the enemy is not necessarily an immoral or evil person. We do not kill the enemy because of any individual moral offense. There are countless stories in which the soldier discovers the enemy he confronts to be someone who was previously a personal friend. The moral quality of the other has not changed; rather, his political character has changed. Combatants can remain personal friends even as they kill each other as political enemies. We are also aware of accounts that move in the other direction. Now, the soldiers on the battlefield discover their common humanity; they are not just enemies, but share a single moral universe in which all are innocent. This is seen in the famous example of the Christmas truce in the World War I.[14] Political meanings are as contingent as any others. A slight change in perspective and enemies become brothers created in the image of God. But then a new change of perspectives casts them as enemies again.[15]

We also know, as a commonplace, the phenomenon in which people who were enemies become allies and even friends. At that point, they cannot imagine what sustained their relationship of hatred as enemies. This is how many Americans experience the Germans or Japanese

---

[14] See S. Weintraub, *Silent Night: The Remarkable 1914 Christmas Truce* (2001).

[15] See N. Ferguson, *The Pity of War* 343–44 (1998) (arguing that "disproportionate attention" has been paid to the Christmas truce).

today—presumably, the same is true in the opposite direction as well. We think it was some sort of terrible mistake, some sort of mass illusion brought about by evil men: Hitler or the emperor. Or consider the quick integration of the Warsaw Pact countries of Eastern Europe into the common European project. Outside of the political, we cannot imagine a set of meanings for the sake of which individuals sacrifice and kill. But that is no different from observing that from outside the aesthetic, we cannot imagine that some marks on a canvas can be worth much effort or sacrifice, or that from within the original position we cannot imagine love.[16]

This same phenomenon of political meaning is behind the observation that democracies do not go to war against each other.[17] What they do not do is fight those whom they cannot imagine as enemies. They can be quick to commit force, however, and extremely vigorous in the force committed, against those whom they do imagine as enemies.[18] This makes perfect sense because the democratic community is often one with an intense sense of its own way of life, that is, it "stands for something," and sees that meaning challenged by an enemy. There is a link between the American commitment to popular sovereignty and the size of the American defense budget. The latter is not just a product of the power of a military-industrial complex.

Politics is a way of seeing the world that is as tenuous—and as tenacious—as any other symbolic form. It does not take much, just a slight change in the angle of perception, to see the world in a way in which

---

[16] The autonomous character of political meaning explains, in part, why different countries, having transitioned to democracy, confront different problems in responding to an authoritarian past. It is often easier to reach reconciliation with an external than an internal enemy. When the authoritarianism was wholly a function of internal political development, in retrospect it tends to be read in moral terms. Members of the same political community reread the political as the moral. When authoritarianism was a function of an external political pressure, it is read more readily in political terms. This makes a political resolution available, without taking up the moral issue. See S. Zizek, *Tarrying with the Negative: Kant, Hegel and the Critique of Ideology* 207–11 (1993).

[17] See M. Doyle, "Kant, Liberal Legacies, and Foreign Affairs," 12 *Phil. & Pub. Aff.* (pts. 1 and 2) 205, 323 (1983); B. Russett, *Grasping the Democratic Peace: Principles for a Post-Cold War World* (1993).

[18] See V. Hanson, *Carnage and Culture: Landmark Battles in the Rise of Western Power* (2001).

political meanings disappear. We are then left genuinely puzzled as to what all the fighting was about. Today, most people think this way of World War I. Americans cannot really understand what's at issue in the Balkans such that so many people are still willing to kill and be killed there. The explanations "make no sense" to us. It is as if we are hearing accounts of religious systems that we do not understand. No one really believes the claims of miracles put forward by *other* religious communities. But, for most people, the presence of different beliefs outside of the community does not shake their own beliefs. It is the same with political meanings. We cannot understand why the various groups in the Balkans do not just stop all the fighting, but that does not lead us to consider why we spend so much money on our own defense budget, why we limit immigration, or resist various forms of globalization. Indeed, just the opposite. Because the world remains dangerous, and we "really" do have a political order that deserves protection, we think we should invest more, not less.

Just as political meanings can slip away with a slight change of perspective, they can easily slip back into place. Americans find themselves quickly responding to the language of threat and counterthreat, of national interests and national security. We do not live in a world in which we cannot imagine enemies. Our sense of potential enemies is hardly an empty set: we plot potential defenses against "rogue states" or the "axis of evil," we worry about Islamic states, and about the rise of China as a superpower. As long as that is so, we will continue to live in a political world. At the edge of our imagination remains the possibility that we, or our children, will be asked to sacrifice for the state. Since the events of September 11, 2001, what had been at the edge has moved closer to the center. The imagination of the enemy has been given a new, concrete shape: the Muslim fundamentalist as terrorist.[19]

Politics provides a license to kill and be killed that cannot be justified on the grounds of any moral calculus. The fundamental moral message of the West is that there should be no killing: "Thou shalt not

---

[19] Prior to September 11, 2001, many of the actions of the new administration seemed to be efforts to identify China as the enemy. At least in the short term, the Chinese threat has receded in the face of that identified with terrorists.

kill." But the politics of the West has been a long story of killing and sacrifice. This was not just the story of colonization of non-Western populations, but also of the mass sacrifice by Western states of their own political communities in the wars of the nineteenth and twentieth centuries. As Michael Walzer writes, "surely there has never been a more successful claimant of human life than the state."[20]

The effort to displace politics by morality is a constant ambition of well-meaning people. But measuring politics by morality makes as much sense as measuring art by morality. These are different ways of perceiving meaning in the world; they work in different dimensions. While each can displace the other, neither can be reduced to the other. These are simply incommensurable. From the moral perspective, each individual—citizen or alien—is of ultimate value; from the political perspective, citizen and alien are of fundamentally different value.[21]

Of course, we can measure politics by morality, but so can we measure the moral by the political. We are equally impressed, and confused, by moral measures of the political and by political measures of the moral. Thus, we can condemn the self-centered character of our politics when we consider our moral obligations to others—for example, the destitute in Third World countries. We certainly have moral obligations to aid others materially and to help them secure human rights. Yet, we condemn as politically naive any moral universalism that fails to take account of the priority of our own community. Morally, we should have open borders; politically, we exclude others in order to maintain our own identity, as well as our own well-being. No state is about to take up the question of whether it is just that it has the geography and history that it does—unless of course it is making a claim of injustice and seeking redress from others. But morally, we cannot ignore these questions.[22] Morally, we might believe we should risk ourselves for the sake of others suffering extreme human rights

[20] Walzer, *Obligations* 77.

[21] This distinction has been vigorously pursued in the post–September 11 security measures directed at noncitizens. That noncitizens would be targets of special legal measures has, as one would predict, been far more easily accepted in the United Sates than in Europe. Compare, e.g., *A. v. Secretary of State of the Home Department* [2003] 1 All E.R. 816, with *North Jersey Media Group, Inc. v. Ashcroft*, 308 F.3d 198 (2002).

[22] See D. Luban, "The Romance of the Nation-State," 9 *Phil. & Pub. Aff.* 392 (1980).

abuses; politically we think that we cannot ask citizens to sacrifice themselves for those outside of the community. The crossing of moral and political boundaries produced the odd spectacle of the NATO intervention in Kosovo. This was, in substantial part, a use of political instruments—armies—for moral purposes. It was morally praiseworthy action, but nevertheless lacked a political justification commensurate with the ordinary demands on the military. Thus, despite the morally compelling nature of the end, no one was allowed to sacrifice for that end. We saw the first war fought under a "no-casualties" rule—one could kill, but not sacrifice.[23] Of course, every army wants to minimize its casualties, but that is not the same as conditioning the use of force on a rule of no casualties. The use of an army is no longer a sure sign of a "political action." The intervention in Kosovo was not a war, but a police action intended to enforce a moral norm.[24]

The most basic right in the liberal state is the right to life. This is the point from which Hobbes would construct the entire political order; it is the premise of Rawls's original position as well. We may not be differentiated in our capacities for reason behind the veil of ignorance, but we are differentiated in our understanding that we each die our own death. Yet, there is something politically naive about liberalism's privileging of life itself. This flies in the face of the obvious character of the political as a specific domain of meaning constructed by the imagination. That set of meanings only begins with the threat of death: not the natural death of old age, and not the death brought about by violence. Rather, the political begins when I can imagine myself sacrificing myself and killing others to maintain the state. The modern state has fully arrived not when it defends me against violence, but when it conscripts me into its armed force. It fully reached the limits of its own self-conception with the appearance of nuclear weapons of

[23] See P. Kahn, "War and Sacrifice in Kosovo," 19 *Phil. & Pub. Pol.* 1 (1999).

[24] In Afghanistan, the military returned to a political role of confrontation with an enemy and sacrifice for the state. This was not a humanitarian intervention, but a "war on terrorism." Thus, the political leadership did not hesitate to make clear that casualties—deaths—were expected. In Iraq, the Bush administration has not been successful in offering political justifications—the threat of an enemy possessing weapons of mass destruction—but has been reluctant to rely upon moral justifications. The cost has been far too great to justify the war as a form of humanitarian intervention.

mass destruction.[25] In the age of mutual assured destruction, we are effectively all conscripted from the moment of birth. We cannot simply dismiss the political perspective from the world in which we live. Or, if we try, are likely to be surprised by the recalcitrance of the world to our efforts at reform.[26]

Nowhere in the liberal accounts of the state does anyone die. There is only protection from the state; there is no dying for the state. Protection from the state, as well as protection from abuse by private persons, is important, but it is hardly a complete account of political experience. It is as if it were thought that with the displacement of the state of nature, death itself had disappeared from the individual's life. The state, however, has not substituted peace for violence. Rather, it has displaced violence by power, unexplained suffering with sacrifice, and chaos with history. Of course, it has not really "displaced" anything at all, since we were never anywhere but where we remain, or anything but what we are: subjects with a political identity.

To see sacrifice as the core of the political strikes the liberal theorist as characteristic of fascist political theory. But even liberal political orders rest upon an understanding that the state can call upon the individual to kill and to be killed. States disagree over the content of the political way of life, but they do not disagree over the state's right to call upon its citizens to defend that way of life.

THE FORMS OF POLITICAL DISCOURSE

If the political is an imaginative construction that begins in an awareness of the possibility of sacrifice, then politics cannot defend itself on the grounds of reason. Neither should it have to. Politics is a way of being in the world for subjects who are neither pure reason nor pure interest; nor are they some uneasy combination of the two. The political imagination can be reduced neither to the abstract reason of rights, nor to the maximization of satisfaction. It is a way of being for subjects

[25] See P. Kahn, "Nuclear Weapons and the Rule of Law," 31 *N.Y.U. J. Int'l. L. & Pol.* 349 (1999).

[26] Consider Kennan's complaint about the legalization and moralization of U.S. foreign policy. G. Kennan, *American Diplomacy 1900–1950* (1951). After September 11, 2001, one hears far less talk of globalization as the end of the nation-state.

who imagine themselves as citizens. Of course, citizens have moral and economic concerns that they bring to political institutions, just as they bring with them aesthetic and romantic concerns. The ends for which political institutions can be deployed, however, are not the elementary parts of a political life, as if politics is an aggregation of individual concerns or an overarching system for maximizing realization of these individual ends. The political imagination presents a distinct form of self-understanding. Traditionally, politics has had its own discursive form: rhetoric. The justifications of politics are arguments within politics. They are rhetorical performances.

We have to distinguish among the logics of three discursive types that operate within the polity. First, there is the logic of liberalism, the ideal of which is to subject basic political arrangements to a kind of formal reasoning. That reasoning generally operates on two levels: the derivation and the application of rights. The derivation of rights can aspire to take the form of deduction, as in Kant's argument from the idea of a will formed by pure reason alone, or Rawls's argument from the original position, which he initially describes as "ideally . . . strictly deductive."[27] Each of these models aims for a logical objectivity in the sense that each purports to be that which everyone would say under the conditions proposed. Those conditions are designed to make a universal claim. Rejection of the argument represents either a rejection of reason itself or an insistence on an unjustified inequality. The primacy of reason seems so obvious to us that the effort to link morality to reason, and both to law, is often just assumed.

Arguments for the application of rights can also take the form of deduction. In part, application can mean extension of rights: having recognized a right to X in some privileged population, and recognizing some other group of individuals as citizens, then all are equally entitled to the same rights. For example, if the rights of all citizens are to be respected, and if blacks are equal citizens with whites, then blacks are entitled to all of those rights that whites enjoy. The key move in this deduction is to characterize an entitlement possessed by some group as a right: for example, due process, employment, food, shelter, medical care. Once we agree on the rights, then the deduction follows. This

[27] J. Rawls, *A Theory of Justice* 121 (1971).

creates a Whiggish view of history that understands political development as the extension of rights where they had not previously been recognized.[28] This same distinctive logic appears in the administrative character of the modern bureaucracy. Administration consists in the extension of a set of legally defined rights to a population, the members of which are similarly situated with respect to the rights at issue. That extension is not to represent judgment with respect to the creation of a right, but only the perfection of the internal logic of the already established right.[29] If application is to take a deductive form, that same logical form provides a ground for criticism of the work of those who are to administer rights. Courts are to hold administrative agencies to this test: agencies are to apply, not invent, rights. For this reason, even those who are skeptics on the logical derivation of rights—the work of political and moral theory—can be enthusiasts with respect to the deductive form of the application of rights.

Opposed to the deductive form of reasoning is the form of legal argument. Not deduction but analogy fuels legal reasoning.[30] Analogy creates sameness across difference; it is the form of reasoning by which dissimilar subjects are treated as the same. Analogy bridges a gap of difference that deduction cannot do alone: analogical reasoning provides the minor premise of a deduction. In legal reasoning, all of the labor is in the construction of that minor premise. The major premise can become merely tautological: for example, like cases must be treated the same. We must come to see the present case as the same as, or different from, some other that has already been established.

By coming to see sameness and difference, we learn how to orient ourselves in a world of law. Once we know the applicable categories and classifications, deduction can take over. But that is always the end of the legal argument. The real work is done in establishing those

[28] This, for example, is just the logic of *Lawrence v. Texas*, 123 S. Ct. 2472 (2003) (recognizing a right of homosexuals to engage in sexual intimacy with partners of their choice).

[29] See *J. W. Hampton, Jr., & Co. v. United States*, 276 U.S. 394, 409 (1928). ("If Congress shall lay down by legislative act an intelligible principle to which the person or body authorized to [act] is directed to conform, such legislative action is not a forbidden delegation of legislative power.")

[30] See E. Levi, *An Introduction to Legal Reasoning* 2–4 (1949); P. Kahn, *The Cultural Study of Law* 51–52 (1999).

categories. For example, if sexual orientation is a category like race, then we know as a matter of deduction that the government may not act on this basis without a compelling reason. The legal chore is to figure out whether sexual orientation is such a category. No deduction is going to answer that question. Instead, the category is approached analogically, placing it alongside the category of race and other categories that have and have not been treated like race. Analogical reasoning works at every level of legal argument from the specification of rights (does free speech include a right to contribute to political campaigns?) to application to an individual case (was this search "reasonable?"). In law, deduction and analogy are inseparable.

Political rhetoric works in yet another dimension, which is not reducible to either deduction or analogy. For this reason, the space of legal decision making is always trying to exclude political rhetoric, just as that of political rhetoric is wary of law.[31] Political rhetoric works in the language of sacrifice. It is about the realization of the idea of the state in the individual citizen's body. It invokes participation in a transtemporal community that is the mystical corpus of the state. In the United States, this is the popular sovereign.

The touchstone of American political rhetoric is the Gettysburg Address. Lincoln's direct theme is sacrifice: they "gave their lives that [the] nation might live." Birth and death of both the individual and the nation are at issue. Sacrifice is the point at which the two are linked. "Our fathers brought forth . . . a new nation, conceived in liberty," but it is the responsibility of the present generation to provide the nation a "new birth of freedom." The task of the living is to continue the work of those citizens who have already sacrificed. "It is for us the living . . . to be dedicated here to the unfinished work." This work is not only noble, it is sacred. This language of sacrifice links each generation to its predecessors and ultimately to the revolutionary origins of the nation in a collective threat of political martyrdom.[32]

---

[31] As I explain below, constitutional adjudication before the Supreme Court does not fall within the ordinary character of legal decision making.

[32] See P. Kahn, *Legitimacy and History: Self-Government in American Constitutional Theory* 52–55 (1992). Benjamin Rush reported that Benjamin Harrison said to Elbridge Gerry just after both had signed the Declaration: "I shall have a great advantage over you, Mr. Gerry, when we are all hung for what we are now doing. From the

Rhetoric reminds us that the birth of a nation depends upon individuals taking up political meanings as matters of ultimate concern, and that the maintenance of the nation may require the same of the contemporary generation. Jefferson's metaphor of a "tree of liberty . . . refreshed from time to time with the blood of patriots and tyrants" remains an important part of our rhetorical tradition.[33] Kennedy's Inaugural Address, for example, was directed at a "new generation of Americans" and demanded of them that they "[a]sk not what your country can do for you, but what you can do for your country." These words were spoken in the middle of the Cold War, when the possibility of killing and being killed for the state was a palpable reality for the entire population. Kennedy rhetorically reminds the nation of the obligations of political sacrifice. Very soon thereafter, he brings the nation to, and then through, the Cuban missile crisis. If we can no longer imagine responding to such rhetoric, then the political meaning of the world has disappeared. We may still have rights, law, and administration, but we will not have a political community. Sacrifice, of course, need not be a matter of death. Roosevelt's first Inaugural Address, speaking to an economic, not a military, crisis equally invokes the theme of sacrifice: "If we are to go forward, we must move as a trained and loyal army willing to sacrifice for the good of a common discipline."

This rhetorical demand, while not our everyday mode of discourse, nevertheless remains a constant possibility. If we understand ourselves as living under the potential demand for sacrifice, we understand the forms of political discourse that will explain and justify that sacrifice. This will not be the language of deductive or analogical reasoning. We do not ask whether the nation has the order of rights correct before we commit ourselves to its political maintenance; we do not wait on the pronouncements of the courts to legitimate that commitment. When we look back at the nation's history, we accept it all as our own. We speak of that history as a continuous manifestation of popular

---

size and weight of my body, I shall die in a few minutes, but from the lightness of your body, you will dance in the air an hour or two before you are dead." Quoted in J. Ellis, *Founding Brothers: The Revolutionary Generation* 5 (2001).

[33] Letter of Thomas Jefferson to William Smith, Nov. 13, 1787, in *Jefferson on Democracy* 20 (S. Padover, ed., 1939).

sovereignty, even as we acknowledge its moral failures. Our political commitments do not turn us into moral hypocrites, but neither do they easily align with our moral standards. For the most part, we want the state to act in a moral manner, but we do not condition our sense of political identity on satisfaction of that standard. Again, the point is not that we should be satisfied with injustice or that we should willingly sacrifice ourselves for whatever the state demands. As citizens, we do not lose the capacity for moral and political disagreement. The state may commit moral travesties that compel us to withdraw or even to revolt. Similarly, our ambitions for political reform do not disappear. Nevertheless, we recognize the possibility of a demand for sacrifice. We imagine the demand arising under some set of circumstances, and we cannot imagine how we could decline that demand.

When we say we will sacrifice for the rights of others, we are usually expressing a willingness to sacrifice for the endurance of the political community that has organized itself in such a way as to recognize certain rights. It is not the rights, but the political character of the community that grounds the sacrifice. We quickly realize this when nonmembers seek out aid in protection of their human rights. Members of different communities may have equal claims to rights, but they do not have an equal claim on my life. The boundaries of that claim are the boundaries of the polity.

Political rhetoric addresses our capacity to understand ourselves as the embodiment of an idea of the nation. American political rhetoric tells us that we—each of us—are the popular sovereign, that our bodies constitute its body. Thus, when Martin Luther King Jr. proclaims "I have a dream," he reminds his listeners that it is "deeply rooted in the American dream." He claims for the black community their rightful patrimony from "the architects of our republic [who] wrote the magnificent words of the Constitution and the Declaration of Independence." King's dream would have us all children of this family, sitting down "together at a table of brotherhood." To get there, King speaks of "creative suffering" in this struggle. He exhorts his listeners to "continue to work with the faith that unearned suffering is redemptive." Earlier, in his letter from a Birmingham jail, he locates the movement's practice of civil disobedience in the long Western tradition of martyrdom, connecting politics and sacrifice: "We had no alternative except to . . . present our very bodies as a means of laying our case before the conscience of the local and the national community."[34]

Political rhetoric appeals to the individual's sense of an intergenerational privilege and burden. Burke is working in this rhetorical tradition when he writes, in *Reflections on the Revolution in France*, of "the whole chain and continuity of the commonwealth," in which each generation is linked to those who came before and will come after.[35] But Burke focuses on the wrong point. It is not the connection of past and future that defines the political—the point he defends against the excessive faith in reason that he believes to be at the heart of the French Revolution—but the willingness to sacrifice for the idea of the nation. This identification of the self with the nation unites the *political* character of the French revolutionary with Burke's own conservative defense of the nation. Sacrifice unites revolutionary founders with subsequent defenders. Traditions are more malleable than conservatives believe, just as revolutions are less rational than revolutionaries believe. American law can quickly model itself on the British common law after the Revolution, just as Napoleon can succeed to power after the French Revolution. Conversely, the British constitutional system has been subject to repeated "rational" interventions, limiting the power of the House of Lords and expanding the electorate.[36] Disputes over the sources and character of political order occur against a background of ultimate belief in the polity. That belief supports a practice of sacrifice.

Political rhetoric is not a matter of making claims of right. It is most certainly not the language of administration by an efficient bureaucracy. Of course, such claims will be made within a rhetorical presentation. But there is no logic that moves us from such claims to a willingness to sacrifice. There is no deduction of practical reason that concludes with my death. Sacrifice is a matter of reading the state in the body. Future generations of citizens, for example, could be thought to have no more claim upon us than the people of a foreign nation have presently. Yet, this is not how we see it. Political rhetoric reminds

---

[34] M. L. King Jr., "Letter from a Birmingham Jail" (Apr. 16, 1963).

[35] E. Burke, *Reflections on the Revolution in France* 83 (J. Pocock, ed., [1790] 1987).

[36] See the Reform Acts of 1832, 1867, and 1884 and the Parliament Act of 1911.

us that we are participants in a political project, not subjects who need moral and logical arguments to persuade us to take up a burden against our own self-interest.

Political rhetoric affirms that in the life of the nation, we never die. We are assured of a kind of secular resurrection: he who believes in the nation shall never die. Calling it secular, however, only refers to its institutional form. In itself, it is a form of faith as deep as that of any religion. Political rhetoric is the contemporary language of transubstantiation; it is the direct inheritor of the religious language of sovereignty. In Christ, and then in the monarch, the sovereign did not die, despite the death of the corporeal entity that is the finite body. In the popular sovereign, we do not die, despite the death of the body. The popular sovereign is the contemporary mystical corpus of the state.

We confuse the language of rights with political rhetoric because so much of our particular political self-understanding appeals to the idea of rights.[37] For the American nation, rights are the product of the self-formation of the popular sovereign. They are *our* rights not because they are universal rights, but because we, as a sovereign people, have bestowed these rights upon ourselves. If the popular sovereign speaks the nation into existence, then rights are the content of this speech. But it is for the speaker, not the speech, that we sacrifice ourselves. We sacrifice because *we are* the popular sovereign—that, at least, is the content of our political belief. Rights are valuable, but they are never more valuable than the individual whose rights they are. Your rights cannot be more valuable than my rights, but I have no rights once I am dead. This is just the problem of the political over which Hobbes stumbled: how can a community founded in the promise of life demand the death of its members?[38] Life is a necessary condition of the Kingdom of Rights.

This hardly means that we are indifferent to the specific character of the "way of life" that the community represents. That the community represent a way of life that we judge to be both just and good is a matter of utmost importance to us. It is with nations as it is with other

[37] See R. Primus, *The American Language of Rights* (1999) (arguing that rights language is just a way of emphasizing political importance).

[38] See above at 231.

objects of our love. The moral character of the object of our love matters because we are concerned, on its behalf, that it be as good as possible. But our love is not a product of, or conditioned by, that moral character. Because we love the nation, we want its history to be one of progress toward moral ideals. Those moral ideals, however, never displace our political relationship to the nation.

We argue endlessly over reform of the state. But we do not similarly argue over its existence. Nor do we generally argue over our own attachment to *this* state. We are concerned about the character of the polity, but that concern does not generally question its ultimate value to ourselves. There are, however, exceptional moments when faith in the state collapses. Just as there are limits on what we will do for the beloved, there are limits on what we will do for the state. Because politics and morality work in different dimensions, politics can always be judged from a moral perspective. We can never know in advance whether the political or the moral demand will prove to be stronger under particular circumstances.[39] But then we can never know whether the political or narrow self-interest will prove stronger in any actual set of circumstances. Political meanings are only one form of self-understanding. There is no set of rankings by which we can order these relations or measure their relative power.

Scholarship tends to discount the rhetorical voice while contributing to the deductive and analogical forms of reasoning within the state. But politics without the support of rhetoric is stripped of the discursive form that creates and sustains a way of seeing the world. Stripping politics of rhetoric is the equivalent of stripping love of poetry. We can identify the elements of contract in marriage; we can have judicial resolutions of marital disputes. But we would be deeply mistaken to think that relationships of love can be sustained in a world of administration and law.

Just as we cannot explain the reason for our love, we cannot explain the nature of our self-understanding as citizens of a particular polity. We do not choose our political allegiance, except in the relatively rare

---

[39] See discussion of *Antigone* in chap. 5. When politics and law conflict, we similarly cannot know in advance which will prove stranger. On the devices within law, which seek to assure its apparent victory, regardless of actual outcome, see Kahn, *Reign of Law* 167–74.

circumstances of naturalization. We find ourselves already to have a political self defining the community that can demand our sacrifice and direct our killing. We respond to the rhetoric of this community, not others. Responding to this rhetoric, we realize who we are. When we no longer respond, we have become someone other. Hearing the rhetoric of other nations is similar to listening to the liturgy of a religion different from one's own: we wonder how anyone can fail to see the illogic of the rhetorical claims.

We can only explain the experience of the political by appealing to unqualified terms. We say that politics is a matter of "ultimate" meanings. We imagine a pure experience of the political as the point at which debate ends, and action follows. The language at that transitional point is rhetoric, not logic. I imagine a pure rhetorical moment when the citizen understands that the state demands his sacrifice, and there is nothing more to be argued. There are no excuses to be made, no reconsiderations of the justice or legitimacy of the claim.[40] There is only silence and then the act itself. The silence is subsequently filled in by the rhetorical speech of commemoration. The political exists as a distinct, meaningful phenomenon as long as we can imagine this experience. This experience is not simply the excitement of working together in a group. Camaraderie contributes to political life, but it will not take us to the experience that is the construction and maintenance of the history of the nation through individual sacrifice.

Justice Holmes captured this sense of the depth of the political in his writings about his experience as a soldier in the Civil War. He refers to a "faith that is true and adorable which leads a soldier to throw away his life in obedience to blindly accepted duty," and speaks of the soldier's capacity for sacrifice as a "miracle."[41] This is not a matter of reason, or a matter of legal reasoning. Yet Holmes also claimed that something approaching the same character of ultimate meaning could be obtained in "the remoter and more general aspects of the law." Here too, he thought, one could catch "an echo of the infinite" and connect oneself as subject with the universe.[42]

---

[40] This is the point at which the discourse ethics of Habermas fails as a model for the normative character of the political.

[41] O. Holmes, "The Soldiers Faith," in *The Occasional Speeches of Justice Oliver Wendell Holmes* 73 (M. Howe, ed., 1962).

[42] O. Holmes, "The Path of the Law," 10 *Harv. L. Rev.* 457, 478 (1897).

Holmes never clearly explains the infinite in the law. Most of his writings about law are hardly inspiring essays of political rhetoric, but rather work in the familiar forms of deduction and analogy. Nevertheless he was right to suggest a link between the discursive forms of rhetoric and our law, particularly as expressed in the Supreme Court opinion. Lincoln, the better rhetorician, expressed this link early in his career when he spoke of substituting the text of the Constitution for the scared bodies of veterans of the Revolution, who were then reaching the end of their lives. Those veterans were a "history bearing the indubitable testimonies of [the revolutionary battles'] own authenticity, in the limbs mangled, and the scars of wounds received, in the midst of the very scenes related." With their passing, the country faced a crisis of patriotism, unless a new "political religion" of reverence for the law could take the place of the suffering body.[43] The Constitution, Lincoln tells us, is not just an order of rights and the formation of an institutional structure: it is the material embodiment of the meaning of the Revolution as an act of popular sovereignty. It is the Revolution as a fact present in the ordinary lives of the people. This was Lincoln's belief, and, in this, he was not alone. The miracle of American politics is located at the intersection of Lincoln and Holmes, for what they see is that Americans have managed to attach the ultimate claims of politics to their nation as a legal order. For us, law has a political meaning that, as Holmes said, provides an "echo of the infinite."

Together Lincoln and Holmes illustrate the fact that the different genres of political discourse do not operate exclusively of each other. While there is some institutional separation—the bureaucratic, legal, and executive voices—there is also considerable mixing of the genres. The executive branch always has a dual role as both head of the administrative state and political leader of the nation. With regard to judicial opinions, we have particularly to distinguish the constitutional rhetoric of the Supreme Court from the ordinary legal reasoning of courts adjudicating private disputes or criminal matters.

Today, the constitutional discourse of the Supreme Court may be our most important source of political rhetoric. There is a certain

---

[43] See A. Lincoln, "The Perpetuation of Our Political Institutions: Address before the Young Men's Lyceum of Springfield, Illinois, January 27, 1838," in *Abraham Lincoln: His Speeches and Writings* 76–85 (R. Basler, ed., 1948).

irony in this given that the Court originally justified judicial review—the evaluation of statutes for their constitutionality—by claiming it to be an implicit aspect of the judicial role of saying "what the law is."[44] Politically, judicial review functions in a different dimension from the adjudication of ordinary disputes. The Court shows us, on a regular basis, the high political rhetoric of the nation. When the Court decides, it speaks in the name of the sovereign people. That rhetoric serves to tell us who we are, and who we are not. Ideally, it aims to do so by telling us who we have been in order that we might remain the same sovereign subject in the future. The Court's role is to elaborate the character of this political subject who is the citizen.[45]

Because our constitutionalism is a matter of political rhetoric rather than the elaboration of the logic of rights, American legal scholars—unlike those from virtually everywhere else—are quite comfortable speaking of the political role of the courts. Our law bears a political burden quite uncharacteristic of the function of law elsewhere. Thus, one of the most important works of modern constitutional theory bears the subtitle: "The Supreme Court at the Bar of Politics."[46] The foundation of the legitimacy of the Court is not located in the "science of law," but in politics: not in the ordinary politics of the electoral cycle, but in the high politics of revolution and constitutional self-construction. Only in America would a legal scholar so easily claim to speak in the voice of We the People—a remarkably political claim for the elite scholar.[47] Only here does the national political identity focus so clearly and quickly on a legal text. Our deepest politics, that

---

[44] *Marbury v. Madison* 5 U.S. (1 Cranch) 137, 177 (1803). Interestingly, most nations that have recently adopted a practice of constitutional review have not followed *Marbury*, but recognize this as a practice quite distinct from the ordinary legal affairs of the courts. For this reason, they have created special constitutional courts that are separate from the rest of the judiciary. See, e.g., A. Sweet, *Governing with Judges: Constitutional Politics in Europe* 32–37 (2000).

[45] In this sense, *Bush v. Gore*, 531 U.S. 98 (2000), represents a failure of political rhetoric. Instead of showing us who we are as citizens of a constitutional democracy, the Court chose to treat the case as a matter of ordinary legal reasoning, reducing it all to analogical reasoning within a deductive form of the application of rights.

[46] A. Bickel, *The Least Dangerous Branch: The Supreme Court at the Bar of Politics* (2d ed. 1986).

[47] See, e.g., B. Ackerman, *We the People: Foundations* (1991). See also, J. Rubenfeld, *Freedom and Time: A Theory of Constitutional Self-Government* (2001).

which defines our political self-understanding, merges into our understanding of ourselves as a people under the rule of law. For the Constitution is law as an expression of popular sovereignty. This is the American political myth: through the Constitution we participate in a sovereign act of self-government.

Not only does our constitutional law bear a unique political burden, but our ordinary politics has been substantially depoliticized. Increasingly, we see a politics that never reaches the domain of political rhetoric. Liberal democracies manage disagreement through a kind of depoliticization of ordinary politics. Campaigns debate issues of administration and management; citizens come to believe that not much turns on which way the contemporary debates are resolved or which party wins any given election. The outcome of an election is not seen as a matter of political ultimates. The less that turns on any single outcome the better. This hardly means that politics has itself disappeared from our self-conception. It means simply that we are looking in the wrong place.

There is always a danger that an ordinary debate will become a full-blown political confrontation. Parties may believe that they can mobilize more support if they suggest that the opposition is the enemy. There is the temptation to violate the implicit norms of civility without which liberal debate cannot survive. But equally there is a strong inclination toward self-policing. Opposing parties in a liberal political order, particularly one structured around competition between two parties, must be committed to behave in such a way as not to invoke the friend/enemy distinction. Political disagreement is not treason; those against whom one campaigns are not the enemy. American politics, for example, is univocal in its condemnation of anything that looks like "class warfare," as well as on the need for a "bipartisan" foreign policy. No one challenges the Constitution itself, although there are disagreements over interpretation. Politicians tend to claim that a proposal will not work or that what purports to be a plan of rational action for the public good is "really" only a means of advancing "special interests." Special interest groups, however, are not the enemy.

For us, the Constitution bears our character as a particular political community. The defining political question we ask about any particular law or official act is, is it constitutional? By this, we ask whether it is consistent with our national identity embodied in the Constitution. If it is not, it needs to be excised from the body politic. Such a provision only appeared to be a law; it was not really a part of us at all. It was, we say, an action only "under color of law."[48] This question of constitutionality is surprisingly close to the surface of our political life. It is institutionally represented in the Supreme Court, but the question can be raised in literally any court. Every citizen believes that he or she has a right to take issue with a law or government action, and to try to push the challenge to the Supreme Court. Before the courts, citizens and government make equal claims to represent the sovereign people. When the government loses its case, accordingly, we say that the people have won.

Of course, most citizens do not understand this process in a legal sense. They suspect that its technical character might overwhelm them. They know that the process requires professional guidance and institutional support. Yet they intuit the possibility as a right of political membership. They know—again as a matter of faith, not study—that somehow the Supreme Court has the final word over the political life of the nation, and that not even the president is above the law. They have faith in the Constitution and in the Court. These are there not just in an emergency but as the institutional guarantors of the whole. Citizens imagine that each of these objects of their faith is there for them personally. They form the background conditions of their day-to-day lives.

The citizen's belief in a right to take an issue to court for constitutional adjudication is symmetrical with his knowledge that he can be called upon to sacrifice for the polity. These are two sides of the same ultimate belief. Sacrifice for the state is, for Americans, sacrifice for the Constitution. This was the fundamental truth that Lincoln expressed at Gettysburg. Accordingly, the Constitution must appear as personal, as defining a meaning for the individual. This is what our highest political rhetoric tells us: that the nation is the Constitution, and that the Constitution is ours. The Constitution calls us to our perfect political selves—"I have a dream"—and it calls upon us to be willing to sacrifice for its sake. When Ronald Dworkin, our leading

[48] See, e.g., *Ex parte Young*, 209 U.S. 123 (1908).

jurisprudential thinker, identifies the Constitution with a set of moral principles, he depoliticizes the text and denudes us of our political identity.[49]

If we come to the point where we can only subject political rhetoric to the critique of the language of rights and the logic of administration, then what we have known as the political life of the nation will be over. We may continue as a bureaucratic arrangement of social-welfare programs, but the issue will always be whether some other form of organization—global or local—can accomplish the same ends more efficiently. We may continue as a structure for the maintenance of legal rights, but the distinction between human rights and constitutional rights will disappear, and the question will be whether transnational courts or domestic courts can do a better job of following the logic of rights.

The state may continue as an ethical community. We lead our lives within many such communities—from neighborhood to church to club to union to professional association. Yet we have no reason to think that the national grouping will represent a particularly strong ethical community. In fact, the communitarians, who do generally confuse political and ethical communities, find that the national community cannot generally compete in this respect with local groupings.[50] If the nation-state is nothing more than another source of communal identification and of the satisfaction to be found in working in a group, then national citizenship is destined to become a weak factor in a world increasingly subject to globalization.[51] The process of European unification, for example, has been accompanied by an increasing localism.[52] We may see this phenomenon on a larger scale

[49] R. Dworkin, *Freedom's Law: The Moral Reading of the American Constitution* (1996).

[50] See, e.g., M. Sandel, *Democracy's Discontents: America in Search of a Public Philosophy* (1996); R. Putnam, *Bowling Alone: The Collapse and Revival of American Community* (2000).

[51] See, e.g., T. Franck, "Clan and Superclan: Loyalty, Identity and Community in Law and Practice," 90 *Am. J. Int'l. L.* 359 (1996).

[52] Consider also recent political devolution in Britain and France. See F. Tuytschaever, *Differentiation in European Law* (1999); D. Curtin, "The Constitutional Structure of the Union: A Europe of Bits and Pieces," 30 *Common Mkt. L. Rev.* 17 (1993).

as globalization leads to a revalorization of local communities. Already, we have seen a resurgence of federalism claims in the United States at just the moment of an increasingly global order of trade and communications. NAFTA and *United states v. Lopez* may be two sides of a single process in which the loser is the nation-state.[53]

The position I am arguing for is in sharp contrast to Bruce Ackerman's defense of a cyclical dualism in American political life.[54] Constitutionalism for him includes long periods of satisfaction with existing political arrangements. During such times, individuals pursue private interests. Little is demanded of them politically; government institutions pursue a reformist agenda within already established fundamental norms. On occasion, however, there arises substantial dissatisfaction with these norms. Then individuals give up their private lives and become mobilized, public citizens. They reawaken the popular sovereign in order to bring about a change in the fundamental norms. If they are successful—and Ackerman lays out criteria of success—they settle back into their ordinary state of satisfaction within a largely private life.

What matters to Ackerman are political events and institutional changes that have an objective, identifiable character. His aim is to remind us of these objective characteristics, and to establish them as legal criteria for interpreting the content of the Constitution. For this reason, his central thesis has always been that constitutional amendment can occur outside of the formal procedures set forth in Article V. He asks us, as well as courts, to focus our attention on political formations, rather than text, in interpreting the Constitution.

My concern is not with judicial interpretations of the Constitution. Rather, my focus is on the political self-understanding of the citizen. Here, Ackerman's dualism does not quite capture what is at stake. One would not say of persons of faith that they practiced a kind of dualism—for the most part, they led lives within secular forms of family and market, but at extraordinary moments they appealed to their

---

[53] *United States v. Lopez*, 514 U.S. 549 (1995) (limiting national authority over state policies); see J. Guehenno, *The End of the Nation-State* (V. Elliott, trans., 1995).

[54] See Ackerman, *We the People: Foundations*.

faith. Rather, one would say that faith abides, that it forms a kind of background condition to ordinary activities, and that it provides a ground of personal identity. Ultimate meanings are ultimate not because they are always present at hand, but because we understand their potential presence. We live under their threat and promise.

We live our lives within the dualism identified by Lincoln. This is not the Ackermanian dualism of the sometime patriot. Ackerman's dualism is only a variation on the traditional liberal dichotomies of reason and interest, or public and private. Lincoln's dualism is the Revolution and the Constitution. These are not related to each other as different moments of political experience in the life of the nation; they are not to each other as sleeping is to wakefulness, or private life to public action. Rather, each purports to be the truth of the other; they are reciprocal images of each other. Thus, if we ask about the legitimacy of the Constitution, the answer we inevitably hear is that it is the product of the popular sovereign. It is the self-formation of We the People. That process of self-formation is exactly what we mean by Revolution. But if we ask after the truth of the Revolution—how do we know that this particular set of actions was indeed a revolution?—the only answer we have is the Constitution.[55] We know the People acted by virtue of their product. Had there been no product, we might decide we were looking at a coup or a majority faction in the Madisonian sense. We see the People only through the Constitution; we see the Constitution because we understand the People expressed themselves in the Revolution.

The citizen understands the self as a part of the popular sovereign not just at moments when issues of constitutional import are open, but also when they are answered. Constitutional authority rests on the citizen's self-conception as a member of the popular sovereign. This is not hidden; it is celebrated in the constitutional deliberations of the Supreme Court and it is proclaimed constantly as the fundamental character of our political faith. Living under the rule of law is not

---

[55] That the end of the Revolution did not exactly coincide with the creation of the Constitution is of no significance in the domain of myth and rhetoric. Lincoln, for example, dates the creation of the nation ("four score and seven years") from the Declaration of Independence.

some lesser form of political life, awaiting the possible rebirth of the national political spirit in a constitutional moment of either Arendtian or Ackermanian dimensions. Rather, it is itself the celebration of a national political life as a form of popular sovereignty. The political rhetoric of the nation may be routinized in the constitutional rhetoric of the Court, but it is also maintained there as a constantly available resource.

In our secular faith, we affirm an identity with all of those who sacrificed themselves for the conception and maintenance of the nation. Believing in the Constitution as that which can demand our sacrifice, we affirm an identity with all who came before and will come after. We know who we are as subjects of a political community that exists in an imaginative space beyond reason and interest. The power of the Court extends no further than its power to hold up the ideals of this community and proclaim them to be the truth of the popular sovereign. The Court speaks in the name of the popular sovereign when it announces its opinion. If it is to succeed, it must be believed: "If the Court's legitimacy should be undermined, then, so would the country be in its very ability to see itself through its constitutional ideals?"[56]

The Court sees a world in which there has been a single, two hundred-year project of ordering the polity to match the Constitution. It sees, in short, a world of embodied ideas. It reads the polity through the Constitution. Indeed, represented and representation change places in its readings. It no longer reads the text of the Constitution as much as it reads the polity. The polity itself becomes a text to be read and the truth of that reading is the Constitution.[57] Word has become flesh. The Constitution is the word and we are the flesh. This is the relationship that we have to explore if we are to understand the subject's imaginative construction of the self as citizen.

---

[56] *Planned Parenthood of Southeastern Pennsylvania v. Casey*, 505 U.S. 833, 868 (1992).

[57] See *Youngstown Sheet & Tube Co. v. Sawyer*, 343 U.S. 579, 610 (1952) (Frankfurter, J., concurring) ("It is an inadmissibly narrow conception of American constitutional law to confine it to the words of the Constitution and to disregard the gloss which life has written upon them.")

A CLASSICAL VIEW OF THE MODERN
POLITICAL IMAGINATION

All modern Western states—as well as those that model themselves on the West—purport to be democratic: this has been the age of "people's republics." They trace their conceptual origins to the age of revolutions.[58] The coming into existence of the modern state required the destruction of a premodern order in which the state was seen as a part of a natural—or divine—order. Authority in the state was an instance of the same norms that ruled everywhere and at all times. There were, of course, competing interpretations of natural authority in its political manifestations; there were diverse views of the relationship between the natural and the divine. Nevertheless, all behavior, political and otherwise, was subject to the same norms. The task of moral and political reasoning was to decipher that normative order and make it operative in one's behavior. Law—public and private, international and national—should express this order. Real law, accordingly, was "natural law," which set forth a single rule for the individual and the state.[59] Reasoning through the state, one quickly met God, the sovereign; one most certainly did not meet a sovereign people. Just for this reason, the appearance of the people was announced by revolution.[60]

The modern state claims to express popular sovereignty; it claims to embody the people as a single, intergenerational community. No Western state purports to represent a divine order, an order of nature, or even a privileged class among the people in general. Governments base their authority on a claim of representation. They represent not simply the majority of the electorate, which brought them into office, but the people who retain sovereignty. Facing the state, the citizen is to see him- or herself. The state appears as a purely human construction, and the author of that construction is the people. These propositions are

[58] See H. Arendt, *On Revolution* 49 (1963) (on the irony of the French displacing the American revolution in Western consciousness).

[59] See e.g., H. Grotius, *De Jure Belli Ac Pacis Libri Tres* in 2 *Classics of International Law* (J. Scot, ed., and F. Kelsey, trans., 1925).

[60] See Arendt, *On Revolution* 40 (Louis XVI's belief that he confronted a revolt was corrected by the Duc de La Rochefoucauld-Liancourt, who announced "cést une révolution").

descriptive, but they do not describe facts about a political order. Rather, they describe the beliefs about that order characteristic of what we might call the "nonskeptical citizen." These propositions are also normative from that citizen's point of view—every political order *should* express the will of the popular sovereign. They operate at such a level of generality, however, that they can be used by both supporters and opponents of a particular government or a particular policy. They do not tell us where or how the will of the people is expressed. Nevertheless, these propositions describe the basic structures of belief within which modern political argument goes forward.

The modern state of popular sovereignty is the nation-state—a term that has generated considerable confusion. Too often, it is read with the emphasis on the word "nation." On this reading, it refers to the principle that every nation should gain political institutionalization as a state. If so, the nation precedes the state, and the state is a means for the realization of this national identity. This Wilsonian reading has increased currency in the contemporary period, despite the fact that it continues to generate the same practical conundrums that have always attended it: there are far more nations than there are possible states. The nightmare of a Wilsonian world of nation-states is global chaos as existing states fracture into smaller and smaller geographical units that map national identity.

The Wilsonian conception of the nation-state is actually the opposite of the distinctive, modern experience of the nation-state. That experience put the emphasis on the second term, "state." The idea was that a nation could be created out of a state, not that the state must track the preexistent nation. The political self-formation of a state would itself create a nation, quite independently of a prepolitical, ethnic nation. Wilson was trying to bring order to the old world, and to that end he deployed what seemed to him an Old World conception of politics. About America, Wilson had no doubt that nationhood followed statehood.[61] This belief remains central to the American self-conception.

---

[61] See W. Wilson, *Constitutional Government* 23 (1890) ("Every man in a free country is, as it were, put upon his honor to be the kind of man such a polity supposes its citizens to be."); idem, *Constitutional Government in the United States* (1917).

The nation-*state* was an Enlightenment idea, resting on a conception of the free, self-formation of a collectivity. Citizens would form a nation by virtue of their common political activity as members of the same state. This idea of the nation-state made possible the belief that a nation of diverse immigrants could form a vibrant state. Citizens would find a common identity in and through this political project of state-formation. A political conception of the self would form the basis of individual identity. That which one was prior to, or apart from, this political self-formation is reconceived as the "private." Ethnicity, family, and religion are prepolitical phenomena that are subordinate to the public. A nation of diverse immigrants finds a common ground in public politics. That, at least, is the modern ideal.

What begins as revolutionary self-construction, when contrasted with the premodern political order, appears in the postrevolutionary period as the rule of law. Self-construction takes the form of imposition of a constitutional order through an act of popular sovereignty. This act appears, especially in retrospect, as one of deliberative choice. It must be guided by a conception of an ideal order of the polity and an understanding of the just demands upon and among the citizens. For this reason, the modern rule of law, beginning with the construction of a constitution, is always informed by political and moral theory. The modern state is the state of law because law in a system of self-government is seen as theory become reality.[62] Law is, therefore, both the subject of deliberation and the object of choice. This double-character bridges Berlin's distinction of negative and positive liberty. The revolutionary origin of law—revolution as breaking the bonds of existing authority—captures the idea of negative liberty. But law as the choice to be what reason tells us we should be captures an idea of positive liberty.

The American political order was the first truly modern state because it imagined itself to be founded simultaneously on a revolutionary act by the popular sovereign and on "inalienable truths." Political

[62] This perceived need to understand constitutional self-formation as more than the politics of special interests explains the recurrent appeal to forms of dualism in American constitutional theory, from Bickel's distinction of principle from policy to Ackerman's distinction of ordinary from constitutional politics. See Bickel, *The Least Dangerous Branch*; Ackerman, *We The People*.

theory was an inseparable part of autonomous political construction. The popular sovereign does not just vote: it forms itself under a substantive vision of what the state should be. This is made explicit in the Declaration of Independence and again in the process of constitutional construction. Not accidentally, our greatest public work of political theory remains *The Federalist Papers*. As the first modern state, America is paradigmatic of the task of politics in the modern period: every state is to be made, or remade, on the basis of deliberation and choice.[63] This is the revolutionary project of modernity. Liberalism is so compelling in the modern state precisely because of this linkage of state construction to political theory. The original position is a reminder of the importance of theory in our own revolutionary origins.

This project of state construction will always draw on the reigning normative discourse. For us, this is the discourse of liberalism. But liberalism cannot explain the citizen's experience of the nation-state; it cannot explain the citizen who finds there an authority that can demand his sacrifice. To think otherwise would be as if we thought we could explain the passion for a sport by looking at its rules, or religious faith by looking at theological doctrine. Political self-construction in the modern nation-state is a way of being in the world. That way of life in and through politics is not grasped by examining its rules, but only by understanding the personal and communal identity that it sustains. The truly interesting question is not whether we can theorize a better set of rules—we can always develop a more rational system of justice. Rather, the most pressing intellectual inquiry is to understand whether and how the experience of political meanings acts as a constraint on the domain of possible rules.[64]

Even if we emphasize the role of liberal political theory in this project of national self-construction, much more is at stake than determining the appropriate content of the legal order. Looking at the law, we will never see the violent character of the modern state. We will never

---

[63] See *The Federalist No. 1*, 33 (A. Hamilton) (C. Rossiter, ed., 1961); P. Kahn, "Reason and Will in the Origins of American Constitutionalism," 98 *Yale L.J.* 449 (1989).

[64] See P. Kahn, "American Hegemony and International Law—Speaking Law to Power: Popular Sovereignty, Human Rights, and the New International Order," 1 *Chi. J. Int'l L.* 1 (2000).

reach the phenomena of killing and being killed for the state. The immense capacity of the nation-state to sacrifice its citizens in war was the great political discovery of the nineteenth century. That discovery begins with Napoleon's armies inheriting the popular enthusiasm of the Revolution; it was further revealed in the American Civil War, when democratic armies based on mass conscription confront each other for the first time. As the conception of citizenship and political participation broadened, so did the conception of the reach of military service. The people's state is supported by people's armies.

The end point of this development linking popular sovereignty to popular armies was a breakdown of the distinction between combatant and noncombatant. If all are equal parts of the state, then all can be appropriately sacrificed for the life of the state. What is at stake is a matter of ultimate meaning for every citizen.[65] Defeat of the popular sovereign becomes unimaginable because politics is no longer a means to some other end, but an autonomous activity constitutive of the citizen's world of meaning. There is no measure of its worth outside of itself. To take up arms in the name of the people becomes a force without limit, both in the official actions of the state in pursuit of "vital national interests" and in the revolutionary opposition to what is perceived as an "illegitimate" government. Revolutionary opposition is always pursued in the name of the people. Modernity could not be the age of people's republics without validating a revolutionary tradition that always makes possible a challenge to the government's claim to represent the popular sovereign.

The modern nation-state replaced the chivalrous conduct of a warrior class with a popular ideology that supports universal, political sacrifice. None of this will appear if we identify the self-formation of the nation-state with the liberal project of reason. We need to understand how the modern state could express itself simultaneously as the rule of law and armed force, as law and violence. This question is answered only in part by tracing the historical development of the nation-state, noting its dependence on centrally controlled standing

---

[65] W. Mead, "The Jacksonian Tradition and American Foreign Policy," *The Nat'l Interest* 1, 10 (Winter 1999/2000). ("Jacksonian America views military services as a sacred duty. . . . An honorable person is ready to kill or to die for family and flag.")

armies and its institutionalization of legal forms.[66] Whatever the historical causes, law and war are maintained as linked concepts in the modern citizen's imagination, that is, in his understanding of the state of which he is a part as citizen-soldier.[67] One of the lessons of the 1960s was that disrespect for the citizen-soldier is a wholly unacceptable position within the factions characteristic of American political competition. The veteran can never be blamed for the mistakes of government. He or she is the literal embodiment of the popular sovereign, which is all of us.

We can use Aristotle's concept of the "four causes" to gain a better understanding of the connection of law and war—ideology and sacrifice—in the modern nation-state. Aristotle believed every object or event can be explained from four different perspectives. The *efficient cause* is that course of action that brings an object or event into being. The actions of the craftsman are the efficient cause of that which he produces. The *formal cause* is the principle of order that gives shape or meaning to an object or event. It is the plan or design that the craftsman attempts to realize in the object of production. The *material cause* is that out of which the object is made. For the craftsman, it might be wood or stone. And the *final cause* is the end for which the production is pursued. For the craftsman, it may be earning a living; for the artist, it may be the experience of the beauty of the object itself.

Applying the Aristotelian schema to the modern nation-state, we can ask, what process brought it into being? What is the principle of order that it realizes in its institutional arrangements? What is the material that bears this order, and for what end is it maintained? Different answers to these questions will be reached as the position of the inquirer changes. The historian will investigate different causes from those that appear to the economist, and both will be different from those of the constitutional lawyer. My concern here is not with the variety of scholarly answers, but with those answers that are maintained in the citizen's self-conception, that is, the ordinary per-

---

[66] See W. McNeill, *The Pursuit of Power: Technology, Armed Force and Society Since AD 1000* (1985).

[67] See, e.g., R. Ferguson, "Holmes and the Judicial Figure," 55 *U. Chi. L. Rev.* 506, 526–27 (1988).

son's understanding of himself as a citizen with obligations and responsibilities to the state as well as rights against it. Characteristic of the modern nation-state is an ideology that I will refer to as "the autonomy of the political."[68] This is the belief that the state is its own cause in each of these dimensions. This ideology grounds the self-understanding of the citizen who locates the origin of the state in revolution and understands its fundamental principle of order as the rule of law. Revolution and Constitution are fixed points of his own political self-understanding. Both are expressions of the autonomy of the political.

The Efficient Cause of the Nation-State: Revolution

The efficient cause combines ideas of agent and agency: it is action by a subject. For the modern nation-state, the act that brings it into existence is revolution. The collective entity that carries out the revolution is the popular sovereign. A revolution is different from a coup just in this claim that it is action by the popular sovereign. Revolution is not an empirical fact but a politically and culturally formed collective self-perception. There is no revolution, then, without a narrative in which the popular sovereign is the hero.

The narrative of revolution begins with the establishment of a kind of negative freedom. The people must free themselves, before they can form themselves.[69] The revolutionary breach is the paradigmatic political act, successfully creating a new identity by identifying an enemy. It breaks the bonds of authority by which the polity is subordinate to a political power that is now conceived as external to the people themselves, regardless of whether that power is actually a foreign state. What had been political authority now appears as mere

---

[68] Less felicitously, but more accurately, I should speak of the "autochthony of the political." This would also distinguish my usage from the concept of autonomy used by contemporary social-systems theorists. See, e.g., N. Luhmann, *Ecological Communication* (J. Bednarz, trans., 1989). In contrast, my conception of autonomy deliberately links the legal to other forms of political self-understanding. Indeed, I am suggesting that the American constitutional discourse is misunderstood if law is seen as its own autopoetic subsystem. Constitutional law is embedded in a broader political understanding of self and nation.

[69] See J. Rousseau, *The Social Contract* 5 (C. Sherover, trans., 1975). ("Man is born free and everywhere he is in chains.")

violence.[70] This is really nothing more than a performative utterance: existing authority becomes the enemy when the People declare it to be. Declaring that authority to be the enemy, the People constitute themselves as an historical presence.

Revolution is successful when the moment of negative freedom is followed by an expression of positive freedom: the organization of a new constitutional order. Unsuccessful revolution is not revolution at all, just as an unsuccessful effort in any craft or art is not the cause of any product. Actor and act are tightly bound together through the form of an efficient cause: an unsuccessful revolution not only fails to produce its product, it fails to mark an appearance of the popular sovereign. Absent revolution, the People as popular sovereign are not present at all. Wherever the People appear, they succeed. This means that only in retrospect can we distinguish between a revolutionary act of the People and the violent illegality of a mob. A civil war may appear to an outsider as a contest between factions, but from within the nation-state, it will appear as a contest over the locus of the popular sovereign—that is, each side will purport not just to represent but to *be* the People. The resolution of that claim will be achieved only through a competition of sacrifice.[71]

The nation-state brings itself into being by an act of popular sovereignty. Other events may be the occasion for the popular sovereign to act, but the act itself cannot be reduced to other causes or events. We make a category mistake, however, if we believe the People to be a subject apart from these acts of negative and positive liberty, as if first there is a subject who then decides to act. Popular sovereignty is only a particular way of viewing the state. It has no other form, place, or time apart from the state itself. The popular sovereign is the nation-state conceived as efficient cause of its own existence. We will not find it anywhere else but in a narrative of efficient causes by which the state is first brought into existence and then maintained as the particular state that it is.[72]

---

[70] The Declaration of Independence, for example, sets forth how authority had become violence in the prerevolutionary period.

[71] See below at 275–76, on war and sacrifice.

[72] In fact, the relationship of the popular sovereign to maintenance of the state is always difficult to conceive because of the absence of the explicit appearance of effi-

Accordingly, the nation-state is the product of no subject's actions apart from its own self-creation. Those who participated in the creation of the state acted as the sovereign People. Apart from this, they would have had no authority to create a set of political institutions or make a set of political decisions that bind their successors. They could do so because, viewing those past actions, the citizen sees only an expression of the popular sovereign of which he or she remains a part. For this reason, the popular sovereign, even as it is understood to be the efficient cause and thus the "originator" of the state, always has a transtemporal character that resists chronological time. It is timeless because it is nothing more than a form of self-perception within the state.

This ideology of self-creation through an act of popular sovereignty cuts across the variety of modern constitutional forms. Modern states purport to find their source only in themselves. For this reason, the political project of modernity cannot simply be imposed on a polity from without: one state cannot impose a constitutional order on another. Instead, each has to be brought to a set of conditions in which it can create itself. This paradox was already present in the quandary that victory over others presented for the revolutionary armies of France.[73] Were they to impose a republican political order or to allow the self-determination of the "liberated" People? More recently, it has been present in the question of how to re-form Germany and Japan after World War II, and post-Cold War states of Europe today. It also meant there could be no smooth transition to a postcolonial order: decolonization had to include a revolutionary principle of self-construction. Just this conundrum faces the United States as an occupying power in Iraq today.

The popular sovereign is, therefore, the state conceived as the efficient agency of its own construction. Imagining political creation as an act comparable to the divine Creation ex nihilo, we imagine a subject—the popular sovereign—capable of having or expressing such an act of will. This popular sovereign shares many characteristics with

cient causes. This leads to theories of "tacit consent" under which the popular sovereign is always acting in its very failure to act.

[73] See C. O'Brien, "Nationalism and the French Revolution," in *The Permanent Revolution: The French Revolution and its Legacy 1789–1989* at 36 (G. Best, ed., 1989).

the divine sovereign of Western monotheism. First, it is omnipotent: all political forms are open to its choice. Second, it wholly fills time and space: it is equally present at every moment of the nation's life and in every location within the nation's borders. Third, we know it only by its product. We do not first become aware of the popular sovereign and then ask what it has accomplished. We know that it must exist, because we perceive the state as an expression of its will. We deduce the fact of the subject from the experience of its created product. Finally, we cannot be aware of this sovereign without experiencing it as a normative claim that presents itself as an assertion of identity. We understand ourselves as a part, and as a product, of this sovereign. In it, we see ourselves.[74]

Can there be a modern nation-state without a revolutionary tradition of action by the popular sovereign? Obviously, states do find themselves with diverse national narratives, and one should not impose the norms of our own tradition on the self-perception of others. Yet there is reason to believe that absent the narrative of popular sovereignty as self-creation, a state is more likely to face a crisis of legitimacy. That crisis can take the form of an exclusionary nationalism: absent the revolutionary narrative, popular sovereignty is more likely to take the form of an antimodernist ethnonationalism. Alternatively, contemporary states may try to avoid both revolution and ethnonationalism by turning to global regimes of law and trade, but these moves are likely to provoke claims of a democracy deficit. Since 1989, Europe has been struggling with both of these problems.

The Formal Cause of the Nation-State: Constitution

To move from efficient to formal cause is to move from revolution to constitution. The formal cause of this state is that order realized in the revolutionary act of popular self-creation. The constitution expresses the principles of order that give the state its identity, distinguishing it

---

[74] The possibility of constitutional amendment presents some of the same conundrums as post-Creation intervention by God. Ultimately, these are metaphysical problems about the relationship of law and freedom. In American constitutional culture, they show up as a tension between conceiving of amendment as a possibility for reform and correction or as the institutionalization of the further possibility of revolution. See Kahn, *Reign of Law* 63–64 (on amendment as reform, not revolution).

from what other popular sovereigns have done or might do. Without a constitutional moment, the revolutionary act of popular sovereignty could only destroy the old order. That, however, would not be seen as an act of popular sovereignty at all, but perhaps that of a mob.

The constitution may begin as a document or formal plan, in the same way that a blueprint may provide the formal order for the construction of a building. Just as the blueprint provides the unity of the construction, the constitution holds the diverse parts of the state in a single, unified project. A state that operates under the rule of men, not law, has no unity over time; it is as various as the interests of those who come to rule. It may have no unity over space, dividing into local spheres of influence. Conversely, constitutionalism always suggests unity within diversity. For this reason, constitutional inquiry often becomes a theory about the unity of the legal order, that is, a search for the grand principle that explains the whole.[75] More concretely, this idea of unity in diversity takes the form of the central constitutional doctrines of separation of powers and federalism.

To emphasize constitutionalism and the rule of law is not to make a normative claim for a particular form of political organization.[76] The content of law varies dramatically across political borders, as well as across time. A parliamentary order is no less a matter of law than a presidential order; a common law order no less than a civil law system. Alone, the concept of formal cause does not tell us anything about membership in the political community—does it include women and minorities?—nor does it tell us anything about the content of claims of legal right. Both of these have changed substantially in the course of American history. Yet already in 1803, Chief Justice Marshall was able to describe the American political order as "a government of laws, and not of men."[77] The limits on the political order imposed by the idea of a formal cause are not a function of the idea of law alone. They are a function of surrounding beliefs, of where and how we are prepared to see that order.

[75] See, e.g., A. Amar, *Intratextualism* 112 *Harv. L. Rev.* 747 (1999); J. Ely, *Democracy and Distrust* (1980); L. Tribe, *American Constitutional Law* 1–2 (1988).

[76] Compare L. Fuller, *The Morality of Law* (1964).

[77] See *Marbury v. Madison*, 5 U.S. (1 Cranch) 137, 163 (1803).

The point of the identification of constitution and formal cause is to make clear that the modern state is always a project of theory, as well as of practice. Beliefs about the best order of the state will fuel a debate about the appropriate character of law within the state. The modern state has, accordingly, invited a continuing argument in political theory about the appropriate order of law. Conceived as a project of self-construction, there is literally no way to stop debate over the question, what should we be? This question inevitably connects the political and the moral orders. Just here, we find the powerful connection between liberalism—the dominant form of contemporary moral theory—and modern constitutionalism. The content of the rule of law gives the polity its formal identity.

A formal cause has an ambiguous status: as formal, it may be considered abstractly, but as a cause it has no existence apart from its material embodiment. We cannot search for the formal cause of the state in some abstract ideal of justice, some divine plan, or some natural order. Instead, we must look to the way in which the state is organized, the way in which it maintains its own institutions and relationships between rulers and ruled. In this respect, the nation-state is more organic than artificial: we cannot separate the form from that of which it is the form.[78] Citizens do not seek the plan of the state in some external source; they too must study its law. This does not mean that abstract considerations of justice are irrelevant. We appeal to justice to criticize law, to work toward the reform of law and, at times, to decide among possible interpretations of law. We also recognize, however, that a claim that a law is not just is not the same as a claim that a proposition is not law.[79]

The contrast of perspectives of efficient and formal causes is found behind many of the debates about the nature of law. An account that

[78] There is an inevitable movement in constitutional history from a period in which a constitution is conceived as a product of art to one in which it is understood on the model of an organism. This is the move from making a constitution to maintaining one. See Kahn, *Legitimacy and History* 32–64.

[79] Some legal systems may include a moral norm of justice as a positive legal standard. See J. Coleman, "Negative and Positive Positivism," reprinted in *Ronald Dworkin and Contemporary Jurisprudence* 28 (M. Cohen, ed., 1983); J. Coleman & B. Leiter, "Legal Positivism," in *A Companion to the Philosophy of Law and Legal Theory* 241 (D. Patterson, ed., 1996).

focuses on efficient causes will tend to present arguments about the legitimacy of law that rely on an account of origins, that is, on "pedigree." On this view, a legal system is legitimate when it is the product of the people's consent. An account focusing on formal causes will offer a justification of the legal order based not on consent, but on the rationally compelling character of law's claim to justice. Popular consent may be necessary, but it is not a sufficient condition of the normative claim of law. For that, the people must act in a rational and just manner. An account of efficient causes alone will not, for example, deal with the problem of majority tyranny. Neither will without reason, nor reason without will, can account for the modern nation-state. Reason and will work together as formal and efficient cause in the state's self-understanding, and as arguments of justification and legitimacy for legal authority.

We bring this double-approach—appealing to both efficient and formal causes—not just to the whole of the constitutional order that is the nation-state, but to every particular legal regulation as well. We can always explain why something is law by pointing to the institutions responsible for its production. Hart's "rule of recognition," for example, arises largely out of this general concern with efficient causes.[80] In the modern state, the efficient causes of legal rules are nothing apart from the state understood as a self-governing set of institutions. We speak of law as a product of congressional or parliamentary action—or perhaps the action of courts—but not as the product of lobbying by special interests. When we do speak of lobbying, we are standing outside of the autonomous operation of the constitutional-legal system. We might do so as political theorists or as political activists. From within, the state appears to create and maintain its own order.

Legal rules do not come from nowhere. We read in every legal regulation a narrative of the state's self-creation. Even a just rule that has not been produced by this particular set of efficient causes is not law. The state continually creates and maintains itself by creating law. Of course, the capacity of these institutions to express the popular will may be questioned; they may be criticized for their representational

[80] See H.L.A. Hart, *The Concept of Law* 92–93 (1961).

failures. But such criticism simply asks whether the institutions realize their own internal norms.

Laws, however, are not contracts. Laws are not only legitimated by an account of their origins, they are also justified. Justification is not a matter of pedigree, but of reasonableness. Law always appears as an effort to bring reason to an otherwise unreasonable world. To interpret the law, to understand its character and reach, we assume that it expresses a rational policy: irrationality is ruled out in advance.[81] Accordingly, we imagine every law as the product of an ideal legislative process in which the participants acted on the basis of their best understanding of the demands of reason. A particularized history is replaced by universal reason.[82] This is reading the law through its formal cause.

The Material Cause of the Nation-State: The Citizen's Body

The material cause of the modern nation-state is the citizenry considered as the bearers of popular sovereignty. The popular sovereign has a material existence only in the bodies of the citizens. Modern states do not attach themselves to a natural geography, although all have a geography. Nor do they attach to prepolitical organizations of family or other corporate forms. The unit of membership is the individual. Even in a federal state, the national political order is not simply a coalition of subparts. If it is, we have a federation, not a single nation-state.

The modern nation-state attaches directly to the individual who understands herself as a citizen.[83] This is not the private individual who

---

[81] Thus the minimum-rationality test of constitutional law. *Williamson v. Lee Optical of Oklahoma* 348 U.S. 483 (1955); see also R. Unger, *What Should Legal Analysis Become?* 36–37 (1996) (on rationalizing legal analysis).

[82] See, e.g., J. Thayer, "The Origins and Scope of the American Doctrine of Constitutional Law," in *Legal Essays* 1 [1908] (1972) (on the ideal legislature); Unger, *Legal Analysis* 72. ("Rightwing Hegelianism is . . . the secret philosophy of history of the rationalizing legal analyst.")

[83] In U.S. history this is the message of *McCulloch v. Maryland*, 17 U.S. 316 (1819), and numerous federalism cases. It is why it is constitutionally easier for the federal government directly to regulate the behavior of individuals than to try to regulate that behavior through directions to the state governments. See *Printz v. United States*, 521 U.S. 898 (1997).

chooses to be a member of the polity, already having a substantive individual identity. It is, rather, the individual who has no cognizable character prior to membership in the polity.[84] A material cause has no identity apart from its formation; it is pure potential. From the perspective of modern politics, the citizen apart from the state is nothing at all. She has no existence apart from the distinctive shape of the political order. The stateless person lacks something essential to her very identity: a political life. One mark of the emergence of a distinctly contemporary conception of the international rule of law is the shift in the characteristic paradigm of the individual: no longer the citizen, but the refugee. Under traditional international law, to injure a citizen was to offend the rights of his or her state. An international legal norm that takes its point of departure from the stateless refugee can appear to the nation-state as pure moral demand, as mere aspiration that makes little contact with political reality.[85]

While in liberal theory the idea of the private precedes the public, in the modern state the private is a function of the public. Citizens may have rights to privacy, but they have them as a function of law. Claims to a private self beyond or apart from the law are simply noncognizable from within the polity. In every direction we look, law is there. A liberal state restrains its exercise of power in order to leave room for the private. It nevertheless reserves the power to wholly absorb the private: property can be appropriated, as can life itself when the political circumstances require it.

A nation-state comes into existence when there is a popular sovereign that expresses itself by imposing a formal order on itself and there is no popular sovereign until it achieves a material existence in and through individual citizens. Unless conceived as a material first principle, the popular sovereign is always caught in logical paradoxes of inclusion and exclusion.[86] Those affected by state action, as well as

---

[84] Interestingly, the Fourteenth Amendment attaches citizenship to "[a]ll persons born or naturalized in the United States." U.S. Const. Amendment XIV, § 1.

[85] Contemporary American responses have been to shift the geographical locus of interaction with the refugee to territory outside of the United States proper. The nebulous identity of the refugee is matched now by the indeterminate status of law in these "stateless" geographic regions. See *Sale v. Haitian Centers Council, Inc.*, 509 U.S. 155 (1993).

[86] See L. Brilmayer, *Justifying International Acts* (1989).

those with a substantial interest in that action, always include both more and less than those formally recognized as citizens. There is no reasoning to the boundary between those within and without the state; there is only the fact of the existence of the popular sovereign as borne in the bodies of individuals who conceive of themselves as citizens. In our secular faith, we affirm an identity with all of those who sacrificed themselves for the conception and maintenance of the nation, as well as with all who will take up this burden in the future. We are all a part of, and constitutive of, that organic body that is the mystical corpus of the state. We know who we are as subjects of a political community that exists in an imaginative space beyond the universalism of reason and the particularity of interest. This political faith exceeds the capacity of reason to explain or to justify. It is, nevertheless, at the foundation of a national project that includes the idea of self-government under the liberal rule of law.

If citizens refuse to see themselves as the material bearers of the popular sovereign, then the nation-state can quickly become a mere abstraction. Formally, it may continue, but its political life ceases for its population. We saw this happen in the collapse of the Soviet Union and its satellite states after 1989. Without individuals willing to invest themselves with the meaning of the existing state, those states simply had no power to sustain themselves. Citizens came to understand themselves as members of new popular sovereigns, in some instances hollowed out from within the existing states. In the modern nation-state, geography follows popular sovereignty. The material reality of the state is not its geographic reach, but the bodies of its citizens. This does not mean that modern states are uninterested in territorial claims. These claims are often inseparable from the claims of identity of the people who live there. A claim to land, without such a link, appears anachronistic—a remnant of an earlier understanding of territoriality.

Since the French Revolution, the preferred term of individual identity has been "citizen." To be a citizen is to recognize the coincidence of self and state. The boundaries of the modern nation-state have been constituted by the willingness of individuals to take on this set of political meanings as their own. This idea of materiality supports both inclusion and exclusion. On the one hand, the modern state has remained particularly open to immigration, since ethnicity is not itself a condition of the material cause. On the other hand, the same idea of self-construction has made the state particularly wary of the possibility of admitting immigrants who were not thought to be capable of taking on this material identity. This produced the American pattern of openness linked to exceptions, the largest of which was, of course, the black slave population.[87]

The constitutive character of citizenship as a material cause is not fully captured by either the idea of consent or that of birth. The totalizing character of a citizenship is fully revealed only in the willingness of the citizen to sacrifice for the state. The modern nation-state makes a potential claim on the life of every citizen. All understand that political identity can be a matter of life or death. In this sense, every citizen is a potential subject of conscription, despite the fact that formal conscription law may be limited to those of a certain age or gender. The universal claim of the nation-state is directly expressed in the policy of mutual assured destruction—the entire nation is deployed as a potential target. Nuclear policy is not exceptional: The history of twentieth-century warfare demonstrates the quick capacity of the nation at war to devote all of its resources to that endeavor, as well as the easy transgression of any international legal rule protecting noncombatants.

The nation-state is the sole source of its own existence and it exists only as a meaning borne by citizens willing to invest their bodies in its continued existence as an order of law. In the act of sacrifice, the body is understood as wholly in-formed by the idea of the state. The extravagant character of American consumerism may have misled many into thinking that ours is no longer a sacrificial political culture. The reactions to September 11, however, suggest that this is not so. September 11 itself stands for the risk of life that attaches directly to political identity. The victims were targeted for no reason particular to themselves apart from that identity.[88]

The power of the nation-state rests, in part, on the willingness of individuals to understand themselves as citizens, to take up as their own self-identity that of the state. Seeing themselves as citizens, individuals

---

[87] A direct expression of this idea of the political immateriality of the black population was *Dred Scott v. Sandford*, 60 U.S. 393 (1856).

[88] Of course, the victims included many non-Americans. In part, this was collateral damage—the targets were symbolic of American power. In part, however, it was a

have shown themselves willing to devote themselves completely to the continued existence of the state. Indeed, there was a glorification of war throughout the nineteenth and twentieth centuries as the moment at which the ordinary person could overcome the limits of his own particularity. The act of sacrifice remained what it has always been: a taking on, in one's own body, of a meaning that informs and sustains a larger community.

The modern nation-state has shown itself to be an extremely effective instrument of sacrifice. It has been able to mobilize its population to make sacrifices in order to sustain the state's own historical existence. In this sense, the nation-state stepped into the place of religious belief, offering the individual the hope of transcending the limits of his or her own finitude. Modernity has been an age of political faith even more destructive than the age of religious faith that preceded it.

The modern American has shown himself willing to sacrifice for the Constitution. He has understood the modern battle as a test of whether a state "dedicated to a proposition" can survive. Modern war has quite literally been a test of the national will. We know that will only as it takes a formal shape—the rule of law—and achieves a material embodiment in the citizen. Thus war has been a test fought out in the very real bodies of its citizens. War has been the act of sacrifice for law and a means by which law has continued its historical existence. War casts on the microdrama of the individual the entire drama of the state.

The Final Cause of the Nation-State: Constitutionalism without End

The final cause of the modern nation-state is nothing more than the perpetuation of the state's own existence. The state is not trying to achieve any end apart from the realization of its own existence. It is a means to no other end than its own continued existence. Its continued existence is not one end among others; it is that end for which all others can be sacrificed.

---

matter of targeting the West more generally. This suggests a shift in the character of contemporary political identity, which I discuss in the conclusion.

Every modern state claims to realize a just order. Nevertheless, this justice is not an end that exists apart from the state itself. The state is not a transitional moment in a move toward something else, whether a vision of abstract justice or economic well-being. The modern nation-state could not subordinate itself to another state it believed to be more just, or to one it believed to promise greater wealth. If contemporary states look to a global order for both justice and well-being, there has been a fundamental transformation of the nature of the state, of the meaning of the political, and of the character of citizenship. This would no longer be a politics of popular sovereignty, although it might indeed be more just.

The modern nation-state has understood itself as a temporal project without limit. Its history is simply to continue without end. Of course, states do end, but not on their own terms. They do not "use themselves up"; they are a limitless resource. The termination of the state is not necessarily signaled in defeat by external forces—a state can exist in a privative mode if it continues to inform citizen self-identity. We know what it means to be an "occupied state." States end when the idea of the state fails in the imagination of the citizen.

Self-defense is a necessary element of the nation-state, because the state recognizes no value higher than its own continued existence. This is the point at which war and domestic law intersect in the modern period. War is the defense of the rule of law because law is the state understood as an order of meaning. Through war, the state expresses the necessity of its own existence. This is not a necessity external to the state, but one form of the principle of political autonomy characteristic of the modern nation-state. The nation-state knows only itself; it knows that it must continue without end.

An age of people's republics needs an international law of war much more than the age of premodern states. There are no principles of restraint on the use of force that are implicit in the state that understands itself as the expression of popular sovereignty under the rule of law. A state that understands itself as an expression of a divine or a natural order can look to meanings outside of itself to limit its actions. A state based on family or class can subordinate the political to the continuing interests of those prepolitical elements of the civil order.

But the state under law knows only itself—without end and without limit. The autonomy of the political leaves no way in which to assign a measurable value to those outside of the state. Those who are not allies are enemies or potential enemies.[89]

The turn toward international legal regulation of war at the beginning of the last century rested in substantial part on the awareness of this lack of internal limits. Recognizing that the modern state was capable of waging war without limits, some limits were sought.[90] International law was the perfect vehicle for expressing this concern precisely because of its ambiguous authority: a rule of international law can express a concern without enforcing a commitment. Thus, the articulation of rules to limit warfare was always far more successful than actual efforts to disarm.[91] It is one thing, for example, to say that submarine warfare is illegal and quite another to limit the size of the navy. The twentieth century was marked by the simultaneous expansion of international law regulating the use of force and of war itself. Indeed, this reciprocal relationship between law and war—more law and more war—is the great puzzle for international legal scholarship.

The autonomy of the political characteristic of the modern nation-state was carried to its logical end point with the development of nuclear weapons and the policy of deterrence based upon mutual assured destruction. This policy has been the lived background condition of several generations of citizens in modern Western nation-states, even as they have argued about liberal values and the limits of the state. There has been a puzzling conjunction of liberal beliefs with an experience of politics as a source of ultimate meaning, and thus of ultimate threat. The state expresses a willingness to destroy not only itself in

[89] President Bush has recently invoked this theme in warning states that they must take sides in the "war on terrorism."

[90] See, e.g., Convention with Respect to the Laws and Customs of War on Land, July 29, 1859; Convention Respecting the Laws and Customs of War on Land, Oct. 18, 1907.

[91] See, e.g., International Treaty for the Limitation and Reduction of Naval Armaments, Apr. 22, 1930, 112 L.N.T.S. 65, 88; U.N. Charter Art. 26. ("In order to promote the establishment and maintenance of international peace . . . with the least diversion for armaments of the world's . . . resources, the Security Council shall [submit plans] . . . for the regulation of armaments.")

its full material extension—all citizens—but to end history itself: if not this state as a particular political formation, then nothing at all. This is just the logic of the modern nation-state. If the nation-state cannot continue, then there is no reason for history to continue. There is not some higher end, whether humanity or the planet. In every dimension—all four causes—the nation-state could see only itself. Our liberalism operates within, not apart from, the autonomy of the political. Its locus is in the domain of formal cause—constitutions and the rule of law. It is misunderstood if seen as the sole perspective from which to judge political meanings.

Citizenship as a willingness to respond to the demand for sacrifice for the continued existence of the state is not the privilege of an elite, or even the male privilege of the battlefield. It is an ultimate meaning of life for each individual within the nation-state. An autonomous order of meaning is always comprehensive, that is, it offers a point of reference from which all else can gain meaning, including family, church, and nature. From the political perspective, these are objects and activities within the state, not a private order apart from the state. This is not the only perspective from which we can view our commitments and values. We can judge the political from the perspective of the moral; we can judge both from the perspective of romantic love. In this competition of incommensurable perspectives, the political has been particularly successful in Western experience, but it has never been without challenge.

Law and war have not been antithetical forces, but common expressions of the modern political culture of the sovereign nation-state. That state writes itself into existence by drafting a constitution. It expresses the historical permanence of that law by defending it at all costs. It demonstrates its own ultimate significance in the life of the individual citizen through the act of sacrifice that war entails. The sovereign people's state applies these principles without limit. All citizens become appropriate subjects of sacrifice and all history becomes coterminous with the continuation of the state. The dominance of war in the modern era has been a measure of just how seriously we have taken our politics—even a liberal politics. It has had an ultimate significance measured by the ultimate sacrifice of millions.

CONCLUSION: LIBERALISM, THE NATION-STATE, AND INTERNATIONAL LAW

We need all of these elements to understand the modern nation-state—and the United States is paradigmatically that modern nation-state. Together they constitute the autonomy of the political, which is a complete system of meaning that is its own source and end. This autonomy makes the state an ultimate value from the perspective of the citizen. It is a normative order closed in upon itself in the same way that a religious order does not rest on yet some higher end or justification. Not even the well-being of individuals serves as such a higher end. Instrumental justifications of the political that rely on well-being will always fail at the moment of conscription. Yet, without the potential of a demand for sacrifice, we are not speaking of modern politics at all. What modern politics demanded of us has always been too much and too terrible to find its reason elsewhere.

This is the political matrix within which our liberalism operates. Liberalism is the morality of the nation-state, which is itself an illiberal structure of ultimate value.[92] Modern politics has lived within the same conundrum that has characterized theological speculation in the West for thousands of years: is the source of value of the Ten Commandments the fact that they were spoken by God or were they spoken by God because they were right? If we think liberalism is spoken because it is right, then we may think we can do away with the sovereign voice, and even with the particularity of the state. Liberalism becomes a program seeking to transcend the political conditions of its own existence. This is the contemporary phenomenon of globalization of a liberal order of law. It is law without politics.

Yet we can no more adopt half of the synthetic proposition that defines the political order of law—the popular sovereign speaks a liberal order of law into existence—than the religious faithful could adopt half of the synthetic proposition of their belief. That God spoke was not a matter of indifference to the faithful. What God said was important, but never more important than that he said it. The question

---

[92] "The essence of the contradiction inherent in patriotism is that one's country is something limited whose demands are unlimited." S. Weil, *The Need for Roots* (A. Wills, trans., 1955), quoted in Walzer, *Obligations* 87.

politics answers is not only, what should we do? but, who are we? If we are not made in God's image, if we are not a part of the popular sovereign, we must be something else. The liberal would say we are reason struggling to control interest. I have tried to show that we are always more than that. We are word become flesh; we are loving and political beings.

The political form of this conundrum of source and content—of efficient and formal causes—has had the virtue of opening political order to political theory. By raising the question of what it is the sovereign says, the political order became a field of construction within which arguments of political science have had a role. The state can always be made a better expression of itself. It is never out of place to raise questions of the adequacy of representative institutions, to ask about the justification of criminal law, or to challenge the character of wealth-distribution. We construct our own political order, and the justifications must convince us. This is true not just at the limits—that is, moments of revolution—but also in the ever-present question of reform. Noting the power of a politics of sacrifice does not make us mindless automatons of state authority.

The legal order of the nation-state appears as an "experimental" order open to endless reform. But this openness to reform should not be mistaken for a lack of commitment to its substance at any moment. Politics is an endless project, but the state is simultaneously an ultimate value to be defended at any cost. Only a politics of ultimate meanings could see reason in the practice of mutual assured destruction. This is no longer the morality of liberalism, but the threat of a political sovereign that has become a vengeful God. If we believe in such a God, we cannot say that this is a vice of the system of belief. Rather, it is simply the way the world is. Our politics appears to us as simply the way the world is: not in the sense that we cannot reform its content, but in the sense that we find ourselves with a political identity.

Those who preach law as an answer to state violence fail to recognize the extent to which the state under law has been more, not less, willing to wage war without limits than were its predecessors. From a political point of view, there is no point at which the modern nation-state can admit that defeat is a more reasonable choice than further sacrifice. Of course, individuals may come to doubt the ultimate value of the political; they may abandon their beliefs, individually or collectively. Nor does this mean that every deployment of force must be pursued to a successful conclusion; it is not the case that the life of the nation is at issue in every such deployment. Any government policy, including a military action, can be seen as merely a mistake, having little to do with projection or protection of the popular sovereign. For many, if not most Americans, Vietnam came to be seen as such a mistake. Just as any particular law can be seen as mistaken, so too can any particular appeal to force.[93] While actions by the popular sovereign, as Rousseau already saw, are always correct, it hardly follows that all government actions are those of the popular sovereign.[94] The government itself can be resisted as unrepresentative. These claims and counterclaims structure a debate; they do not tell us how any particular debate will come out or how any particular set of decisions will come to be seen historically.

It is this ideological dynamic of sovereignty, rather than technological developments, that explains why international legal limits on the use of force were rarely effective in the modern age. The international law of war was an effort to establish "reasonable" limits, as if we could deliberate about how much force was adequate: enough to accomplish the essential ends of the state, without unnecessary destruction or violence. The central idea in legal regulation of war was the idea of proportionality, a kind of measuring of action and response designed to prevent unnecessary suffering. Yet at the core of the modern nation-state is an idea of infinite value. Nothing can be balanced against the continued life of the state. Proportionality is, therefore, a dysfunctional idea, just as the distinction of combatant from noncombatant has proved dysfunctional.[95] It is useful only in instances in

---

[93] This parallel between a mistake of law and a mistaken recourse to force—both understood as failures of popular sovereignty—fuels the repeated efforts to seek judicial review of the use of force, despite the courts' extreme reluctance to take up this task. See *United States v. Curtiss-Wright Export Corp.*, 299 U.S. 304, 319–22 (1936); R. Schoen, "A Strange Silence: Vietnam and the Supreme Court," 33 *Washburn L.J.* 275 (1994).

[94] See Rousseau, *The Social Contract* 45; see above at 266 on unsuccessful revolution as an empty category.

[95] See above at 275; see also P. Kahn, "Nuclear Weapons and the Rule of Law," 31 *N.Y.U. J. Int'l. L. & Pol.* 349 (1999).

which the limit imposes no burden: if no benefit is gained, or if the same benefit can be gained at lower cost, proportionality can be invoked. Proportionality can only mean "do no more than is necessary to win." If the state is of unlimited value, then there are no limits on the amount of force that can be used to defend it. Nuclear weapons are the end point of a discourse on proportionality for the modern state. An effective rule of proportionality would require a neutral perspective that could view both sides of the conflict as equal. But that perspective is just what the modern nation-state denies.

Until the contemporary development of the legal doctrine of jus cogens, it had been believed that all international law gave way in the extreme instance of self-defense. The Germans called this *kriegsraison;* the English spoke of a doctrine of military necessity.[96] No state had to accept a legal rule that led to its own demise. The emergence of jus cogens norms is the best signal of the beginning of a new era of international law and thus of a new perspective on the nation-state. Such norms necessarily displace the state from a position of ultimate value. A norm that cannot be violated even as a matter of the defense of the state must rest on a value greater than that of the continued existence of the state. Such a norm depends on a transnational perspective not available within a system of sovereign nation-states. There were simply no political resources in that system by which we could get beyond the state.

The two proposed sources of jus cogens norms are an idea of the ultimate moral value of the prepolitical individual and of an apolitical nature. A state has value, on this view, just to the degree that it furthers the value of individual human dignity and/or preserves the natural environmental order.[97] The state becomes a means to ends that are defined quite apart from, and prior to, politics. The actual extent to which such transnational supernorms operate in contemporary inter-

[96] See C. Jochnick and R. Normand, "The Legitimation of Violence: A Critical History of the Laws of War," 35 *Harv. Int'l. L.J.* 49, 63 (1994); B. Carnahan, "Lincoln, Lieber and the Laws of War: The Origins and Limits of the Principle of Military Necessity," 92 *Am. J. Int'l. L.* 213 (1998).

[97] As is likely to become increasingly clear over the next generation, these norms are in substantial tension—one cannot celebrate equally the individual subject as agent and the order of nature. See P. Singer, *Animal Liberation* (1975) and *Practical Ethics* (1997).

national law, however, remains controversial—at least once we look beyond the self-serving statements of the contemporary proponents of international law. To the classic international lawyer, who believed that state consent is the sole ground of all international legal norms, the idea of jus cogens makes little sense, just because it suggests a ground of law beyond the consenting agent.[98] That a state would agree to conditions of international law that would threaten its own survival was a possibility ruled out in advance.[99]

Contemporary international-law scholars tend to take up the perspective of formal causes, arguing that the issue is not the origin of the rule, but the rationality of the rule.[100] If states agree to recognize human rights, the justification of such a norm is a principle of the dignity of the individual. If they agree to protect the environment, the justification is a concept of a stewardship or the preservation of nature for future generations. Viewed from such a "principled" perspective, there is no reason to give priority to the state. To do so confuses origins with meaning. It is as if one limited the meaning of a mathematical equation to those meanings present to the mind of its discoverer. There are reasons inherent in the law that we find operative at any moment. The role of the scholar is to make clear the principles that have informed the development of the law and to demonstrate their impli-

---

[98] The classic statement of this view is that of P. Weil, "Towards Relative Normativity in International Law?," 77 *Am. J. Int'l. L.* 413 (1983).

[99] Modern examples of this debate go back at least to the Kellogg-Briand Pact; they surface again in the debate over the place of self defense under Article 51 of the United Nations Charter. Appealing to a model of efficient causes, the traditionalists argue that a promise not to use force must be limited by a doctrine of necessity as measured by the state's own political perspective. The state alone can set the parameters of its vital interests. See P. Kahn, "From Nuremberg to the Hague: The United States Position in *Nicaragua v. United States* and the Development of International Law," 12 *Yale J. Int'l. L.* 1 (1987).

[100] Formal sources doctrine continues to recognize the priority of consent in the doctrine of the "persistent objector." A state may not be compelled to give agreement to a norm, no matter how many other states do or how compelling other states find the norm. The relative ranking of priorities is a matter ultimately for the state itself to decide. But see T. Stein, "The Approach of the Different Drummer: The Principle of the Persistent Objector in International Law," 26 *Harv. Int'l. L.J.* 457, 459 (1985) (persistent objector status has rarely been invoked).

cations. Law, thereby, overcomes the limits of its own originating sources. Those who gave consent may have had only the vaguest idea of the full reach of the principles to which they gave consent. Their consent can, accordingly, come back to haunt them.

The international-law judge or scholar who adopts this perspective can easily speak of norms of international law that subordinate state interests. Indeed, the analytic danger is now just the opposite of that which arises from the perspective of efficient causes. Adopting the viewpoint of formal causes, every norm can expand into a universal norm of compelling force. Jus cogens becomes a category that threatens to encompass every norm of international law. It appears as either an empty set or a set of indefinite expansion.

A new generation of international lawyers, academics, and transnational activists would abandon state sovereignty and its vision of the irreducible quality of the political. In its place, they would put human rights and global markets. This cosmopolitanism of rights is the contemporary version of the traditional liberal misunderstanding of the political. The liberal sees the individual—through the social contract—as the efficient cause of the state; he fails to see the origin of the state in the transgenerational, collective actor that is the popular sovereign. He sees the final cause of the state as only individual well-being, the satisfactions individuals can obtain before death. He does not see the endurance of the nation-state as an end in itself. He sees the material cause of the state in property—the liberal state is an organization of ownership. He does not see the instantiation of the popular sovereign in the body of the citizen. The autonomy of the political for the liberal is reduced to the argument over formal causes. Here, he says that the rule of law should be guided by public reasons, which all reasonable citizens should accept. Because liberal politics only has a determinate content at the level of formal causes, it moves effortlessly to a cosmopolitan claim: universal rules of law for reasonable people everywhere.

But the argument over formal causes is not the politics of nation-states. Although not without relevance to that politics, it is hardly the source of political identity. Formal causes alone are wholly inadequate to explain the core political phenomena of distinguishing citizen from alien and of imagining the possibility of sacrifice for the state. Not surprisingly, the development of a rights-based international law has made little contact with much of the world. This is the problem not just on the killing fields of the former Yugoslavia; it is the problem in the United States as well. Never in history has a whole population been so exposed to the threat of political sacrifice as we have been for the last half century. Even the end of the Cold War has not substantially changed this, as we see with the new threat of terrorist use of weapons of mass destruction. This is the essence of democratization of the experience of the political. It may also be completely immoral. This is just the point. Political meanings are not moral meanings. They are their own ultimate values.

We will know that we are entering a new era when we have decommissioned the last of our nuclear weapons. We will not do so until we no longer can imagine ourselves as the enemy of a potentially threatening political force. We still cultivate as a political matter the category of "the enemy." We maintain a defense establishment, not because we are seriously engaged in the contemporary phenomenon of humanitarian intervention, but because we believe that we face potential enemies, an "axis of evil."

The United States has greeted many of the recent developments in international law with a substantial degree of skepticism. It has declined to participate in many; it has halfheartedly acknowledged some.[101] It is likely to believe that behind the articulation of the values of international law is a political agenda: potential adversaries using law to gain a tactical advantage against the United States. These political perceptions are not going to be legislated out of existence at a global conference called by the United Nations.

Yet even in the United States, recent political life may have been less a source of identity and ultimate meanings than it was in the past. Sacrifice seemed very far removed from our ordinary understanding of ourselves. Many thought of politics as the practice of lobbying by special interest groups. We no longer lived with the draft. We created

---

[101] Consider the Bush administration's rejection of the Kyoto Accords and of the proposed International Criminal Court, as well as its termination of the ABM Treaty, and its refusal to extend the enforcement regime of the Convention on Biological Weapons.

specialists in military affairs, just as we created police and firemen. We did not imagine our armies defending us so much as carrying out moral missions to help others. The nation seemed secure from threats, and therefore it did not seem to need to threaten others. On September 11, 2001, we saw that that was hardly the whole story. The country quickly and easily fell back into a political register of friends and enemies, of sacrifice and killing, of ultimate values made real in the bodies of citizens.

The moralists among us—and we are all moralists on occasion—will always be dismayed by the tenacity of politics. That tenacity can only be explained on its own terms. I have tried to explain this quality by developing the ideas of political autonomy and ultimate values. That account does not offer a justification for our political belief. Indeed, it denies the possibility of such a justification. On that issue, all that can be said is that it is a part of the human condition to read the self as bearing a meaning, that the fear of death and the effort to find satisfactions before death are not an adequate imaginative field. We construct meaning on an erotic field because this meaning-giving function of the imagination is the source and locus of our own identity. This is an identity we share with others because we are mutually and reciprocally engaged in its construction. It is not consent but eros that links us to the polity and to each other. We do not decide that it should be this way. We are already a product of the meanings we create.

There has operated through much of American political life an unexpressed understanding that we do indeed practice a religion of patriotic faith. The displacement of religions of faith by a religion of politics represented a shift in the locus of the ultimate from the eternal to the historical. No longer seeking to escape time through a divine presence, we instead confront time through the construction of history. Modern politics has been the investment of history with ultimate value. The nation-state has been the vehicle for the construction of meaning in time, even as it represented itself as an organization of space. From within the nation-state, history has a beginning—revolution—but no end. That may be as close to the eternal as modern man can come.

Reason does not construct history, politics does. Such constructions are always the work of an embodied imagination that is neither reason nor interest. Too much reason will leave us without what we need most: a sense that we are an idea become flesh, that this dying body can be the vehicle for an enduring idea.[102] When we read ourselves in this way, we create the state and we sustain history. When we deny others their own readings, even when we do so in the name of reason as a part of the great project of liberalism, we fail to recognize who they are. We may still treat them as perfect, rational agents. Real people, however, do not live by reason, but by the faith that fuels the imagination.

We can never be comfortable with our own political life. Politics creates friends and enemies; it lives with the potential of sacrifice and killing. Reason will always seek to moralize politics and thus to make life safe under a regime of rights. Death appears as the worst of fates to reason, because reason has no source of individualization other than interest. To the desiring body, death is pure negation. For those of faith, it is not death but meaninglessness that is the danger. If we are to be sympathetic to the politics of others, we must be so in the name of politics: every political form, including our own, will fail the test of reason and morality.

Finally, a word of caution. I have argued that only an appreciation for the autonomy of the political can ground an understanding of what is at stake for us in our liberal *politics*. Liberalism itself has far too narrow an understanding of the context within which it operates. To say that politics has been an autonomous system of meaning is not, however, to say that it is the only source of meaning that we have. It is not even to say that every political association must take up the same meanings as those that characterized the modern nation-state. The structures of our experience are historical, not essential; they are contingent, not universal.

We find ourselves within a number of incommensurable symbolic worlds of meaning, each of which is autonomous and complete in the same sense that political meanings have been. We are not bound to political meanings as if they were our natural habitat. We can stand apart and locate meaning in a nonpolitical domain—for instance, family, religion, science, aesthetics. Because each is equally autonomous

---

[102] See P. Berger, *The Sacred Canopy* 22 (1967).

and comprehensive, each will subordinate political relationships to other values. There is no single ordering, no truth of the self. We are as capable of being revolted as enthralled by our politics. Families do not always willingly give up their children for the ends of the state. With the claim of great meaning comes the possibility that it will be judged great evil.

CONCLUSION

■ ■ ■ ■

THE FUTURE OF THE NATION-STATE

In the last chapter, I described the autonomy of the political in the American nation-state as a structure of meaning that bridges the sacrificial and the representational. The sacrificial character of politics is carried forward in our idea of the popular sovereign as a single actor, of which every citizen is a part: the lingering mystical corpus of the state. The representational character of our politics is located in the Constitution as the rule of law. Aristotle's scheme of four causes provided a means of analyzing the character of a politics of ultimate value that is simultaneously the rule of law. That same analysis suggests the lines of possible fracture. If any one of the four causes of political autonomy gives way, the modern nation-state as a structure of meaning may collapse. Arguably, all of these lines of fracture are operating today.

If citizens see the state as a means to nonpolitical ends, or if they do not see themselves as the material embodiment of the sovereign, then the sacrificial dimension is not likely to survive. If they see the efficient cause of the political order as markets, geography, or global forces beyond the control of deliberative choice, they will not see the state as the autonomous source of its own construction. If they do not understand its formal character as an expression of their own ideal of political reason, then they may see no single, formal order at all. A political order without unity is not one with which the citizen can identify.[1] These changes are all familiar elements of contemporary accounts of the democratic polity.

---

[1] See R. Dworkin, *Law's Empire* 189. ("[A] citizen cannot treat himself as the author of a collection of laws that are inconsistent in principle.")

Contemporary politics is often described as a site of competition between special interest groups. Citizens understand their own relationship to the state to be mediated through factions that express their specific economic, moral, or ethnic interests. They do not understand themselves as citizens first of all, but see themselves as having multiple interests extending across markets, families, religions, ethnicities, and other social formations. Each of these can define an interest group that seeks to advance an "agenda" through influencing the decisions of political representatives and institutions. Once the state is no longer seen as an end in itself, the citizen's self-understanding of his or her relationship to the political will be mediated through nonpolitical conceptions of self-interest. Thus, ultimate political meanings give way to a multiplicity of particular interests. Many of those interests are the same as those advanced through markets. Politics appears, in substantial part, as an alternative means for accomplishing market ends. No one sacrifices the self for the market. That does not mean that market models cannot be a part, even a substantial part, of an idea of political freedom—especially of the liberal idea of liberty. Something like this surely played a role in the recent velvet revolutions of Eastern Europe. But the market model needs to be connected to an idea of the political to understand what is at stake. To accomplish that, we must look beyond the market as a mechanism of production and distribution.

Markets and market models of interests are one form of stress on the autonomy of the political; expert knowledge is another. If governance is a matter of bureaucratic and administrative expertise, then it is not the expression of a form of life that can be constitutive of citizen identity. The legal order cannot be understood as the product of self-construction by a popular sovereign when the knowledge relevant to political administration is thought to be in the possession of experts. We cannot mutually deliberate about national fiscal policy if we want to run a modern global economy. Individual citizens might have opinions, but opinions—even when they become the collective voice of public opinion—are not a ground for action in this domain. Increasingly, the task of government is to deploy the sciences of administration and management in order to draw upon technical fields of knowledge—for example, environmental science, economics, medical science, engineering—in formulating specific policies. Areas in which opinion is thought to matter are seen as areas that should be returned to market orderings. This depoliticization is not resisted by politicians who portray their own responsibilities as essentially acting as adjuncts to the market.[2] They set their ambitions at little more than maintaining economic growth.

The autonomy of the political, accordingly, is vulnerable to new forms of expertise and new forms of self-understanding. From both directions, there is a kind of reconceptualization of the subject as only the bearer of opinions, no longer the embodiment of an idea of the state. Opinion is linked to interest, and interest to the body. This is a linkage as old as Plato's divided line of Book 6 of the *Republic*. The autonomy of the political cannot survive in a world of opinion. That the autonomy of the political is vulnerable, however, hardly suggests that it is already an anachronism. It is far too early to proclaim the death of politics.

THE POSTPOLITICAL DOMESTIC ORDER

If we have outgrown the autonomy of the political, then perhaps the conditions of a liberal order—a postpolitical order stripped of its attachment to a popular sovereign—are now emerging. Reducing politics to the dimension of formal causes, liberalism asks the question of principles, what principles should determine the basic structure of the legal order? Contemporary liberals seek political prescriptions in an idea of pure speech that never makes contact with the embodied meanings that characterize the politics of the nation-state. If liberalism is the politics of pure representation, then perhaps it is the appropriate political order for an age increasingly characterized by the fluidity of its representational forms. For many, that fluidity is the promise—or the threat—of the Internet.

The political life of the nation-state has always existed in some tension with the experience of an economic life based on private choice

---

[2] A good example of the phenomenon was the Thatcherite revolution in Britain in the 1980s. This accomplished a substantial reorientation of the means of production toward a market order—a reorientation based on claims of economic expertise—but also a substantial depoliticization of British society. See L. Siedentop, *Democracy in Europe* 64–80 (2001); see also J. Habermas, *Legitimation Crisis* 68–72 (T. McCarthy, trans., 1973).

within free markets. Well-functioning markets operate without regard to the character of the subject who is purchasing or producing. The neoclassical market is one of "faceless buyers and sellers, households and firms that grind out . . . rules from their objective functions (utility, profit) [and] meet . . . for an instant to exchange standardized goods at equilibrium prices."[3] Economics can be a quantitative science because the quality of the subject is irrelevant. Indeed, when issues of personal identity enter into considerations of market distribution, we speak of market failures that may require government interventions.[4] In this respect, markets parallel the rule of law. Justice under law also operates without respect to the identity of the subject. We speak of a failure, and seek remedial measures if the outcome of a legal dispute is driven by concern for the character of the parties. This is true even if we have reasons for preferring one party to another as a moral matter: the good do not necessarily win their lawsuits against the bad. Nor do they necessarily win their bidding wars.

We do not ordinarily check the moral character of the agents with whom we pursue market transactions—unless we believe that character will bear on an issue of market performance. If we are concerned about the impact of market transactions on areas of life governed by other norms—for example, environment, health, or global justice— we have those concerns regardless of the particular character of the subject of a market transaction. Character is not a substitute for a concern with pollution. Because of this indifference to character, markets and legal rules tend toward globalization. Similarly, there is a tendency to think of the extension of markets and of the development of the rule of law as mutually supportive aspects of a single process, although there is often debate as to their relative priority in transitional contexts.[5] Within a political perspective, however, we are con-

---

[3] Y. Ben-Porath, "The F-Connection: Families, Friends and Firms and the Organization of Exchange," 6 *Population & Dev. Rev.* 1, 4 (1980).

[4] See, e.g., Title II (prohibiting discrimination in places of public accommodation) and Title VII (prohibiting discrimination in employment) of the Civil Rights Act of 1964.

[5] Compare R. Posner, "Creating a Legal Framework for Economic Development," 13 *World Bank Res. Observer* 1 (1998), and A. Sen, *Development as Freedom* (1999). See also O. Lee Reed, "Law, the Rule of Law, and Property: A Foundation for the Private Market and Business Study," 38 *Am. Bus. L.J.* 441 (2001).

cerned with questions of identity—our own, that of our political leadership, and that of our political rivals. Politics, for this reason, does not tend toward globalization. Or, if it does, it is likely to appear as hegemonic, an empire.

The systemic indifference of the market to the subject's identity appears not only in transactions, but in the self-conception of the subject as market actor. The ideal subject of the market is one who takes an experimental attitude toward the self. This is obvious with respect to production: markets will not work unless individuals are willing to respond to market demands and opportunities. Markets require a fluidity of capital, human and fixed. The producer must maintain a certain distance from his or her capital if the market is to function properly. Indeed, provisions for incorporation, including bankruptcy law, provide legal security for this necessary nonidentification. They allow an individual to have "multiple personalities" in a market, without uniquely identifying with any one of them.

A similar fluidity marks the consumption end of markets. Individuals are to experiment in their spending decisions. Subjects seek to maximize the return on their purchasing power, which means that they must be open to competitive offers. The fluidity of consumer identity implies a reshaping of one's own conception of the self over time. We see this constantly as products unknown at one point become necessities a short while later. Competition may push markets toward a kind of stability as more efficient producers gain market share, but there is a countervailing destabilization as individuals change their understanding of themselves and their needs in response to innovation.

The fluidity of identity in markets, however, has always been conditioned by wealth. At one extreme is the multinational conglomerate that finds itself in diverse areas of production linked only through investment decisions. As corporations come to control more wealth, their identities tend to diffuse. At the other extreme is the individual with minimal resources who is locked into a particular identity—a fixed job, perhaps, and a limited range of consumption choices. The wealthier the person, the more his or her personal life can take an experimental form. The wealthy can celebrate the diversity of identities that their capacity for eclectic consumption—of travel, cuisine, culture, dress, entertainment—makes possible. This class increasingly conceives of itself in global terms, while the poor may increasingly conceive of themselves in local—particularly urban—terms. The idea of a national political identity is under stress from both directions.[6]

For many, the great allure of the Internet is its promise dramatically to mitigate these wealth effects that have previously limited the possibilities for the individual. Whether or not that mitigation is realized by the average user, the promise has had a powerful impact on liberal theorizing about an emerging global order. While wealth is required to create the infrastructure of the Net, on the Net itself experimentation seems costless. That experimentation can extend directly into personal identity. By making possible purely symbolic exchanges on a global and instantaneous basis, a literally free market is created. Individuals can consume and produce anonymously and endlessly; they can selectively enter symbolic exchanges revealing only a part of their identity or they can adopt new identities. The boundaries of self and fiction blur, because the cyberself has no being apart from the symbolic representation of itself.

Authoritarian regimes are concerned about controlling access to the Internet because they fear it will make available information necessary to the construction of a more liberal political order. In liberal states, the politics of the Net presents a quite different problem. The question here is whether the construction of the subject through participation in the Net will undermine the conditions of political identity that have operated since the age of revolutions began two hundred years ago. Popularly, this is represented as an aspect of the contemporary phenomenon of globalization, as if the issue is simply the displacement of state borders through instantaneous worldwide communication. The real question, however, is whether the politics of material instantiation can survive in an age in which personal identity is increasingly thought of as an ephemeral symbolic construction.[7] Can popular sovereignty survive the Net?

In cyberspace, the flesh is stripped from every idea. Free from the body, we would not have politics in anything like the shape we have known it. The Greeks already understood this. In their representation

---

[6] See S. Sassen, *Losing Control? Sovereignty in an Age of Globalization* (1996).

[7] See J. Geuhenno, *The End of the Nation-State* (V. Elliott, trans., 1995).

of the gods, there is much personal rivalry, there is even fluidity of identity, but there is no politics. I have argued that politics—and, more broadly, love—begins when the body stands for something. The vulnerability of the body puts that representation at risk. Politics is an effort to realize and maintain meaning in the face of the mortality of the body. The Net promises to separate itself entirely from instantiated meanings, holding forth a world of pure symbols in which the body can have no presence and thus can make no demands.

The cyberworld promises to achieve a postpolitical world: a world as close to that of the Greek gods as we are likely to attain. In this world, ideas have become information. Information only exists in relationship to other information: the network displaces the body as the locus of material existence.[8] For this reason, cyberspace blurs the distinction between entertainment and work. Life on the Net seems simultaneously both. Information on the Net increasingly takes the appearance of a television format. Accessing the net through AOL, for example, puts one in space that looks and feels like entertainment, regardless of the reason that one may have arrived there.

This entertainment quality extends the fluidity of the market conception of the subject. The cyberself, by blurring the line between work and entertainment, is an even further development along this line of increasing negative freedom. The immediacy and self-contained character of entertainment means that there is no investment of the self in the activity. Today, I may be entertained by one chat room, tomorrow by another. I may happen to be someone who prefers comedy to tragedy, but as long as I see both as forms of entertainment, I would not think that I am doing violence to my self-conception were my tastes to change, any more than if I were, for instance, to suddenly discover that I really enjoy Japanese food. This conception of a free—because uncommitted—self will make not just political meanings difficult to maintain, but any form of meaning that makes a claim upon individual identity.[9]

---

[8] See J. Mnookin, "Virtual(ly) Law: The Emergence of Law in LambdaMoo," 2 *J. Computer-Mediated Comm.* 8 (1996).

[9] See C. Taylor, *The Ethics of Authenticity* 39 (1991) ("[U]nless some options are more significant than others, the very idea of self-choice falls into triviality."); see also A. Bloom, *The Closing of the American Mind* (1987).

The mutually supportive triumphalism of markets and networks sets the conditions for much of contemporary liberalism. There appears to be an endless capacity of the subject for reformation when he or she is nothing but a temporary stopping point within multiple networks. In this idealized future, network and market would merge into a single domain in which subjects have no before that constrains them and no future that will remember them. If networks are our future, so then is liberalism. Yet the fact remains that we die. We must get off the Net at some point. We cannot be everything without risking becoming nothing. If we can be anything without cost, then we may find that nothing at all calls us. A networked age will, therefore, produce a reaction that takes up again the investment of the self—the real, physical self—in some meanings rather than others. At these points, the representational content of meaning will be displaced by the immediacy of instantiation—that is, the coincidence of being and meaning.

In the United States, we have seen the emergence of several forms of meaning that compete with the fluidity of markets and networks, but occupy neither the traditional place of work nor that of politics. First, there has been a substantial turn toward the family, stripped now of a connection to politics. Despite the high incidence of divorce, the familial ideal is being redrawn on ever more romantic lines. Second, there has been a resurgence of religious fundamentalism. Finally, there has been a turn toward multiculturalism. All three take up issues of substantive identity in a postpolitical world.

The romantic family stands in some tension with the loving family that I described in chapter 5. The latter understands the family as a locus for the production of meanings that have a substantial temporal dimensions. The child was the instantiation of an idea: the generation of the child was the birth of history. Family was the source of both public and private life. On this view, the life of the nation is equally the well-being of the familial.

The contemporary ideal of the romantic family has been shorn of temporal extension, but not because, as liberalism would have it, its consensual nature is emphasized. In place of historical presence, we have affixed a norm of romantic love to the ideal of the family. One consequence of this has been an emphasis on the nuclear family. Extended families are an antiquated social form, both in practice and theory.[10] Family now means parents and children. In this new family, children are not taught to maintain a memory of their familial line. Children have themselves become the center of familial meaning. For this reason, nontraditional couples make a powerful claim that they too should be allowed to establish this romantic relationship to the child. We have invested ourselves in an ideal of childhood, finding in it a kind of innocence that is to reflect back upon the meaning of adulthood. This innocence is no longer an empty space to be filled by adult meanings. It is complete in itself, as is every form of the romantic.

The result has been a massive transfer of the romantic to the familial order. The attachment to children is modeled on the attachment between lovers. It is a meaning that is fully embodied, yet without explanation. Innocence is a condition of speechlessness. The child of the romantic family—unlike, for example, Isaac—represents nothing outside of herself. The child's claim upon us is as immediate as Aristophanes' romantic idea of our other half.[11] The relationship of parent to child appears as an ultimate value, against which nothing else can compete. The family becomes an image of an autochthonous social group, in need of no other source of meaning. Its meaning is not translatable. Indeed it is not expressible in any language accessible to others. This is an erotic attachment that needs no justification and supports no explanation. It is a world unto itself.

Of course, the romantic family is no more descriptive of actual families than is the loving family. Both serve as ideal types, as cultural paradigms through which we attempt to understand ourselves. We are disturbed by the high incidence of divorce and separation not just because it limits the child's opportunities for self-construction, but because it violates this romantic ideal of the family. Similarly, we are not disturbed by the enormous investments of families in their children, as opposed to investments that are redistributive, because this romantic ideal permits of no limits. Children are of ultimate value not because of what they represent, but simply because of who they are.

---

[10] Tracing the genealogy of the family has, however, become a web-based type of entertainment.

[11] See chap. 5 above.

Again, I must emphasize that these paradigms are hardly exhaustive of the normative or descriptive character of family or personal relations. Contemporary social life is deeply fractured and deeply contested. Individuals, couples, and families not only may draw on diverse ideals, but they can do so in a self-reflective manner, critiquing and reformulating the ideal even as it informs their self-understandings. The point is not to give an exhaustive account of the contemporary family, but to point to certain trends and to suggest their connection to an underlying contestation of the modern experience of the political. The romantic family is one such trend.

To the romantic family, the demand of the nation-state upon children and familial resources appears as a kind of invasion, a pure cost. This contest over the body of the son is as old as the story of the sacrifice of Isaac. To the romantic family, that demand for sacrifice— whether from the sovereign polity or the Lord—will simply make no sense. Still, the romantic family hardly represents a selfish ideal: individuals are willing to make enormous sacrifices for the family. It is, however, a deeply antipolitical ideal. Its antipolitical character is not captured by the liberal conception of the private. The romantic family generates its own set of values that span the distinction of the private from the public. Families want their children to succeed in a public world. The romantic family creates a public space; it includes public display and public relationships. The romantic has itself become a public value. There is the displacement of patriotism by compassion as the public order places the child at the center of its image of itself.[12]

The romantic family stands opposed not only to traditional political meanings, but also to traditional forms of religious practice. American culture long maintained two forms of public life: state and church. From the perspective of the state, religion was a private matter. From the perspective of the individual citizen, however, membership in a church was often the most public activity in which he or she engaged. At church, one regularly gathered in a public space with friends, neighbors, and relatives. The church was at the center of a rich communal

---

[12] The conflict and tension over these values is well represented by the experience of the Bush administration. It campaigned for office in 2000 on a platform of "compassionate conservativism." Post September 11, 2001, patriotism has displaced compassion as the primary public virtue.

enterprise. Like the political community, this tended to be a text-centered, discursive community. The public space of devotion was an important space for the loving family. Through familial participation, the child was located in a religious history and space that existed alongside of a political history and space. These were equal dimensions of the child's public identity: membership in a congregation of faith and membership in a political community. Both communities were defined by the double-character of representation (there were doctrines to learn and interpret) and instantiation (participation was material and not just formal). Just as the state could not be indifferent to the production of children, neither could the church. Both saw the child as the embodiment of an idea and celebrated the initiation of the child into the community.

The romantic family has no need for the public space of the religious community. The contemporary family maintains its own internal meaning that is quite independent of organized religious practice. This does not necessarily mean that families are abandoning churches.[13] Rather, fewer believe that religious identification is a necessary condition of familial well-being. The ultimate character of the romantic bond within the family stands in place of the external support of a community of representation, whether church or state.

When we look at trends in religious participation, we find that the representational forms of Protestantism have been on the decline, while those faiths that take up a nondiscursive form of meaning have been rising.[14] Christian evangelicalism is not a matter of a specific doctrinal content. Rather, it claims an immediate experience of the divine in and through the body: one must be "born again." This religious experience does not require interpretation, but only openness to the Holy Spirit.[15]

[13] In 2000, it was still the case that 40 percent of American adults attended church on a typical weekend. See Baran Research Online, *www.baran.org*. On the long-term decline in church attendance, see B. Beckwith, *The Decline of U.S. Religious Faith 1912–1984* (1985); W. Root and W. McKinney, *American Mainline Religion: Its Changing Shape and Future* 148–50 (1987).

[14] See R. Perrin et al., "Examining the Sources of Conservative Church Growth," 36 *J. Sci. Stud. of Religion* 71–72 (1997).

[15] Similar forms of fundamentalism are on an upward trend in both Judaism and Islam.

As with the romantic family, evangelical forms of religious experience deny the representational character of meaning. Truth is not an object of representation, or a quality of propositions. Truth is an experience that sustains itself without explanation. Religious fundamentalists pursue the immediacy of presence, the transformation of the body into meaning itself. Experience and meaning—being and the good—are inseparable in romance and fundamentalism.

The turn toward ethnic identity is another aspect of the rise of new forms of instantiated meaning. For many, the attraction of ethnic identity lies in the denial of the modern, liberal project of self-construction. Ethnicity confronts the subject as given. It makes a claim on individual identity that attaches in a nondeliberative fashion. What holds this community together is not propositional truth, but a mutual recognition of identity supported by history, language, cultural practices, and family. One discovers this identity as the truth of an embodied self; one discovers it as a good. Again, fact and value coincide. For this reason, it is extremely difficult to express the normative substance of such an ethnic-cultural identity in propositional form. Such expressions sound either racist (appealing to broad generalities about particular groups) or trivial (appealing to the symbols of cultural difference such as food and dress). If trivial, they seem incapable of supporting the importance some people attach to them; if racist, then they might be capable, but should be resisted. Both reactions miss the point, because both seek the representational truth of ethnicity, of which there is none. Neither is there a biological truth. We cannot locate meaning here in either of these directions. Ethnic identity is not just a matter of symbols, but neither is it specifiable in a set of tenets. Rather, it is experienced as a form of instantiated meaning. It is continuous with the romantic family and religious fundamentalism. It too creates its own community of faith.

Against this conception of ethnicity, we do find a liberal counterclaim. Now, the turn to ethnicity is seen as yet another expression of the fluidity of the self. Individuals are to take up the question of which part of their cultural inheritance they will *choose* to make central to their identity. Ethnicity is thought of as nothing more than another set of networked meanings. Individuals with multiple cultural heritages are fortunate to be able to think of identity as a choice among networks. Those without such complex heritages should, nevertheless, have the same freedom of choice. Not surprisingly, we find books on "liberal nationalism," arguing that cultural identity should be understood as a matter of choice, not destiny. Other liberal works on multiculturalism defend a form of cultural identity that is itself always open to re-formation by its members' choices.[16] Multiculturalism, like religion and family, has become yet another site of battle between representational and instantiated forms of meaning, between choosing and being chosen.

Multiculturalism is less of a threat to the rise of the Net than a compensatory form of response. Those who identify with a particular cultural background are, for the most part, not interested in withdrawing from contemporary markets and networks. They are interested in maintaining an identity despite the fluidity of their participation in these networked forms of meaning. Across an entire range of experience, made accessible by markets and networks, values will be shared. This, indeed, is just what we see as subcommunities come to feel that the growth of networks and markets allows them to differentiate themselves without putting at risk their participation in these larger structures.

The future of politics, if this is the model, will look very different from the past politics of nation-states. Those political forms will survive that are compatible with the larger process of creating global networks. These might be small communities that can maintain a distinct identity or transnational ethnic communities that demand little of their members. There is likely to be a kind of reciprocal relationship between the two as the local ethnic community simultaneously sees itself as part of a larger ethnicity. This will be a politics stripped of the political; it will be politics as ethos. That ethos will not be as dangerous, deadly, or demanding as the political has been in the recent past. It cannot be, for it exits in a state of codependence with a global order of networks. This will not be a politics that defines friends and enemies, or for which sacrifice becomes the paradigmatic political act. The very idea of a politics of multiculturalism means that the distinct groupings do not

---

[16] See Y. Tamir, *Liberal Nationalism* (1993); W. Kymlicka, *Multicultural Citizenship* (1995).

see themselves as forming boundaries beyond which others will appear as potential enemies. This is a politics that takes place within a context of rights, not across a qualitative divide of self and others.

One hundred and fifty years ago, Americans went to war over secession. Thirty years ago, Prime Minister Trudeau called out the troops in response to a militant secessionist movement in Quebec. Today, Canada has no interest in going to war over Quebec. Thus, the Canadian Supreme Court could take up the question of secession of Quebec and treat it as a matter of procedure.[17] The issue is to be managed by appeal to the norms of a transnational legal order. Even to conceive of the problem in this way is to sever law from the autonomous political character of the nation-state. The Canadian Supreme Court does not imagine law as the expression of popular sovereignty. Rather, it understands law as the fulfillment of a doctrine of rights. There is a confidence that were secession to occur, the result would be two liberal societies fundamentally agreeing on legal rights and linked through markets and networks.

The post-nation-state polity will no longer be one dedicated to any proposition at all, except the proposition that information wants to be free and thus all should have access to the internet. National political identity will diminish as we become simultaneously more global and more local. There is little space left for the modern nation-state in this vision of the future. Were this the only future we face, we would have to ask whether the demise of the nation-state is cause for mourning. What would we lose by splitting apart our representational and our instantiated forms of meaning? There is no way to tally up the benefits and costs of this transformation. Nor is there much we can do about it if such a transformation is coming. We can stop neither the growth of networks nor the development of new communities of faith. Still, it is too early to confidently proclaim the end of an autonomous politics of ultimate meanings, at least in the United States. For when we turn from internal developments within the liberal nation-state to external developments, we find that we are still committed to a modern—not a postmodern—conception of political citizenship, which continues to shape the perception of risks and possibilities.

---

[17] *Reference re Secession of Quebec* [1998] 2 S.C.R. 217.

POLITICS IN THE POSTPOLITICAL STATE

One form of the postpolitical is the movement toward a transnational understanding of rights coupled to a thin cultural or ethnic identity. That identity is thin precisely because it develops in response to the fluidity of the self imagined and sustained by markets and networks. The multicultural state has no intention of abandoning that fluidity. Indeed, it protects fluidity through a doctrine of rights—rights to information, to network access, to speech, and to educational and market opportunities. We can call this the European model, although it is surely present in North America as well.

In many places, however, the politics of ethnicity marks a turn toward traditional forms of sacrificial, political action. Just as we saw a violent form of Québécois separatism in the 1970s, we have seen the continuing violence of the Basque separatist movement, as well as the Balkan wars of the last decade, the armed confrontation of India and Pakistan, and the continuing threat of violence in many of the states that emerged from the former Soviet Union. It hardly looks as if the Palestinians and the Israelis are about to affirm a common vision of transnational rights in order to create a multicultural state or federation.

To many in the West, these violent political movements seem aberrational precisely because so much of the individual's self is now invested in transnational markets and information networks. There is a confidence that a politics that distorts access to these transnational phenomena is not likely to be successful. Populations will demand that their political leadership pursue integration into this system of networks.[18] The politics of nation-states will therefore fail in the dimension of final causes, and a more general failure will follow. This passes as the optimistic attitude toward the future: the era of state sovereignty is ending, and the sooner the better.

Much of the West experienced something of the exhilaration of political autonomy in the transformation from authoritarian to democratic regimes in the last generation. For the most part, however, that

---

[18] See T. Freidman, *The Lexus and the Olive Branch* (1999).

exhilaration was a temporary phenomenon.[19] In many of these places—from Latin America to Eastern Europe—politics has now been normalized, which means politics is understood as an aid to markets and information networks. The measure of political success is found in nonpolitical ends—most importantly, an increasing GDP and decreasing unemployment. Little is thought to turn on electoral results, as all of the major parties converge on a center that shares a common vision of the conditions under which markets and networks can flourish. It did not take long to convert the communist parties of Eastern Europe into political parties with the same centrist agenda.

Yet we can hardly proclaim the Europeanization of the world. The transformation of the West into postpolitical forms has required the creation of wealth in the fluid forms of markets and networks, as well as the rise of alternative sources of meaning: the romantic family, the ethnic community, and even fundamentalist religious groups. One cannot study the shape of the political and moral imagination in the West, observing its transformation through an age of nation-states into a postpolitical phenomenon, without coming to understand this as a unique story that derives its force from norms internal to this very tradition. This is not the story of the world historical spirit working itself pure. Rather, it is the story of the interaction of values that have their own history. It just happens to be our history. In affirming these values, we affirm our own character, not a universal virtue. Even here, these developments are not satisfactory to everyone.

Politics is not likely to disappear from the rest of the world any time soon. Moreover, the politics that exists is not necessarily going to follow Western patterns, moving toward its own demise. Much of the world does not match the cultural, economic, or social conditions of the West. Those conditions—epistemic, economic, and religious— worked together to create the possibility of that ideal of individual autonomy that is so powerful today. Outside of the West, these conditions do not exist and are not likely to exist within the imaginable future.

---

[19] See B. Ackerman, *The Future of Liberal Revolution* (1992) (offering a strategy for maximizing the political effectiveness of popular mobilization in light of its "temporary" character).

We are unlikely to bring about a single harmonious order simply by extending markets and networks to the rest of the world. These structures do not create their own meanings—or, if they do, it will be a long, slow process. We can see a harbinger of the difficulties in the contemporary dispute between the Israelis and the Palestinians. There is a body of elite, Western opinion that believes that resolution of the conflict is long past due, and that the resolution lies in both communities participating in common markets and information networks. Sovereignty is seen as an antiquated idea that fails to correspond to contemporary reality. Yet the negotiations between the parties stumbled over conflicting claims of sovereignty to the most local and symbolic of all places. The unresolvable point was not in cyberspace, but rather the space of Muhammad, Abraham, and Jesus. As I write this, the communities are again engaged in that most political form of symbolic action: sacrifice on a field of battle. They are motivated not by the anonymity and freedom of the network, but by an understanding of friend and enemy that "makes no sense" in a global era, which is only to say that its sense must be understood within the terms of the political.

Of course, we can say that it would be better if the Israelis and the Palestinians could live peaceably together, engaged in mutual enterprises of wealth- and information-creation. Yet, this is only to reject the terms within which many of them live their lives. It is like saying it would be better if someone had not been born with a physical handicap. It would be better, all other things being equal. But other things are never equal. If a handicap figures in who I am, that is, in my understanding of myself, to say I would be better off without it is to say it would be better if I were someone else. Each of us, however, is fully invested in the self we are. We imagine ourselves as others only from within the self that we already find ourselves to be. We cannot say that some lives are not worth living, because each is of ultimate value to the subject whose life it is.[20]

We can wish that the Palestinians and Israelis were not killing each other. But we cannot make them other than they are. We cannot deny

---

[20] It is quite a different issue to ask whether we should allow individuals to judge that their own lives are no longer worth living.

the forms of meaning in which they find themselves. We can encourage change; we can contribute to the conditions that might bring about change. We can even try to intervene to stop the fighting. But when we intervene, regardless of whether we think we are acting on moral grounds, we will be understood to be acting on political grounds. We are taking sides in a political dispute, even if the position we take is one that is opposed by both of the parties. We will become friend or enemy to the parties.[21]

If the rest of the world is not necessarily going to follow the West into a postpolitical life, the West will be forced to understand its own postpolitical order as itself a kind of politics. We will be forced to consider the boundaries of our own postpolitical perception; we will understand politics to start on the other side of those limits. The content of our political life may increasingly look multicultural and we may speak the language of human rights, but our political investment in that content will remain as strong as ever: not a depoliticization of the world, but a reshaping of a politics of ultimate value. This has already happened to a substantial extent. Western multiculturalism is becoming its own political form, supporting a claim of ultimate value. This is a kind of paradoxical politics of the antipolitical. The new political divide will be between those who participate in the politics of multiculturalism and those who are perceived as its enemies.[22] Multiculturalism is absorbing that most basic element of our political rhetoric: "freedom." It is, thereby, attaching to the popular sovereign itself.

Of course, the politics of the antipolitical is hardly a new phenomenon in American history. American exceptionalism has always claimed to be just this: a celebration of a national political identity founded on the rejection of the always already corrupted forms of the political tradition. Our political self-understanding has always claimed a kind

[21] For this reason, international criminal tribunals, including that at the Hague trying ex-Serbian leader Slobodan Milošević and others, are always accused of administering "victors' justice." See, e.g., J. Dower, *Embracing Defeat: Japan in the Wake of World War II* (1999).

[22] Accordingly, the Islamic fundamentalist as terrorist is carefully specified. Because Islam too must be respected in the politics of multiculturalism, the enemy is not Islam. The terrorist is the enemy because he attacks "our liberty" and liberty is understood on the model of multiculturalism.

of purity from politics. The transformation of ethnic nationalism into a national multiculturalism is a new version of this older story.

Our postpolitical, multicultural society will remain a nation-state within a larger political world for the indefinite future. Enemies will not disappear, but their identity will shift. We are likely to witness some reconfiguration of nation-states as the territorial compromises of the past two hundred years come to be seen as inadequate markers of friends and enemies. This is the story of Europe. The emergence of Europe over the last generation is as significant as the emergence of a single United States in the nineteenth century. The political fracture of Western Europe—war between France and Germany—is no longer a possibility. It is as unimaginable as a renewal of sectional conflict in the United States.

Politics is a form of meaning in a fractured world in which potential enemies are perceived. Ours remains a fractured world of multiple potential enemies. We need no reminder of this after September 11, 2001. Suddenly, we find ourselves "at war" with an enemy that seems at times to threaten from every direction. Effectively, this means that we will continue to live a double-life: we will witness the rise of post-political forms of meaning right alongside the continued political life of the nation. We find ourselves today simultaneously responding to the most traditional political calls for sacrifice and battle, while being told that we should continue our ordinary lives within global markets and information networks.

This will produce odd juxtapositions of the global and the national, a discourse of universal rights that fails to match our political discourse of sacrifice. Politics will seem to be an aid to markets, yet markets will remain subject to ultimate political demands. We will teach our children the historical meaning of citizenship—patriotism—even as we prepare them to be members of a global order. Militarily, we will continue to be confused about the ethics of intervention in the political disputes of others. Intervention may be the moral thing to do in many situations where gross abuses of human rights are occurring, but we do not demand that citizens sacrifice themselves for the moral good of strangers. This is just the case with the intervention in Iraq, the justification of which seems always to move back and forth between eliminating the threat to ourselves—weapons of mass destruction and support for terrorism—and acting on behalf of the suffering Iraqi population.

The point is not that sacrifice is too much to ask of the citizen. We ask it all of the time. Rather, we require that the demand for sacrifice satisfy a set of political meanings. It is not the state's end to advance moral meanings, until and unless there is a political identification with those ends. There is, however, nothing inconsistent about a state taking up as its own ends the liberal morality of human rights. Where we go wrong, however, is in thinking that the universal ambition of these rights eliminates the political character of the community that adopts them as its own. Here, we would do well to remember the universal moral ambition of Christianity and the way in which it was pursued by political communities.

Political action is about the life of the nation. Political sacrifice sustains a distinct set of meanings against forces of historical dissolution. When sacrifice bears the meaning of the state, the fact that it may cost a life is not a separate part of some other calculation. Politics and morality may intersect across a wide domain, but they are not the same.

When we look at the rest of the world, we will continue to look with political eyes. Conversely, an effort to remake the world in our own image will be seen by others as an assertion of power. It will be seen as a kind of neocolonial intervention, which will be met by political resistance. Politics exists in this tension of power and counterpower. It may be reassuring to think that we can intervene abroad in the name of moral truth rather than political power. But this is a distinction that is without difference. History has taught us this lesson in Southeast Asia, Somalia, Lebanon, the Balkans, and throughout the Middle East.

We cannot ask others to accept our history as their own. This was the mistake of colonialism, which thought that it could simply extend European history to other communities. It could not. Instead it created the conditions for a new history of opposition. Much the same can be said of recent, well-meaning forms of neocolonial intervention. This does not mean that we have to value others' history.[23] To us, those

---

[23] See C. Taylor, *Multiculturalism: Examining the Policies of Recognition* 64–73 (A. Gutman, ed., 1994).

histories may seem to lead to moral and political pathologies. We say this, however, always from within our own world. We need to recognize this as a statement that implicitly identifies friends and enemies, a statement that sets the conditions for potential political conflict.

Only a naive multiculturalism believes that the moral point of view can be brought to politics in order to reconcile differences. Citizen/noncitizen remains as compelling a distinction for us as that between those who are a part of the family and those who are not. Nothing follows from asking the question whether either distinction can support itself in a world limited to moral justifications. Liberal moralizing will not end politics as long as we see ourselves as members of historically defined political communities. We invest ourselves with the meaning of those communities. We take this investment to be one of ultimate value.

The question for intellectual inquiry is not whether politics is morally just, or even how to make it morally just. Politics is always more and less than morality. No political order is a just order from our moral point of view. Politics invests ultimate value in ideas that are morally irrelevant—for example, history and territory. But this is only to say that the construction of meaning in a political world is not the same as that in a moral world. The issue for reflection is to understand the shape of the political world of value as it has been constructed by the imagination, and then to consider the ways in which such structures of meaning can respond to contemporary events and the changing shape of contemporary values.

We have no reason to think that history has come to an end in the simultaneity of markets and networks. We have every reason to think that the rise of this transnational simultaneity will itself be seen as another historical moment in the life of the political community. It may spawn the double-movement toward transnational institutions and localism. These movements, however, will come to describe the content of a Western political imagination, which distinguishes it from others. The perception of difference is always the ground of political identity.

Aristotle told us that we are political beings. We will get nowhere if we pretend we can simply reform politics out of existence. But neither are we doomed by our political destiny. The problem is no different in form from that of thinking about the juxtaposition of morality and markets. We cannot simply condemn markets from a moral point of view and think that anything will change. We are not free simply to imagine better—that is, more just—systems of production and consumption if we want to act or even think in a serious way. Neither, however, are we doomed to live with uncontrolled markets. Action always requires more than theory. Without understanding the conditions within which action occurs, however, we are no more likely to be successful political reformers than reformers of markets.[24]

This means accepting political competition. We make the mistake of dreaming of a postpolitical world in the same way that we dream of a world without illness. We think that because politics makes a world through sacrifice and violence that we can assimilate political action to other forms of bodily injury. It would be better, we think, were we free of all injury from any source, physical or political. The United Nations Charter speaks of a world free of the "scourge of war." Who among us does not want our children, our loved ones, to be free of the violence of politics? But that was no less true in 1914 as millions of young men pursued a sacrificial politics on the battlefields of Europe. Politics is not illness and sacrifice is not injury. We only see it that way when we suppress the political perspective.

Politics has been a form of construction of meaning. We are not wedded to any symbolic form as if it were an unalterable aspect of our nature. But neither is it a secondary characteristic of an otherwise complete subject. The subject we find ourselves to be includes a political imagination. Whether we are capable of stripping away that political imagination is not a question the theorist can answer. Politics has not been just one form of meaning among others; it has been that in which many in the West have for a long time located an ultimate meaning. We are not going to replace this dimension of the absolute with access to more and better goods or information.

---

[24] Stanley Fish and Richard Posner have both attacked the "practice of theory," arguing for a kind of pragmatism, focusing on particular, contextualized decisions. See S. Fish, "Truth but No Consequences: Why Philosophy Doesn't Matter," 29 *Critical Inquiry* 389 (2003); R. Posner, *The Problematics of Moral and Legal Theory* (1999). While I share their skepticism of any easy link between theory and reform, I do not share their rejection of large-scale theory. We need to understand frames

The shift from a religious to a political worldview was a monumental change in the history of culture. Are we now at the point where a dramatic shift is possible to a new form of the absolute? I do not see the resources for this shift. The romantic family cannot support this world alone. Neither religious fundamentalism nor a renewal of cultural-ethnic identity is likely to be appealing to many in a postpolitical world. Are we prepared to pursue lives in which ultimate meanings do not figure? I do not believe that we will have the luxury of even asking this question. For whatever our answer might be in the abstract, the rest of the world will continue to invest ultimate meanings in their own political forms. If that is so, the era of nation-states may be ending, but that of politics still has a long way to go.

---

of reference—liberalism as a cultural phenomenon—even as we take up particular contested positions.

INDEX